THE COMING OF
THE SAINTS

IMAGINATIONS AND STUDIES IN EARLY

CHURCH HISTORY AND TRADITION

By

J. W. TAYLOR

THE COVENANT PUBLISHING CO. LTD.
121, Low Etherley, Bishop Auckland, Co. Durham, DL14 0HA

2015

First published by Methuen & Co Ltd in 1906
Second Edition 1911
Third Edition 1923
New (Revised) Edition by The Covenant Publishing Co Ltd 1969
Reprinted and reset 2015

ISBN 978-085205-082-8

Printed by
THE COVENANT PUBLISHING COMPANY LIMITED
121, Low Etherley, Bishop Auckland,
Co. Durham, DL14 0HA
www.covpub.co.uk

The Coming of the Saints

In this book, history and legend combine to give us a picture of the earliest missionaries of the Christian Faith, their selfless devotion, their achievements, and in some cases their martyrdom for Christ's sake. The debt owed by the Christian Church in the West to these fearless pioneers is indeed incalculable. It is right that we should appreciate the sound foundations which they laid, and this book helps us to do this.

'Heresy to the heretic and religion to the orthodox, but the bloom of the rose-petal belongs to the heart of the perfume-seller.'

ABUL FAZL

CONTENTS

ILLUSTRATIONS

ACKNOWLEDGEMENTS

Popperfoto for 1, 2, 3, 5, 15b;   F. C. Hocking for 4 and 15a;
Fox Photos for 6 and 12;   French Embassy for 8;
French Government Tourist Office for 7, 9 and 13;
10, 11 and 14 from plates in original edition

FOREWORD TO THE NEW EDITION, 1969

It is with great pleasure that I introduce this new edition of a work written some sixty years ago but full of such original information concerning the Church of the first century that it comes with renewed interest to each generation of readers.

The history of this period is often criticized because it is compounded both of written records and local legends. This book shows with absolute clarity that legends and records dovetail in together, each being substantiated by the other. Of particular interest are the references culled from Churches founded by the saints who were companions of our Lord during His ministry. Such evidences can only be obtained in the places concerned, and the pilgrimages made by the author to the Churches of France and nearby countries have produced most impressive proof of the antiquity of the Church planted among the Celts of Western Europe and Britain.

It is a long time since my namesake, John W. Taylor, carried out these researches, and little has been added to his findings by any subsequent writer. We should have been pleased to meet a person so full of knowledge and understanding of a subject of profound importance to students of early Church history, particularly as the facts that he presents completely endorse the findings of those who believe in the historical primacy of the Celtic Church.

GLADYS TAYLOR

INTRODUCTION

By easy walking stages on land and by sailing-ships or strong sailing and rowing-boats at sea – such as you may pass today as you steam down the Mediterranean – the Saints came journeying from Palestine in the first days of the Christian era.

Strangers and pilgrims, with few or none to notice and keep record of their wanderings, they came to distant countries and to strange peoples.

They wandered about, being often 'destitute, afflicted and tormented (of whom the world was not worthy). They wandered in deserts and in mountains,' and they sheltered 'in dens and caves of the earth.'

We know this because something like it has been the almost invariable experience of missionary pioneers through all the succeeding ages.

We know it because even now the caves and rock shelters along the borders of the Mediterranean, immemorially associated with Christian missionaries and Christian rites, speak eloquently of the hardship and the suffering of the way.

Of genuine history regarding them we have but scant outlines. They were altogether beneath the notice of those who, like Tacitus, deserved the title of historian in their day; yet records of their doings, their successes and their failures must have been handed down through many generations, and these form the very texture of the fabric out of which the legends of the Saints have been elaborated.

Sometimes we can trace with considerable certainty the hidden underlying basis of true history. Who, for instance, reading in our own chronicles of Gildas and William of Malmesbury of the caution and tardiness of the British in accepting the Christian faith, can doubt that the quaint and curious admission of this rests upon some definite sort of information which, though now unknown, is still reliable?

How much is true and how much is false in the old legends it is impossible to say. Those who have altogether rejected them have done so, I am convinced, at the expense of much that is worthy of preservation; for there is a certain harmony not only connecting the various narratives themselves, but connecting these with the voices and the silences of history, that decidedly points to some marked substratum of fact.

As one who has been familiar with these legends for many years, who has always loved them and has occasionally lived in the environment and very atmosphere of their acceptance (as you can do today in the Rhone Valley and at Glastonbury), I have written the following pages.

I may have but little that is new to bring to a well-worn controversy. Indeed, I come to no controversy at all. 'The bloom of the rose-petal belongs to the heart of the perfume-seller,' and I will not risk its beauty and fragrance in the handling and appraising necessary for controversy.

I simply take you halfway back – to the ages of faith, to the belief of a thousand years ago – as I try to tell the happenings of two thousand years ago, and re-imagine the remoter past in the light of the traditions of our forefathers.

Only the broad distinction is necessary as we use the old traditions. I write of at least two comings of the Saints. The first is of Hebrew missionaries whose coming is probable but problematical, and whose identity is solely a matter tradition or of legend or of inference. The second is a later coming – the coming of the Greek; the chief example of this being the coming of Trophimus, the friend and disciple of St. Paul, whose identity as the first missionary priest of Arles is fairly well established.

His coming is confirmed by documents going back as far as the beginning of the fifth century, and is therefore partly traditional and partly historical.

I have not taken upon myself to disentangle history from legend. The modern critic is by no means infallible, and in rooting out the tares, is apt to destroy the wheat also, 'Let both grow together until the harvest.'

J.W.Taylor
Birmingham

REFERENCES

Acta Sanctorum (Joannes Bollandus) . . . . Paris, 1863-1904

Anderson, Rev. J., *Wanderings*, &c. (Collins) . . . London, 1851

Arles et le Baux (Hachette et Cie) . . . . Paris, 1896

Aubanel, *Monuments de l'Eglise de St. Marthe* . . . Tarascon, 1835

Backhouse and Tyler, *Early Church History* . . . . London, 1892

Baring-Gould, Rev. S., *Book of the West*, Vol. II . . . London, 1891

Baring-Gould, Rev. S., *In Troubadour Land* . . . . London, 1899

Bede, *Ecclesiastical History and Chronicle* (Bohn's Library) . London, 1875

Bellows, John, *Letters and Memoirs* . . . . . London, 1904

Biggs, Rev. C., *Six Months in Jerusalem* (Mowbray) . . London, 1896

Borlase, W. C., *Historical Sketch of the Tin Trade in Cornwall* . Plymouth, 1874

Breviary, Roman (for St. Martha's Day, July 29th).

Broughton, *Ecclesiastical History of Great Britaine* 1633

Buchedd Mair Vadlen, ⎫ Hafod Collection: Cardiff,
Buchedd, Martha   ⎭ Library.

Bullen, R.A., *Harlyn Bay*, &c. (Swan Sonnenschein & Co.) . London, 1902

Caird, Mona, *Romantic Cities of Provence* . . . . London, 1906

Caldecott, Rev. W. S., *The Tabernacle* . . . . London, 1904

Camden's *Britannia* . . . . London, 1789

Capgrave, *Nova Legenda Anglie* (Horstman) . . . . Oxford, 1901

Cave, W., *Scriptorum Ecclesiasticorum Historia Literaria, Basilae* . . 741

Clement, St., *Recognitions and Homilies* (Ante-Nicene Library, Edinburgh) . 1870

Conybeare, Edward, *Roman Britain* . . . . London, 1903

Crawford, F. Marion, *The Rulers of the South* (Macmillan) . London, 1900

Cyprian, St., *Letters, Library of Fathers* (Parker) . . . Oxford, 1844

Diodorus Siculus, Hist. Library, Booth's Trans. . . . London, 1814

Duchesne, l'Abbé, *Fastes Episcopaux* . . . . Paris, 1900

Dugdale, *Monasticon* . . . . London, 1693

Edersheim, Rev. A., *Jesus the Messiah* . . . . London, 1896

Edwardes, Charles, *Sardinia and the Sardes* . . . . London, 1889

Edmonds, Richard, *The Land's End District* 1862

Encyclopaedia Biblica . . . . Edinburgh, 1899

Encyclopaedia Britannica . . . . . . Edinburgh, 1875

Encyclopaedia, Jewish . . . . New York & London, 1901-1905

Eusebius, *Eccles. History*, Cruse's Translation (Bohn) . . London, 1900

Evans, Sebastian, *High History of the Holy Grail* (Translation) . London, 1898

Faillon, *Monuments Inédits*, &c. (Migne) . . . Paris, 1859 & 1865

Forbes and Burmester, *Our Roman Highways* . . . London, 1904

Ford, Richard, *Handbook of Spain* (Murray) . . . . London, 1878

France. By the Author of *Mlle. Mori* (Sampson, Low and Marston) . .

. . . . London, 1881

Freculphus, *Patrologia Latina*, Vol. CVI.

Freeman, A. E., *Origin of the English Nation* (Macmillan's Magazine, May) .

. . . . 1870

Gaskoin, *Alcuin: His Life and Work* . . . . London, 1904

Geikie, *The Holy Land and the Bible* . . . . London, 1903

Geoffrey of Monmouth, *British History*, Bohn (Thompson & Giles) . .

. . . . London, 1842

Gildas, *History*, Bohn . . . . . . London, 1885

Giles, Rev. J. A., *History of the Ancient Britons* (Bell) . . London, 1847

St. Gregory of Tours, *History of the Church of France*, Patrol. Latina, Vol. LXXI.

Glastonbury Abbey (Woodhams) . . . . . Wells, 1902

Haddan and Stubbs, *Councils and Eccles. Documents relating to Great Britain and Ireland*, Vol. I . . . . . . Oxford, 1869-1871

Haller and Züscher, *Trierische Geschichte* (Trier) . . . Trèves, 1903

Hare, Augustus J. C., *South-Eastern France* . . . . London, 1890

Harnack, *Expansion of Christianity in the First Three Centuries*, Moffatt's Trans. . . . . London, 1905

Haverfield, "Early British Christianity" (*English Historical Review*), Vol. IX.

Henderson, B. W., *Life and Principate of Nero* . . . London, 1903

Hippolytus (Ante-Nicene Library, Vol. IX) . . . . Edinburgh, 1870

Hodgson, F. C., *Early History of Venice* . . . London, 1901

Houtin, A., *La Controverse de l'Apostolicité*, &c. . . . . Paris, 1901

Hovedon, Roger de, *Chronica*, Stubbs (Longmans). . . London, 1868

Hunt, *Romances of the West* (Hotton) . . . . London, 1872

Hutton, W. H., *Lives and Legends of the English Saints* . . London, 1903

Isidorus Hispalensis, *Patrologica Latina*, Vol. LXXXI-LXXXIV.

Jago, *Glossary of the Cornish Dialect* . . . . . Truro, 1899

St. James and St. Mary, Lives of, MS. Laud, 108 (Bodleian), Early English Text Society. . . . . London, 1887

John of Fordun, *Scottish History* . . . . . Edinburgh, 1871

John of Glastonbury, *Glastoniensis Chronica* (Hearne) . . Oxford, 1726

Joinville, de, *Histoire de St. Louis* . . . . Paris, 1874

Joseph of Aramathie, Early English Text Society 1871

Josephus, *Antiquities* (Whiston) . . . . . London, 1737

Lacordaire, Père, *Sainte Marie Madeleine* . . . . Paris, 1883

Lamoureaux, *Les Saintes Maries* . . . . . Avignon, 1898

Lane, Rev. C. A., *Notes on English Church History*, Vol. I. . London, 1889

Lethaby, W. R., *London before the Conquest*. . . . London, 1902

15

Llyfr Gwyn Rhydderch, Hengwrt MS.

Löher, Franz von, *Cyprus: Historical and Descriptive* . . London, 1878

Maclean, Dr. M., *The Literature of the Celts* (Blackie) . . . .

. . . . London, Glasgow and Dublin, 1902

Malory, Sir T., *Morte D'Arthur*, Revised Caxton Edition . . London, 1868

Mansi, *Sacrorum Conciliorum Collectio*, Vols. I, II, III and IV. . .

. . . . Paris & Leipzig, 1901&c.

Matthew of Paris, *Chronica Majora* (Luard) . . . . London, 1872

Milman, Dean, *History of the Jews* . . . . London, 1863

Mistral, *Mireio*, Preston's Translation . . . . London, 1890

Mommarché, *Rocamadour et ses Environs* . . . . Paris, 1898

Narbey, M., l'Abbé, Supplement to the *Acta Sanctorum*.

New Testament, Greek and Revised Version.

Newell, *History of the Welsh Church* . . . . London, 1895

Nutt, Alfred, *The Legends of the Holy Grail* . . . London, 1902

Palmer, Rev. W., *Origines Liturgicae* . . . . Oxford, 1839

Passing of Mary, Ante-Nicene Library, Vol. XVI. . . . Edinburgh, 1870

Polwhele, Rev. R., *History of Cornwall* and Supplement . . Falmouth, 1803

Pryce, Dr., *Archaeologia Cornu-Britannica* . . . Sherborne, 1790

Rabanus, *De Vita B. Mariae Magdalenae*, &c. Magdalen College Library .

. . . . Oxford

Rawlinson, Prof., *History of Phoenicia* . . . London, 1889

Rees, Rev. Rice, *Essay on the Welsh Saints* . . . . London, 1836

Robert of Gloucester, Hearne's Translation . . . . London, 1810

Rocamadour, *Guide du Pélerin*, Rocamandour 1897

Smith, Dr., *The Cassiterides* . . . . . London, 1863

Spence, Dean, *Early Christianity and Paganism* . . . London, 1902

Spratt, Capt., *Travels in Crete* . . . . . London, 1865

Strabo, *Geography*, Hamilton and Falconer's Translation . . London, 1854-7

Stubbs, *Episcopal Succession* . . . . . Oxford, 1858

Tacitus, *Annals and Life of Agricola*, Bohn . . . . London, 1877

Taylor, C., *Calmet's Dictionary* . . . . . London, 1835

Tertullian, *Patrologia Latina*, Vols I and II.

Transactions of Plymouth Institution . . . . Plymouth, 1901

Trevelyan, *Land of Arthur* . . . . . . London, 1895

Ussher, Bishop, Works of, Vols. V, VI and XVII . . . Dublin, 1864

Véran, M. l'Abbé, *Histoire de Ste Marthe* . . . . Avignon, 1868

Wilkins, C., *History of the Literature of Wales* . . . Cardiff, 1884

William of Malmesbury, *Patrologia Latina*, Vol. CLXXIX.

Williams, R., *Biographical Dictionary* . . . Llandovery, 1852

Wright, *Guide to Glastonbury* . . . . . Glastonbury

Zimmer, *The Celtic Church*, Translation . . . London, 1902

'Ut quod enucleatius ostendendum opere praetium estimo multipharis evangelistarum cathegorias quibus in hoc ipsum consonant, enarrare; ac deinde que post Salvatoris ascensionem circa ejus amicos gesta sunt sicut nobis patres nostri tradiderunt, et in suis etiam reliquerunt scriptis stilo veraci disserere.' – From the Prologus of the Manuscript of Rabanus. See Frontispiece.

[Free Translation]

'In order that the facts might be set forth more thoroughly, I have thought it useful to unite in one narrative the divers accounts of these evangelists, and then to faithfully add those events affecting these friends of our Saviour which took place after the Ascension, according as our fathers have told us and according to the accounts they have left for us in their writings.'

CHAPTER I

THE CALLING OF THE SAINTS

CAPERNAUM

'Awestruck I gazed as John, with lifted finger,
    Pointed and cried, "Behold the Lamb of God!"
Even then He drew me so I could not linger;
    Turned I and followed where His footsteps trod.

What was the spell, the charm, that led me to Him? –
    Him, the despised of all the human race?
Rather I'd ask why men so coldly view Him.
    I cannot tell, but I had seen His Face.

Word of the Father! Who before creation
    Dwelt in the light that no man can conceive.
Yet in our flesh has wrought our full salvation;
    What can we do but wonder and believe?

Rich men may boast their wealth and count it pleasure
    Daily to revel in its stores unpriced;
I have known that which sinks to nought their treasure –
    Known the delight of being loved by Christ.'

St. John, by MARY BEALE

The main theory that I propose to consider and develop in the following pages is one of Hebrew or Hebrew-Phoenician missions extending from Palestine to all the old Phoenician colonies in the very earliest years of Christendom.[1]

It is based on the records of Holy Scripture; it is supported by many old writings and traditions.

But it is more than this. It is a theory of missions conducted by the inner circle of disciples who were brought into immediate contact with Jesus at Capernaum and Jerusalem; men and women who were well known to have been the followers of Jesus, and who therefore, in common with Lazarus (*John* 12:10, 11) and with Saul (*Acts* 9:23), went about in danger of their lives, and were forced to escape from Jerusalem at the earliest opportunity.

It was the mission of a fugitive people to a disappearing race, and therefore but scant records, and these mostly traditional, are all that can be found of its beginning and history. But the results were unmistakable; for before St. Paul had fully set forth upon his later labours all the main Phoenician colonies and trading ports appear to have possessed their nucleus of Christians.

At Tyre, Antioch, and Tarsus, in Cyprus and Crete, at Cyrene and in Sicily, all over the eastern coast of the Mediterranean, we see the Phoenician colonies, where Jews and Phoenicians and their descendants had been working together for centuries, singled out as the initial outposts of Christian effort. And, without any recognition of this association, we find, in tradition, that at all the more distant Phoenician trading ports or colonies – at Marseilles, in Sardinia, in Spain and in Cornwall – traces may be found of Hebrew missionary effort long antecedent to anything which bears the stamp of actual history.

The power of Phoenicia as a nation had been waning for centuries before the coming of Christ, but from 65 BC, when Phoenicia came under the definite protection of Rome, its commercial sea-power appears to have received a considerable access of vitality. From this date the ships of Tyre and Sidon could trade from port to port all over the Mediterranean, and even beyond it, with less danger than at any time, perhaps, since the acme of Phoenician prosperity. Undoubtedly the old colonies had lost much of their strict Phoenician character. Greeks and Romans, as well as Syrians and Canaanites, crowded the large towns and cities, but the Phoenicians still held a strong if not predominant position at all the main seaport towns, and these formed the first bridges by which the gospel of Galilee and Jerusalem passed from the Hebrew to the Pagan world.

Regarding this (Roman) period of Phoenician history Professor Rawlinson writes:

'Tyre and Sidon were great commercial centres down to the time of the Crusades, and quite as rich, quite as important, quite as flourishing, commercially, as in the old days of Hiram and Ithobal.

'Mela (*de Situ Orbis*, i, 12) speaks of Sidon in the second century after Christ as "still opulent." Ulpian, himself a Tyrian by descent (*Digest Leg. de Cens*, tit. 15), calls Tyre in the reign of Septimius Severus "a most splendid colony." A writer of the age of Constantine says of it (*Exp. totius Mundi in Hudson's Georgr. Minores*, iii, 6), "The prosperity of Tyre is extraordinary. There is no state in the whole of the East which excels it in the amount of its business. Its merchants are persons of great wealth, and there is no port where they do not exercise considerable influence."'

St. Jerome (Hieronymus, *Comment, ad. Exek*, xxvi, 7), towards the end of the fourth century, speaks of Tyre as 'the noblest and most beautiful of all the cities of Phoenicia,' and as 'an emporium for the commerce of almost the whole world' (Rawlinson's *Phoenicia*, pp. 550, 551).

In Galilee, on the very borders of Syro-Phoenicia, the Saviour lived during the greater part of His ministry. Many of the people from the sea-coasts of Tyre and Sidon listened to His teaching (*Luke* 6:17; *Mark* 3:8), and were healed of their diseases; and once, at least, He made a journey from Galilee into Phoenicia (*Mark* 7), healing there the daughter of the Syro-Phoenician woman who forced her way into His presence.

Phoenicians appear to have been found in all the chief towns of Palestine about this date and, together with Arabians and Egyptians, are described by Strabo as regular inhabitants (bk. xvi, c. ii, par. 34). The commercial influence of Tyre and Sidon formed one of the four great factors which moulded the special civilization of the epoch. The first in importance, perhaps, was the religious patriotism of the Hebrew, inseparable from the land and its associations; the second was the supremacy and occupation of Rome; the third was the learning of the Greek; and the fourth was the commerce of Tyre. All of these factors seem to have been strongly marked throughout the whole of Galilee.

Permanent garrisons of Roman soldiers were maintained in the larger cities to enforce authority and order; the great highway from Tyre to Damascus traversed the country and brought an unending stream of merchants and traffic, while travellers and colonists of Greek or Hebrew-Greek origin, deeply interested in philosophical and religious questions, studied the Jews, their religion and customs, often disputing hotly with them, but occasionally becoming, to some extent, proselytes and disciples. Of such must have been those early disciples of Ephesus who had been 'baptized unto John's baptism' (*Acts* 19:1-12).

Not infrequently the families of these different nations intermarried. The 'stranger that was within his gates' was often accepted as the husband of an Israelitish maiden, and occasional instances of mixed marriages are found in the history of the period.

Drusilla, a member of the Herod family, married a Roman, Claudius Felix; Eunice, a Jewess, married a Greek and became the mother of St. Timothy. Herod Antipas himself married the daughter of Aretas, King of Arabia, and (according to the History of Rabanus), Mary of Magdala (Mary Magdalene of the Gospels) was the daughter of a Syrian and a Jewess, her father, a Syrian prince or ruler, having married a Jewish maiden who traced her descent from the royal family of King David.

The international connections and sympathies formed by such relationships and interests received a yearly stimulus throughout the whole of Palestine when, at the greater festivals, men of Hebrew origin or faith from all parts of the Roman Empire, 'out of every nation under heaven,' met together in Jerusalem for worship and rejoicing. Parthians and Medes, and Elamites, and the dwellers in Mesopotamia, and in Judaea, and Cappadocia, in Pontus, and Asia, Phrygia and Pamphylia, in Egypt and in the parts of Lybia about Cyrene, strangers of Rome, Jews and proselytes, Cretes and Arabians[2] met together on such occasions in Jerusalem, and must have brought news to many a homestead, both in going and returning, of distant lands and absent friends.

But beneath this bright surface-appearance of harmonious, many-coloured life the restless, unsatisfied longing and ambition of the discontented Jew was a perennial source of difficulty.

Nowhere was the Jewish national sentiment so strong and so popular as in Galilee. 'In the days of the taxing,' presumably in the year that Christ was born, Judas of Galilee headed a struggle for independence which probably involved many members of the various families who afterwards became followers of John the Baptist and of Jesus. All the early disciples were full of the same traditions and aspirations which had animated the followers of Judas. Like them, they were hoping for and expecting a Jewish deliverer and king who would lead them to victory against their conquerors and oppressors. This was their conception of the office of the promised Messiah; this formed the basis of their great hope in John the Baptist and afterwards in Jesus.

So deeply ingrained was this expectation of an earthly deliverer that long after the coming of Jesus, when they had already enjoyed many months, and even years, of teaching regarding the spiritual Kingdom He came to establish – after His passion on Calvary and the wonder of His resurrection – still the disciples came to Him with the ever-present question, not only in their hearts but on their lips, 'Lord, wilt thou at this time restore again the kingdom to Israel?' (*Acts* 1:6).

All of the Galilean disciples were at first and mainly patriotic Israelites, and it was only after years of experience and suffering that they finally understood and grasped the meaning of the Master, 'the Kingdom which was not of this world' – the victory to be gained not by conflict with Rome, but by constant conflict with sin and self, the Hope which belonged to the 'things not seen which were eternal.'

Herod Antipas – 'Herod the Tetrarch' – who was the ruler of Galilee from about AD 1-39, had no easy task to fulfil in governing the mixed races and peoples of which he was the titular head. He was brought into very close relationship on the one hand with Rome and on the other with some of the very men who became afterwards identified with Jewish national aspirations and early Christian teaching.

His life, however, is a record of self-indulgence and of failure. With more honesty of purpose he might have ruled as a loyal and unbending servant of Rome; with more courage he might himself have raised the standard of revolt; with a higher conception of life and more spiritual earnestness he might have listened to and obeyed the teaching of the Baptist; but, crafty and unstable in all his ways, he lost the respect of his people; he literally murdered the religious force and love which might have saved him; and finally, losing the confidence of Rome, was banished, with his kinswoman and so-called wife Herodias, to the distant city of Lyons.

As a boy we are told that he was brought up with Manaen, who afterwards became one of the great Christian teachers of Antioch (*Acts* 13:1). This may have some historical significance, as Antioch (as well as Ephesus) is said to have sent missions to Gaul in apostolic times. He had visited Rome and the Imperial Court before assuming his delegated sovereignty, and it is perhaps more than probable that his steward Chuza and the centurion-governor (both mentioned in the Gospels) came with him on returning to his province.

Later on, he and his wife Herodias came into immediate and startling relation with John the Baptist. The latter reproved the king for taking Herodias as his wife, and was consequently cast into prison. Here he was beheaded by the order of Herod at the instigation of Herodias.

The crime was no secret one, but committed in the full light of a public festivity, and all the gruesome details must have been fully known to the officers of the household, the servants and the assembled guests. The memory of it seems to have darkened all the future life of the king; while his people, who honoured the Baptist as a prophet from God, must have regarded the murder as a sinister and ominous incident in the reign of their ruler.

Full of a superstitious remorse and fear, we read that when Herod heard of the ministry of the Saviour he said, 'This is John the Baptist who is arisen from the dead' (*Matthew* 14:2). On his final banishment such a mind and temperament could hardly fail to carry into exile the memory of his sin and connect it in some way with the darkness and misfortune of his closing days.

Such was the ruler and such the people of Galilee at the coming of the Saviour. Such, broadly and briefly, is the Galilean frame or setting from which emerge, as from a picture, the faces of the earthly disciples 'called to be saints.'

At the coming of the Saviour we find all the known members of His 'family' already identified with the national party, and especially with that highest conception of it realized in the person and mission of John the Baptist.

St. John the Baptist was His second cousin, James and John, the sons of Zebedee, were second cousins also, their mother Salome, or Mary Salome, being (like Elizabeth) first cousin to the Blessed Virgin, while, according to Hegesippus, Cleopas, who married another Mary ('Mary the wife of Cleopas') was the brother of St. Joseph, and though his children would have no direct or blood relationship with our Lord, in the eyes of the world around Him they would have the nearest relationship, and these – James the Less, Simon Zelotes, and Judas Lebbaeus, or Thaddeus – are sometimes more especially called 'His brethren.' In St. John's Gospel (*John* 19:25) Mary, the wife of Cleopas, is directly called the sister of the Blessed Virgin.

Zacharias and Elizabeth, the parents of St. John the Baptist, and Joseph, the husband of the Blessed Virgin Mary, appear to have died before our Lord began His ministry; Zacharias, according to Arabic and Greek tradition, having been assassinated within the Temple courts because of his belief in the Miraculous Conception of Jesus by the Virgin Mary. According to the same tradition our Lord refers to him in the 35th verse of the 23rd chapter of the Gospel of *Matthew*, 'From the blood of righteous Abel unto the blood of Zacharias son of Barachias, whom ye slew between the temple and the altar.' His son, St. John the Baptist, was at the height of his reputation and mission when the public life of our Saviour was just beginning.

At this time Andrew and another disciple (presumably John the Evangelist) were already disciples of St. John the Baptist, and on that memorable morning, when the Baptist saw our Lord, and pointed Him out to His disciples, saying, 'Behold, the Lamb of God!' (*John* 1:36), these followed Jesus, and at His invitation went home with Him and spent the day at His house. So at the very outset of His ministry we find our Lord surrounded first by the members and relatives of His own family, and secondly by their immediate friends, all, or nearly all, being known followers and disciples of St. John the Baptist. And of these friends the first to claim our attention are Peter and Andrew, who were partners with James and John, and Zebedee (their father) in a small fishing fleet on the Lake of Galilee. It is hardly correct, perhaps, to think and speak of them as 'poor fishermen.' They had at least two large boats, or 'ships' as these are termed in our Testaments, and in the first chapter of the Gospel of *Mark,* when Jesus called James and John to follow Him, we read, 'they left their father Zebedee in the ship with the hired servants and went after him.'

From the use made of these ships, too, for long journeys and for night fishing, it is evident that they must have been of considerable size, and that in all probability some of the most important fishing of the lake was done by the men of these two families and the fishermen they employed to assist them in their work.

These partners of the brothers James and John (Andrew and Peter) had their friends also, notably Philip and Nathaniel, and these soon joined the circle of disciples. To each one came the Divine call, clear and unmistakable, and each was obedient to the Voice that called him; but simple human ties of family love and friendship were, then as now, the cords by which their hearts were drawn to the Eternal Love who dwelt among them, and it was the illuminating power of the human love that was in them that opened their eyes to behold His glory – 'the glory as of the only begotten of the Father, full of grace and truth.'

At the time the main narrative of the Gospel opens Andrew and Peter and Philip are living at Bethsaida (*John* 1:44, 45), one of the cities on the Lake of Galilee. James and John (the Evangelist) are almost necessarily their neighbours. Mary, the sinner (afterwards known as Mary Magdalene), is at her house in Magdala; St. John the Baptist is baptizing at Bethabara beyond Jordan; Nathaniel is probably living at Cana (*John* 21:2), the little town of the wedding feast and first miracle, while our Lord is still living at Nazareth with His mother and brethren.

If we take a rough map of the Lake of Galilee with the River Jordan running through it, we see that Capernaum is seated towards the northern aspect of the lake, Magdala about midway on its western border, and Bethsaida between the two. Cana lies to the west, about twelve miles off, and Nazareth five miles farther still.

The exact locality of Bethabara (the House of the Ford), called Bethbarah in *Judges*, and Bethany by Edersheim, is uncertain; but it appears to have been below the southern boundary of the lake at the natural ford of the Jordan where the river can be crossed without a boat. It is not improbable, indeed, that there was more than one Bethabara – wherever there was a ford, the House of the Ford might rightly be termed Bethbarah – but the place certainly given this name was the village or resting-place exactly opposite Jericho, from which the Israelites started on their first entrance into the land of Canaan. It was probably here at the old fording-place (Bethabara) that John the Baptist began his ministry, and all classes appear to have been attracted by his preaching. It would even appear that his mission, although essentially a national one, did not altogether exclude those who belonged to another race, for there is some reason to believe that a few foreigners – and notably some Greeks from Ephesus – were admitted by St. John as his disciples. All who were so admitted, whether Jews or Gentiles, were 'baptized in Jordan confessing their sins.'

From the fact that it was at Bethabara beyond Jordan where John was baptizing – quite possibly at the old Bethbarah immediately facing Jericho, where the Israelites had crossed from the wilderness into Canaan, and where our Lord is described as 'going or coming up out of the water' when the Holy Ghost descended upon Him – one cannot help wondering if this baptism of St. John did not essentially consist (after solemn confession of sin) of a ceremonial passage of the Jordan and a re-entry into the land of Canaan. St. John the Baptist stood on the further or 'wilderness' side of Jordan, and those who came to him confessing their sins – not only their own sins but the sins of their nation – may have been solemnly encouraged and commanded by him (if fully intending to keep God's commandments) to pass through the waters of Jordan into the Holy Land, as their fathers had done at first, and claim from God all the blessings and promises given to their forefathers. If so, what memories and traditions would fill the minds of St. John's disciples as they cast off their sins, renewed their covenant with God, and solemnly crossed over into the Holy Land once more, as their forefathers had crossed under Joshua!

St. John remained on the farther or wilderness side 'beyond Jordan.' Who would be their second Joshua to lead them on their journey or fight beyond the passage? One cannot be surprised that after the announcement of St. John his disciples one by one turned their eager eyes from him to Jesus, and seemed almost to forget the Baptist in their expectancy and wonder of all that might grow out of the following of this greater leader – this newer movement and further fellowship.

For a time, during the whole of St. John's ministry, the residences of the little group of Master and disciples remained practically unchanged; but when John was cast into prison (*Matthew* 4:12), the necessity for greater nearness and communion between the disciples and our Lord became increasingly urgent, and so we find our Lord and His mother and the brethren of Jesus leaving their home at Nazareth and coming up to Capernaum, where they would be nearer to their relations, James and John, and to their friends, Peter and Andrew.[3]

Here they evidently took a house, for henceforth Capernaum is known as our Lord's own city. About the same time – perhaps it was because of this – Peter and Andrew, who had as we know been living at Bethsaida, left their old home and took a house for themselves at Capernaum. It must have been a large one, for James and John had rooms with them, while Peter was married, and we are told that his wife and his wife's mother lived with him. Whether it was in this house or His own that Christ healed the bedridden man who was sick of the palsy we cannot tell, but we can gather a good deal of information respecting such a house as that of Peter from the account of the miracle, and from the descriptions of similar old residences in the East. It appears to have been built – like many of our very old inns, colleges, or larger houses – in a quadrangular or four-sided form, containing therefore a court or open space in the centre. At that time staircases inside a house were quite unknown, but there were steps or stairways on the outside, leading to the flat roof of the house, and on the inside of the courtyard another shorter set of steps leading to a lightly covered gallery or veranda which went all round the inside of the building, and communicated with the rooms of the upper storey.

It is supposed to have been from this gallery or from the top of the steps leading up to it that our Lord taught the people who thronged the 'quad,' or courtyard, to hear Him, and so when they not only filled this space, but the gateway out into the road or street, it was impossible for a visitor to find immediate entrance. In the case of the sick man mentioned by St. Mark (*Mark* 2:3), the only course for his friends to pursue was to carry him up the outside stairway to the roof of the house, to break up the light covering of the verandah and then lower him down to the gallery where Jesus was standing.

Shall we for a moment stop and try to imagine one of these evening teachings? The news goes round the city that Jesus is at home, 'and straightway many are gathered together insomuch that there is no room to receive them – no, not so much as about the door, and Christ preaches the Word unto them' (*Mark* 2:2). One sees our Blessed Lord standing at the top of the little steps facing the entrance of the house; around Him are grouped the four chief disciples, James and John and Peter and Andrew, and His brethren, James the Less, Jude and Simon. Behind Him is, perhaps, the open door of the guest-room, and within, the Virgin Mother pondering the scene and all its meaning in her heart. Before Him, stretching out as far as He can see, are the upturned faces of the people, not only filling the courtyard but standing in the doorway directly facing Him, while over all is the roofing of the starlit heavens. There is hardly any twilight so far south: the summer sun sets quickly, and as the darkness gathers one can imagine James and John holding some kind of torch on either side, illuminating the face of Jesus, so that those in the distance can better see His face and understand what He is saying. The crowd is hushed and expectant; many are tired after the hard day's work, but not too tired to stand and look into the face of Jesus – that face touched with the feelings of our infirmities, yet shining with the Divine consciousness of power to heal them – and every ear is open to receive the message as with hands outstretched the gracious words fall from the Master's lips:

'Come unto Me, all ye that labour and are heavy laden, and I will give you rest. Take My yoke upon you, and learn of Me; for I am meek and lowly in heart, and ye shall find rest unto your souls.

31

For My yoke is easy, and My burden is light.'

It is about this Capernaum life that most is known. We are told that Capernaum was a Roman settlement with a castellated fort on a promontory overlooking the Lake of Galilee. It was the centre of Roman government and taxation in Galilee, and possessed a garrison with centurions and other officers.

Civil representatives of the Roman power were stationed there, and its position at the junction of four great roads from Arabia, Egypt, Tyre and Damascus made it an important centre of travel and commerce. The town was a large one, and by its wealth and the richness of its buildings must have held a very distinguished place in the adjacent country. Our Lord Himself spoke of it as 'exalted to heaven'; and although this may have had mainly a spiritual significance, it is not improbable that the height and magnificence of the architecture displayed in many of its public buildings may have suggested the exaltation to which our Lord referred.

At the time of the Roman occupation it had become a notable city, and of the somewhat extensive ruins that still are supposed to mark the ancient site, it is interesting to note that the most important appear to be the remains of a synagogue dating from the Roman period. The building was of white marble, with finely-carved Corinthian columns, and upon the stones which entered into its formation sculptured representations have been found of the seven-branched candlestick, the paschal lamb and the pot of manna. There can be no reasonable doubt that this was the synagogue built at his own charge by the Roman centurion and governor. He was evidently a man of very great wealth as well as of great influence. He was accustomed to say to one man, 'Go,' and he went, and to his servant, 'Do this,' and he did it; and in all probability his own palace was of marble, standing in spacious and well-cultivated grounds.

This, and the barracks or forts where his soldiers lived, and the central synagogue, which he had given to the people among whom he dwelt, would doubtless dominate the city; and as one looked at the blue waters of the Lake of Galilee washing the marble steps which led to the governor's house, flanked, perhaps, on either side by castellated forts of strength and beauty, the white stone gleaming in the brilliant tropic sunshine, and then looked farther at the grove of palm-trees surrounding the residency, and then still farther at the rising ground where the marble synagogue stood in all its clear-cut beauty of outline and of sculpture, the rows of Corinthian columns forming a delicate tracery against the deep blue background of the Eastern sky, one cannot be surprised that our Lord recognized its beauty, that He acknowledged its greatness and exaltation, and was profoundly moved as He foresaw its destruction.

Some may think perhaps that the picture I have drawn is somewhat fanciful and highly coloured, yet it rests on very fair foundation. In any country possessing a beautiful inland sea the banks of the lake would be naturally unusually fertile. The mountain streams running into the lake would provide an abundance of pure water, and the loveliness of the surroundings could not fail to attract the wealthier inhabitants of the country as well as the foreign rulers, both of whom would naturally build their houses at the margin of the lake. The word Gennesareth is said to mean 'Gardens of Princes' and Capernaum appears to be one of the most famous of these gardens.

The governor, centurion, or captain of the guard, quartered in Capernaum, and in the service of Herod Antipas, became, as we know, a friend and disciple of Jesus – a kind man who not only loved the Jews among whom he lived, but loved and took care of his humblest servants and dependants. We remember how his first introduction to our Lord was occasioned by his anxiety for a servant who was ill, and can imagine how Christ, who knew the heart as well as the outward bearing of the man, must have rejoiced to recognize this love and kind consideration.

Another important resident of Capernaum was the nobleman whose son was healed by our Saviour. Some have identified him with Chuza, Herod's servant, whose wife Joanna followed our Lord and ministered to Him. However this may be, we are definitely told that 'himself believed and his whole house,' so that all his family became disciples. Another important resident was Jairus, the chief ruler of the synagogue. He had heard Jesus speak and teach in his synagogue, and had been astonished at His doctrine, for (we read) 'He taught as one having authority, and not as the scribes.' He had also witnessed the healing of the man who had an unclean spirit within the walls of the synagogue, but it was the illness and death of his little daughter, just grown into womanhood, that brought him a suppliant at the feet of Jesus. And when his daughter was given back to him, restored to life and health, after all the attendants '*knew*' that she was dead, it seems that both father and mother could hardly believe it. We read that they were astonished, and Christ Himself had to remind them that she needed food to eat. Whatever knowledge, friendship, or faith existed before between the ruler of the synagogue and our Lord, this would increase it a thousand-fold; and it is therefore not surprising that Jairus, who as ruler had superintendence of Divine service in the synagogue at Capernaum, who could choose the readers of the Law and of the Prophets, and the speaker, if any, to deliver the sermon or address, should hereafter welcome our Lord's ministry in the synagogue service, and ask Him to speak to the people on the Sabbath days. Some of these sermons have come down to us, and one of them is especially remembered as having been spoken by Jesus in this synagogue of Capernaum.

Another householder of the city whose house we read of was Matthew. He was, as we know, a revenue officer, one of the Jews, but in the employment of the Roman Government. As you walked down through the city to the border of the lake you would naturally come to the landing-stage or quay, where the ships of James and John and Peter would be lying moored when the disciples were at home. Close by would be the custom-house, and here the office of Matthew, whose duty it would be to collect the harbour charges for all boats coming in, and probably to levy duty on both exports and imports as they went or came across the lake. So, as we read in the Gospels, it was as Christ 'went forth by the sea-side' that He saw Matthew (or Levi) sitting at the receipt of custom, and said unto him, 'Follow me.' 'And he left all, rose up, and followed him.'

Immediately afterwards we find in *Luke* that Matthew made our Lord a great feast in his own house, and gathered together a 'great company' to meet Him. As the stricter Jews would not associate with tax-collectors in Roman employ, this would be quite a different gathering from those our Lord might meet at the house of Jairus or of Peter or of the Roman governor, and we find it rather critically and contemptuously alluded to as a company of publicans and sinners!

Incidentally it is interesting to note how widespread was the influence of Jesus in Capernaum. No class was beyond it or outside of it. The wealthy and noble, with the governor at their head – the devout Jews under Jairus, the special commercial class among the friends of St. Matthew, the fishing interest brought by the sons of Zebedee, the poor and nameless who always seemed to follow Him, and the sick and maimed who were brought to Him by others – *all*, for a time in this town, seemed open to His teaching and His influence, and though we may not have realized it before, it was really here that Christendom began.

Shall we count up how many we know who either lived in Capernaum itself or within a walking distance from it?

Jesus and the Blessed Virgin Mary.

James.

John.

Zebedee, Salome.

Peter, Peter's wife, Peter's wife's mother.

Andrew.

Philip.

Bartholomew or Nathaniel (Cana).

James the Less ⎫

Simon   ⎬ Cleopas and Mary, wife of Cleopas.

Jude   ⎭

Matthew.

Thomas Didymus.

The Centurion, or Governor, and his servant.

Chuza and Joanna and their son.

Mary Magdalene (the woman who was a sinner, pardoned by our Lord, and who afterwards followed Him through His ministry).[4]

Jairus, his wife and his daughter.

The man with the unclean spirit.

The sick of the palsy.

The widow of Nain and her son (known afterwards traditionally as 'Maternus').

The man with the withered hand.

The scribe who said, 'Master, I will follow thee whithersoever thou goest.'

The woman who had the issue of blood and trusted and was made whole.[5]

The two blind men who followed Him, after the raising of Jairus's daughter, crying, 'Thou son of David, have mercy on us.'

Some thirty-four or thirty-five personally known to us besides the scribes and Pharisees who attended the synagogue; the people who thronged the courtyard at the evening teaching; the 'great company' of St. Matthew's feast; and the multitude who followed Him and desired to crown Him as an earthly king of the Jews.

A special scene of our Lord's Capernaum life, recorded for us by St. John, appears to have taken place at the end of His residence here. It is a notable one, clearly defined in word and act, and it marks a turning-point, a parting of the ways, in one sense a foretaste of the sorrow of the betrayal and crucifixion.

It was a Sabbath morning at Capernaum. The Sabbath began on Friday evening at sunset, and continued until sunset on Saturday. No servile work was done, the Sabbath was kept with the utmost strictness, and no Scottish or old English Sunday could probably give so utter a sense of quiet and calm as that which brooded over the day of rest by the Lake of Galilee. Jesus was preaching in the synagogue, and the synagogue would be crowded to the doors. It was Passover time, and only the day before our Lord had been feeding the five thousand with five barley loaves and two small fishes on the further or eastern side of the Lake of Galilee. Not only would nearly all the town try to come to the synagogue service, but many of those who had been miraculously fed came over the lake seeking Jesus. Through all the ages human nature has not varied much, and from every part we might watch the people thronging towards the central synagogue. Some are coming in boats across the water, others are streaming down from the hill country on the western side of the town, but all alike are full of expectation and of interest, and are probably talking of the great Teacher and of the miracle of yesterday.

To simple and holy hearts Heaven would be very close to earth at such a season, and as they go up to the House of God some are probably repeating the songs of degrees with which the devout were encouraged to draw near to the Temple at Jerusalem – 'I will lift up mine eyes unto the hills, from whence cometh my help.' 'He that keepeth Israel slumbers not nor sleeps.' So, on that Sabbath morning, in many little companies and from all the country round, came throngs of worshippers streaming to the synagogue. In one of the descriptions of this synagogue it is said to have been peculiar in having the carving of the pot of manna over the entrance. While many of the other synagogues in Galilee (the remains of which have been discovered) appear to have possessed carvings of the seven-branched candlestick and paschal lamb, this is the only one on which there are traces of the third sign or emblem of the pot of manna or heavenly food with which the Israelites were fed in the wilderness; and it is definitely stated (Edersheim) that the lintel itself has been discovered, and that it bears not only the device of the pot of manna, but that this is ornamented with a flowing pattern of vine leaves and clusters of grapes.

So the season of the year (the Passover and the special eating of the paschal lamb), the miraculous feeding of the day before, and the carved device over the entrance of the synagogue, all would combine to suggest and enforce the subject of the morning's teaching. What this was we learn from the sixth chapter of the Gospel of *John*. It was Christ the Bread of Life. As in our imagination we follow the crowd within the entrance and stand against one of the pillars of the sanctuary we hear Him saying: 'Not as your fathers did eat manna, and are dead. But the Bread of God is He that cometh down from heaven, and giveth life unto the world. I am the Bread of Life; he that cometh to Me shall never hunger, and he that believeth on Me shall never thirst.'

An angry murmur runs round the seats of the elders. 'Is not this Jesus, the son of Joseph, whose father and mother we know? How is it then that He saith, I came down from heaven?'

Again He speaks: the voice which had stilled the tempest on the

Lake of Galiee, the voice that had raised the dead to life, the voice that had commanded and given food to the five thousand in the wilderness rises once more in conscious power and sovereignty! – 'Verily, verily, I say unto you, Except ye eat the flesh of the Son of man, and drink His blood, ye have no life in you. Whoso eateth My flesh, and drinketh My blood, hath eternal life; and I will raise him up at the last day. For My flesh is meat indeed, and My blood is drink indeed.' 'These things said He in the synagogue as He taught in Capernaum.'

Let us take one last look at Jesus on this memorable Sabbath morning. He is standing on the synagogue steps, for the service is over. 'From that time many of His disciples went back, and walked no more with Him.' Many of those who had been accustomed to stand beside Him and to offer Him outward deference and homage, many of those who had been half-inclined to follow Him – these have hurried away from the synagogue to their homes, and on His face one seems to see for the first time the bitter, pitying grief of the 'Man of Sorrows' who came to His own, and found that His own received Him not. Turning Himself about He sees His Apostles round Him, but even among them he recognizes that one of the last who has joined, Judas Iscariot, a native of Judaea, and not as all the rest from Galilee, is a traitor in his heart; and with that human affection which almost pleads for understanding and for sympathy, we hear Him say: 'And will ye also go away?' Then Simon Peter answered Him, 'Lord, to whom shall we go? Thou hast the words of eternal life, and we believe and are sure that Thou art that Christ, the Son of God.'

Many years afterwards another of those who were present – looking back on a long life and thinking of this and of all that followed – wrote quietly and confidently: 'But as many as received Him, to them gave He power to become the sons of God . . . which were born, not of blood, nor of the will of the flesh, nor of the will of man, but of God' (*John* 1:12, 13).

1. From the earliest times, the ships of Israel sailed with the ships of Tyre, with the result that all, regardless of nationality, became known as Phoenicians. (Ed.)

2. All these regions were inhabited by Greek-speaking peoples of Israel's 'dispersion.' (Ed.)

3. *Matthew* 4:13, 9:1; *Mark* 2:1.

4. In tradition we are told that the mother of Mary Magdalene was of the blood royal of the House of Israel, and therefore distantly related to St. Joseph and the Blessed Virgin (see 'Life of Rabanus,' cap. i).

5. This woman is said by Eusebius to have been a native of Caesarea Philippi, a town to the north of Capernaum. He states (E.H.B., vii, cap. 18): 'Her house is (still) shown in the city, and the wonderful monuments of our Saviour's benefit to her are still remaining. At the gates of her house, on an elevated stone, stands a brazen image of a woman on her bended knees with her hands stretched out before her like one entreating. Opposite her there is the image of a man, decently clad in a mantle and stretching out his hand to the woman. Before her feet and on the same pedestal there is a certain strange plant growing which, rising as high as the hem of the brazen garment, is a kind of antidote to all kinds of diseases. This statue, they say, is a statue of Jesus Christ, and it has remained even to our times; so that we ourselves saw it while tarrying in that city.'

CHAPTER II

THE MAKING OF THE SAINTS

JERUSALEM

'The pathways of Thy land are little changed
    Since Thou wast there:
The busy world through other ways has ranged
    And left these bare.

The rocky path still climbs the glowing steep
    Of Olivet:
Though rains of two millenniums wear it deep
    Men tread it yet.

Still to the gardens o'er the brook it leads
    Quiet and low:
Before his sheep, the shepherd on it treads,
    His voice they know.

The wild fig throws broad shadows o'er it still
    As once o'er Thee;
Peasants go home at evening up the hill
    To Bethany.'

Author of the 'Three Wakings,'
from 'Lyra Angelicana.'

The general ground-plan of Jerusalem is probably fairly well known to all readers of biblical history. Facing southwards, the city terminates on the crest of an extended hill, bounded on the west and south and east by valleys, and therefore having a prominent position from almost every point of view, but especially from the south.

This crest is cut irregularly into two by a central valley (the Tyropoean). On the eastern side of this is Mount Moriah, where the Temple stood. On the western side Mount Zion, the site of the palace of David.

This mountain crest or ridge is of no mean height, and before the repeated destruction of the city (which has considerably altered its environment) the picture it presented was prominent and striking. It and the Mount of Olives, which is somewhat higher, are two of the highest points in Palestine, and attain an elevation of some 2,528 feet above the level of the sea. Ages before the coming of our Lord, long before anything had been built here, we are told that Abraham coming towards it 'lifted up his eyes and saw the place afar off' (*Genesis* 22:2-4).

On the summit of this mountain crest the Holy City was afterwards built, and crowning the special heights of Zion and of Moriah in the time of our Lord would be the palace of King Herod and the Temple.

Sheer down from the Temple heights the rock fell like a solid wall to the Valley of Jehoshaphat, and in the time of our Lord, when this was untouched, anyone journeying from the south or south-east towards Jerusalem would see before him the wide moat of the valley, then the bold and rugged face of the mountain wall, and then, high above this, on the left, the mass of towers and columns marking the regal and public buildings on the Hill of Zion; and on the right the massive wall of the Temple platform crowning the summit of Mount Moriah; while yet again above this he would see the upper part of the Temple itself 'covered with beaten gold.'

Jerusalem was a fortified city, and its walls were literally studded with towers of solid masonry. Ninety of these were in the first wall, fourteen in the second, and sixty in the third: one hundred and sixty-four in all. Four of these – named respectively Psephina, Hippicus, Phasaelis and Mariamne – were really magnificent. All were built of solid blocks of white marble. Mariamne was about 77 feet high; Psephina, an octagonal tower, was 122 ½ feet; Hippicus, a square tower, 140 feet; and Phasaelis, more richly ornamented than the rest, formed a stately palace with battlements and pinnacles rising to a height of 167 feet.

Within these towers, on Mount Zion, stood the palace of the kings, of the most extraordinary size and splendour. The pavements were of rare marble, the chambers countless and adorned with all kinds of figures.

Between the buildings of the palace enclosure one might catch glimpses of numerous open squares of beautiful greenness carefully kept, surrounded by cloisters with columns of various orders. Around were groves and avenues with fountains and bronze statues pouring out water.

Such are the descriptions which have come down to us from those who were present at the destruction of Jerusalem. This occurred only between thirty and forty years after the crucifixion of our Lord, and there is therefore not much likelihood of any great difference between this description and the actual condition during the earthly lifetime of our Saviour.

The wall of the city went round the Temple enclosure on Mount Moriah, and at the north-west corner of this was a massive fortress or citadel built by Herod and called 'Antonia.'

This had every convenience of a palace or small city in itself: spacious walls, courts and baths. It appeared like a vast square tower with four other towers, one at each corner: three of these were between 80 and 90 feet in height; that at the corner next to the Temple was above

120 feet.

The Temple enclosure itself occupied a space of about one furlong square – that is, one-eighth of a mile – on every side.

From this extensive platform there rose a series of marble terraces or esplanades, surrounded by cloisters. The first was the Court of the Gentiles, then came the Court of the Women, and then the Court of the Men of Israel. Finally, on the topmost of the marble platforms, as on an elevated stage, visible from every side except the west, there was the Altar of Burnt Offering and the Temple itself.

'Its appearance had everything that could strike the mind and astonish the sight.'

'Where it was not decorated with plates of gold, it was extremely white and glistening.'

'At a distance the whole Temple looked literally like "a mount of snow, fretted with golden pinnacles".'

These descriptive sentences, all taken directly from authorized sources, will help to convey some idea of the wonder and magnificence of the structure which crowned the summit of Moriah, and which called forth the enthusiasm not only of the Hebrews themselves, but of all who saw it.

When the sun rose upon it over the Mount of Olives and touched the golden pinnacles and gates with living light, no eye could bear the dazzling radiance, and Josephus tells us that 'the head was involuntarily lowered' – as if in the immediate presence of the God of Israel.

Never before or since, in all the history of the world perhaps, did such splendid associations and site and architecture meet. Here had been the place where Abraham made ready to offer Isaac upon the altar; here had been the site of the threshing-floor of Araunah the Jebusite, where the destroying angel stayed his hand and King David offered sacrifice; here was the site of the Temple of Solomon, which had been filled with the visible presence of the Lord of Hosts; and, although times of desolation had intervened, here again, in far greater beauty and splendour, was the wonderful creation of the master-builder Herod – a second Temple, surpassing anything that the world had hitherto dreamed of.

It was, then, to this Jerusalem – gorgeous with the palace of the kings upon Mount Zion – sublime and awful in its claims to Divine enshrining on Moriah – that Jesus came.

Of the tribe of Judah, of the seed of David, before Him, on the one hand, was the magnificent palace and symbol of sovereignty which was, I suppose, indubitably His by right of human inheritance – at all events, we know of no other so directly in the line of succession from King David. On the other hand, there was His Father's House, hallowed by innumerable traditions – hallowed, too, by the holy lives and service of men and women who had worshipped therein, but unhallowed by sins of greed and hate, and even murder, which had been committed within the Temple precincts.

What a wonderful picture do we see of the King of the Jews, who came to His Kingdom – both spiritual and temporal – at Jerusalem!

He came to His own on Mount Moriah, to that beautiful Temple – where by a striking and perhaps purposed coincidence *the Holy of Holies was empty*: waiting for the Word made Flesh to replace the word engraven on stone – and 'His own received Him not.'

On the other hand, it may almost be said that His own earthly inheritance came to Him and asked for His possession. Archelaus had been deposed and banished to Vienne (in Gaul), and though a Roman governor had been appointed, anyone who had the affections and the will of the people in his keeping might perhaps have been acknowledged by

Rome. The band of Galilean disciples who were His devoted adherents were ready at His slightest word to do His bidding; the people themselves came in force to make Him their King. His own earthly kingdom offered itself to Him – 'came to Him' – and more or less distinctly, of His free choice and purpose, He refused it.

So, except for the triumphal procession through the Golden Gate before His crucifixion, there was no public entrance into and acceptance of this earthly sovereignty. His Kingdom was not of this world, and it was rather to His Church of the 'Twelve' and of the 'Seventy,' of the scattered adherents in various places and of the holy women who followed Him, that Christ revealed Himself.

Some of these came with Him from Galilee to Jerusalem; notably, James and John and their mother Salome. With them and in their company came the Blessed Virgin, Cleopas, Mary the wife of Cleopas, their sons, Mary Magdalene and Joanna. Peter also, and indeed all of the twelve Apostles, appear to have been of the final company which gathered round our Saviour at the close of His earthly ministry. So that there were many associations and memories which bound together the old Capernaum life with the later life in Jerusalem. This 'later life,' as depicted for us in the Gospels, shows us the same inner circle of relations and friends surrounding and attending the person of the Saviour, but, fully admitted into the closest fellowship with them, we find the residents of Bethany: Martha, 'the hostess of the Lord'; Lazarus, her brother; and Simon, their traditional kinsman, all of whom delighted to entertain the Saviour and His disciples. And the chief connecting link between these disciples of Bethany and those of Galilee appears to have been St. Mary Magdalene.

For, according to a very old tradition (accepted by such writers and fathers of the Church as Tertullian, St. Ambrose, St. Jerome, St. Augustine, St. Gregory, the Venerable Bede, Rabanus, St. Odo, St.

Bernard and St. Thomas Aquinas), St. Mary Magdalene was none other than St. Mary of Bethany.

If we turn to the first account of the Bethany family in the Gospel of *John*, at the beginning of the 11th chapter, we read as follows:

'Now a certain man was sick, named Lazarus, of Bethany, the town of Mary and her sister Martha. (It was that Mary which anointed the Lord with ointment, and wiped His feet with her hair, whose brother Lazarus was sick.)'

'It was that Mary which anointed the Lord.' This phrase is evidently used by the Apostle to make it clear to his readers the personality of the Mary of whom he is writing.

Now, the only anointing of our Lord which had taken place at this time was that which we read of in the 7th chapter of the Gospel of Luke, when (as we are told) 'a woman of the city, which was a sinner . . . brought an alabaster box of ointment, and stood at Jesus' feet behind Him weeping, and began to wash His feet with tears, and did wipe them with the hair of her head, and kissed His feet, and anointed them with the ointment.'

This seems to have taken place in Galilee, at one of the lakeside cities – possibly Capernaum or Magdala – at the house of Simon the Pharisee; and although no name is given throughout the narrative of St. Luke, the woman of the anointing has always been identified with Mary Magdalene, who (as we read in the very next chapter) from this time followed our Lord and ministered to Him.

So firmly held throughout all the ages has been this traditional ascription, that our own translators who divided the Bible into chapters and texts have not hesitated to use the name of Mary Magdalene in the table of contents, as we see it in many of our Bibles of today.

'It was that Mary which anointed the Lord.' Then Mary of Magdala (or Mary Magdalene) and Mary of Bethany must apparently have been one and the same – 'Mary of Bethany' – in the house of her childhood, the home of her father and mother and sister and brother; 'Mary of Magdala' in the house of her sin, when found and healed by the love of Jesus and finally restored by Him to her kindred at Bethany.

The acceptance of this interpretation and tradition (strangely repugnant as it is to many English minds) is by no means essential to the following of the after-life of St. Mary Magdalene as pictured for us in tradition, but it undoubtedly has a material bearing on this, and appears to throw considerable light on several subsidiary points in the Gospel narrative which are otherwise obscure.

'The house of Mary and her sister Martha' (Mary is mentioned first, as earliest and best known of all the three);

The greater knowledge and love possessed by Mary;

The passing impatience of Martha that her sister (who had sinned) should be preferred before her;

The utter disappearance of Mary of Bethany (if she were not Mary Magdalene) both at the crucifixion and burial of our Lord – all this and more, impossible to quite understand without this explanation, becomes clear and intelligible.

The very terms used by the writers of the Gospels almost forbid any other solution. To the very earliest Christians – the disciples of the Gospels – there are only three Marys known: Mary, the mother of our Lord; Mary, the wife of Cleopas; and Mary Magdalene. Later on we read of another Mary, the mother of St. Mark, but this was after the ascension.

Consequently, when St. Matthew writes of the burial and the resurrection, knowing that St. Mary, the mother of Jesus, had been taken home by St. John and could not have been present at these later scenes, he repeatedly speaks of 'Mary Magdalene and the other Mary,' meaning Mary, the wife of Cleopas. If there had been any possibility of yet another Mary, especially one so loving and beloved as Mary of Bethany, it is scarcely believable either that she could have been absent or that St. Matthew could have used this language.

Of course, there was another anointing – the final anointing of our Saviour – indubitably done by Mary at Bethany shortly before the betrayal and crucifixion. This, which by the hand of any other than hers who was Mary of Magdala, as well as Mary of Bethany, would have seemed a feeble copy of the first anointing, derives fresh beauty when we recognize that it was the same loving heart that once, in deepest penitence, had come falteringly, with the alabaster box of ointment, to the feet of Jesus, that now, three years later, assured of forgiveness, reanoints her Saviour and Messiah with the costly spikenard. No longer weeping, not daring to draw near, but with a rapt and holy confidence, she now not only bathes the feet of her Master in remembrance of her first anointing, but coming nearer pours the costly perfume on His head.

So among the friends of Jesus, 'Mary of Magdala,' 'Mary of Bethany,' 'St. Mary Magdalene' and her intimate associates, Mary, the wife of Cleopas, Salome and Joanna, appear to have had a special pre-eminence, not only on account of their love and devotion throughout the whole of the Saviour's ministry, but also because they alone of all the disciples (save the Blessed Virgin and St. John) appear to have been absolutely faithful in the darkest days of suffering and of agony.

And Bethany, near Jerusalem, the house of Martha and her brother Lazarus and of Mary Magdalene, their sister who had come back to them, naturally became the home of Jesus when He visited Jerusalem. We know that the Saviour and His Apostles stayed here, walking backwards and forwards from Jerusalem, and the tireless feet of thousands of loving pilgrims have ever since been treading in their footsteps and searching for some traces of their presence.

The situation remains much the same – here is the pathway, there the hill; but the surroundings have altered sadly. Where formerly there was cultivation and beauty there is now desolation and decay, and this seems to be increasing.

But when Jerusalem was in its glory, and the village on the slope of Olivet was nestling in the shade of palm-trees and surrounded by olive, almond and pomegranate-trees (as described by some of the oldest travellers), it is easy to understand the restfulness, quiet and beauty of this cool retreat within two miles of the city.

Let me guide you, as we follow the footsteps of our Lord along (to Him) the well-remembered journey. We walk along the 'Dolorous Way' through which our Saviour passed (but in the opposite direction) to His awful crucifixion, then under the 'Ecce Homo' arch, which is supposed to be part of the fortress or citadel of 'Antonia' still standing, and to mark the place where Pilate brought forth our Lord wearing the crown of thorns and the purple robe, and said to the people, 'Behold the Man!' (*John* 19:5).

This fortress of Antonia, which contained the Judgment Hall of Pilate, was at the north-west corner of the Temple enclosure. Almost by the side of this northern wall we pass to the eastern boundary of the city and out by the gate of St. Stephen to the country beyond.

Just outside the gate is the brook Kedron, now generally empty, and almost directly in front of us is the Mount of Olives. A little on our right is the Garden of Gethsemane.

Leaving this behind us, we bear directly eastward for a mile and a half or so over the mountain, for Bethany lies on the farther slope.

At the highest point of the ascent we naturally wait and turn for a moment to note the wonderful view of Jerusalem, and especially of the

Temple, from the Mount of Olives.

On higher ground than Mount Moriah, we look down on the Temple precincts. In the clear Eastern air everything is plainly visible; even individual figures stand out sharply defined and prominent as in a picture. Here, at the offering of the evening sacrifice, the officiating priests, the surrounding worshippers, the Altar of Burnt Offering, the smoke of the sacrifice and even the victim itself – all would be plainly visible, and the low and plaintive chant of the Levites singing the psalms of the day would be heard more or less distinctly when the wind was in the west.

How often, I suppose, did the pious wayfarer pause at such a time as this and, prostrating himself on the grass by the roadside, join his supplications with those of the daily service:

'Let the words of my mouth, and the meditation of my heart, be always acceptable in Thy sight, O Lord, my strength, and my Redeemer.'

Over the brow of the mountain we soon come within sight of the village of Bethany. It lies in a little hollow of the hills. The palm-trees are gone, but the surrounding pasturage is green and good, and together with the tender grey of the foliage of the olive-trees forms a delicate setting for all we try to recall. The quiet house, the two sisters waiting for our Lord, the restored Lazarus who has become the unceasing wonder not only of his hamlet but of the adjoining city, the open tomb in which he had been buried, and the house of Simon, the rich man who had been a leper, and who, after his healing, made the latest happy feast we have recorded in honour of his deliverer and Lord.

All this we remember as we look at Bethany, for all these things are pictured for us in the Gospels. Much beyond this may be left to our imagination. Mary Magdalene already knew most, if not all, of the Apostles, and Salome (the mother of James and John) and Mary, the wife of Cleopas, were now her dearest friends and would frequently be found at Bethany. Joanna, too, who followed Jesus from the beginning with Mary (*Luke* 8:2, 3), would naturally stay at Bethany when coming to Jerusalem, and as a matter of fact we find her accompanying Mary to the tomb of Jesus when the angels appeared to them and told them of His resurrection (*Luke* 24).

Bethany was the earliest as well as the latest home of the Master at Jerusalem, and it was probably here that Nicodemus came by night to hold the converse with our Saviour recorded in the Gospel of *John.*

In fact, all through the latter part of the three years' ministry we may reasonably regard Bethany as a centre of early Christian discipleship and conference such as cannot be found anywhere else since the old days at Capernaum.

Lazarus, we know, had numbers of friends, and it was from Bethany along the lower road and through the Golden Gate of the Temple (now closed) that the palm procession passed when the people 'strawed' their garments in the way and shouted, 'Blessed is He that cometh in the name of the Lord: Hosanna in the highest!'

How marked a centre was Bethany, and what hospitality the little town could furnish when necessity arose, we can gather from the Gospel of *Mark*, who tells us that after the triumphant entry into Jerusalem Jesus and all the twelve Apostles returned to Bethany in the evening and rested here until the morrow. From this it would almost seem that after the raising of Lazarus the whole of the village had become followers of Jesus, and ready to welcome and to honour all who were especially His disciples.

Very different from this was the attitude of the inhabitants of the neighbouring city. Here the Jews appear to have been under the influence of the chief priests and Sanhedrin, and no one dared openly to profess his adherence to the teaching and person of the new Master and Leader, who had claimed to be the Messiah. The only one we are told of who thoroughly did this – the man who was born blind (*John* 9) – was cast out of the Temple, and probably had to claim protection of the Romans. Henceforth, according to tradition, he was known as Restitutus, and lost all place and recognition as a Jew.

Joseph of Arimathea and Nicodemus had residences in Jerusalem, and had both come under the influence of Jesus. They knew Him to be good. In their hearts they were ready to acknowledge Him, but it was only secretly and little by little that they dared to show any real appreciation of Himself, His mission, or His followers.

Nicodemus, as one of the Sanhedrin, had once – as we know – the boldness to speak openly in the Council in favour of our Lord, but his words fell on unsympathetic ears, and only provoked a rude reply. It was not until after the crucifixion that both he and St. Joseph finally cast aside all further concealment and lavished at His grave the honour and hospitality which apparently they had not courage enough to offer during His earthly lifetime. St. Joseph begged the body of our Lord from Pilate. Nicodemus brought a hundred pounds of spices, and together they wound the body of Jesus with linen cloths and spices and laid it in the sepulchre belonging to St. Joseph.

In the history of this we seem to gather traces of the beginning of some friendship between St. Joseph and the Bethany family, for Mary was allowed to follow and to see 'where Jesus was laid.'

But even in Jerusalem itself there was one house which can be identified as having afforded shelter to our Lord and His disciples. This was the house of the 'upper chamber' and the Last Supper, and appears to have been visited by Christ both before and after the crucifixion. In it He not only ate the Passover with His disciples and instituted the Eucharistic feast, but later, after His Passion, it was in this house where the disciples were assembled when 'the doors were shut for fear of the Jews' that Jesus came and stood in the midst saying, 'Peace be unto you: as My Father hath sent Me, even so send I you.'

This house of the Last Supper and of the great Commission is said to have belonged to the father and mother of St. Mark, and Barnabas his uncle (*Colossians* 5:10), probably resided with them when he was in Jerusalem. After the crucifixion and ascension it became the general gathering-place of the disciples. All waited here in prayer until the descent of the Holy Ghost at Pentecost, and it was probably in its courtyard or outside it that St. Peter preached his Pentecostal sermon. We are told that it was situated on Mount Zion, and Epiphanius records that it escaped the destruction of Jerusalem by Titus, and that it was afterwards changed into a church. Strange as it may seem, it is said to be 'the one spot in all Jerusalem of unquestioned identity. Besides being described by Epiphanius, it is spoken of by St. Cyril and St. Jerome, and it has been kept in reverent memory ever since' (Biggs, p. 173).

It was in this house (as we are directly told by St. Luke) that the faithful were assembled when St. Peter was delivered from prison by the angel; and it was probably in the upper chamber here where all assembled for that first Council of the Church when the question of the necessity for circumcision was considered and finally rejected.

From all of this, and especially perhaps from *Acts* 1:15, we may safely gather that this residence – even for an Eastern house – was unusually large and commodious, and that one of the rooms or halls in it – probably that known as the upper chamber – was capable of accommodating a very considerable number of persons, 'about one hundred and twenty.'

Did this number comprise all the early 'Christians'? I think not. The mission and the labours of the 'Seventy' seem to have been largely forgotten by most modern writers. Before Christ suffered on the cross these had gone forth preaching repentance and the coming of the Messiah, and there is some reason to believe that certain of the 'Seventy' or 'Seventy-two' had already taken distant journeys, and were absent from Jerusalem at the time of the betrayal and crucifixion. In the 'Recognitions of Clement' St. Barnabas, who is said to have been one of the 'Seventy,' is reported to have been preaching about this time in the city of Rome itself, and his further labours for the Church, recorded in the *Acts of the Apostles,* are in strict accord with the theory of his previous ministry.

On the east of Jerusalem (as we have seen) lay the village of Bethany; in the centre of the Holy City, on Mount Zion, the house and 'upper room,' or church, of the father and mother of St. Mark – called, after the death of his father, 'the house of Mary, the mother of John whose surname was Mark.'

On the west side of the city, some four miles beyond it, we find (at Emmaus) another residence peculiarly sacred to the 'making of the Saints' – the certain residence of Cleopas and also of St. Luke; for no one but himself could well have been the 'other disciple' described by St. Luke as walking home with Cleopas when the Saviour joined them. With them would necessarily dwell the family of Cleopas, while Salome and her two sons James and John (though evidently staying in Jerusalem or at Bethany on the night of the walk to Emmaus) might very probably share the house with Cleopas and St. Luke. The journey from Jerusalem is thus described by Edersheim:[1]

'We leave the city by the western gate. A rapid progress for about twenty-five minutes and we have reached the edge of the plateau. Other twenty-five or thirty minutes, passing here and there country houses, and we pause to look back on the wide prospect far as Bethlehem. A short quarter of an hour more and we have left the well-paved Roman road, and are heading up a lovely valley. The path gently climbs in a north-westerly direction with the height on which Emmaus stands prominently before us. About equi-distant are, on the right, "Lifta," on the left "Kolonieh." The roads from these two, describing almost a semicircle (the one to the north-west, the other to the north-east) meet about a quarter of a mile to the south of Emmaus. Along the course of the stream, which low in the valley is crossed by a bridge, are scented orange and lemon gardens, olive groves, fruit trees, pleasant enclosures, bright dwellings, and on the height lovely Emmaus.'

Both Cleopas and St. Luke were rather old men – St. Luke, with the exception perhaps of St. Joseph of Arimathea and Nicodemus, the most cultivated and intellectual of all the Christians of that date, by profession a physician, by birth a native of Cyrene, and therefore but little acquainted at first with all that had taken place in Galilee; 'he reasoned' with Cleopas, we are told, 'of all that had happened.'

Later on he became a special friend and confidant of the Blessed Virgin Mary, who evidently told him secrets of her life which were hidden from the other evangelists. Where this special intimacy was fostered is a matter of conjecture, but there is considerable reason to suppose that the unknown house of St. John to which he took the Blessed Virgin (*John* 19:27) may also have been with Cleopas at Emmaus, for it was probably in this house that St. Luke began to write his Gospel.

There were, of course, others besides those I have referred to, living in or near Jerusalem during our Lord's ministry, who are mentioned in the Gospels, and who were brought into immediate relationship with our Saviour.

If we try to make a list of these, as we did of those who lived in or near the town of Capernaum, it will give us not only a collective grouping of the persons already well known to us, but an opportunity to add a few accessory names to whom history or tradition ascribes some personal relationship with Jesus. Of these the most interesting are:

Zacchaeus, who lived at Jericho and who had the honour of entertaining our Lord 'the day' that Jesus 'abode at his house.'

The Ruler, who had 'great possessions' and lived at a little distance from Jerusalem, who came to Jesus having 'kept the commandments from his youth up,' and of whom it is said that 'Jesus beholding him loved him' (*Mark* 10:21).

Whether this 'ruler' became afterwards a follower of Jesus, and was the same as the disciple known in tradition by the name of 'Maximin,' must necessarily be doubtful, but the word αρχων 'princeps,' or 'ruler' (the designation given him by St. Luke) is suggestive of the later name of Maximin. St. Maximin is called by Rabanus 'chief of the disciples after the apostles.'

Simon, the Cyrenian, who bore the cross of Jesus.

Theophilus, who was the friend of St. Luke, for whom he wrote the *Acts of the Apostles,* and who has been supposed by some to be the same as Theophilus, the son of Annas.

Ignatius (afterwards Bishop of Antioch), who as a boy is said to have been the child called by our Lord, and 'set in the midst as He was teaching'; and

Marcella, the traditional stewardess of Martha and Lazarus.

Most, too, if not all the deacons chosen by the Apostles and named in the sixth chapter of the *Acts* were probably taken from among those who had 'companied with the Apostles all the time that the Lord Jesus went in and out among them,' and of these Stephen, the first martyr, and Philip, the evangelist, are especially noticeable as being most active in the preaching of the Gospel.

So the full list would be something like this:

St. Mary, the mother of our Lord.

The twelve Apostles (with Matthias).

Joseph called Barsabas, the colleague of Matthias in the choice after Judas.

Stephen
Philip
Parmenas   'Seven men of honest report, full of the Holy
Timon   Ghost and of wisdom,' chosen as deacons (*Acts* 6:5).
Nicholas
Prochorus
Nicanor

Living in the house upon Mount Zion:

The father of John Mark, who made ready the guest chamber for the Passover.

The mother of John Mark, named Mary.

St. Mark himself.

Barnabas, his uncle.

Rhoda, who kept the entrance.

From other houses in the city:

Joseph of Arimathea.

Nicodemus.

Theophilus.
Restitutus.
Bartimaeus.
The man at the pool of Bethesda.
Simon the Cyrenean.
Ignatius the boy (?)

From Bethany:
Simon.
Lazarus.
Martha.
Mary.
Marcella.
Joanna.

From Emmaus:
Cleopas.
Luke.
Mary (the wife of Cleopas).
Salome.
Sarah (the traditional handmaid of Salome).

And from Jericho:
Zaccheus.

A very similar number, perhaps, to that of the Capernaum district, but representing only a very small proportion of the inhabitants of Jerusalem and the towns adjacent. If, however, we think of this handful of disciples as not only following our Saviour through His later ministry, but partaking in some measure of the agony of His Passion and as witnesses of the mysteries of His resurrection and ascension, we shall at once recognize that most of these are in nearer approach to Him and have drunk more deeply of His Spirit than could have been possible in the old Capernaum days; and if, apart from the mother of our Lord, we are bold enough to think of any names as standing out more prominently in this sacred fellowship, will it not be just those of whom we have been chiefly thinking – the family of Salome, the family of Bethany, and the family of Cleopas and St. Luke? They have already suffered for His sake, and linked to them by this fellowship of suffering are Restitutus, the man cast out from the Temple and, in less near approach perhaps, Joseph and Nicodemus. Some of the future deacons, too, and notably Stephen and Philip, would probably be of their company. All of these have incurred the displeasure of the Jews, and especially of the highest and most powerful class, the priestly circle of the Sanhedrin. Henceforward, whatever others might do, these would be likely more and more to follow the teaching of Christ, to live as in His presence, to let the older ritual and observances pale and pass before the Eucharistic sacrifice, to be filled with love for all who believed in and honoured their Master, and to find their truest fellowship not among their brethren who had disowned Him, but among those, however despised and rejected, irrespective of class or nationality, whose hearts were filled with love and adoration for the risen Jesus.

1. *Jesus the Messiah*, p. 634.

THE FIRST MISSIONARY JOURNEYS

ANTIOCH, ROME, SICILY, SPAIN, GAUL, AFRICA AND THE MEDITERRANEAN ISLANDS

'Come! Pain ye shall have and be blind to the ending.
Come! Fear ye shall have with the skies overcasting.
Come! Change ye shall have for far are ye wending;
    No crown shall ye have for your thirst and your fasting,
Save the kissed lips of love and sweet life everlasting.
    Cry out! for One heedeth who leadeth you Home.'

William Morris

T here can be but little doubt that these, or many among these of whom I have been writing, became the earliest missionaries of Christendom.

Long before the Apostles themselves had left Jerusalem, either before or immediately after the conversion of St. Paul, the chief non-apostolic disciples of our Lord – many, probably, who had been of the number of the 'Seventy' – with or without direct apostolic sanction, began carrying far and wide the news of Christ's Kingdom.

The only names given us in the Bible of which we can be certain are those of St. Luke, St. Stephen, St. Barnabas and St. Philip, but we may safely conclude that all, or nearly all, were Hebrews, for at first they 'preached the word to none but unto the Jews only,' and we know also that none of the Apostles were with them.

We are further told that much of this missionary work was the outcome of enforced dispersion occasioned by the persecution which arose at the martyrdom of St. Stephen.

The passages referring to this are so definite and important that they may well be quoted entire:

'And at that time there was a great persecution against the Church which was at Jerusalem; and they were all scattered abroad throughout the regions of Judea and Samaria, except the apostles,' and 'they that were scattered abroad went everywhere preaching the word' (*Acts* 8:1, 4), and 'now they which were scattered abroad upon the persecution that arose about Stephen, travelled as far as Phenice, and Cyprus, and Antioch, preaching the word to none but unto the Jews only. And some of them were men of Cyprus and Cyrene, which, when they were come to Antioch, spake unto the Grecians, preaching the Lord Jesus. And the hand of the Lord was with them: and a great number believed, and turned to the Lord. Then tidings of these things came unto the ears of the Church which was at Jerusalem: and they sent forth Barnabas, that he should go as far as Antioch, who, when he came, and had seen the grace of God, was glad, and exhorted them all, that with purpose of heart they would cleave unto the Lord. Then departed Barnabas to Tarsus, for to seek Saul: and when he had found him, he brought him to Antioch. And it came to pass, that a whole year they assembled themselves with the Church, and taught much people. And the disciples were called Christians first in Antioch' (*Acts* 11:19-26).

Perhaps few people who are generally acquainted with the Bible recognize who must have been the essential leaders of this great enterprise and how wide-reaching was its influence.

The scattered disciples who were its leaders would necessarily be those who had been living in Jerusalem or its vicinity both before and during the residence and Passion of our Saviour, who were known to have been willing listeners to His teaching and to have been identified in some way with His ministry and discipleship. St. Joseph of Arimathea and Nicodemus, St. Luke and St. Cleopas, St. Martha, St. Mary and St. Lazarus, Joanna who was living with them, and very probably her son; the man who had been born blind and was restored to sight by Jesus, Simon the Cyrenean and St. Philip – all of these (though but few of their names are actually mentioned in the *Acts of the Apostles*) would inevitably become the victims of Jewish suspicion and hatred and be of those who were forced to leave Jerusalem.[1]

The persons with whom we have been familiar in the Gospels have only been temporarily lost. Here we find them again; some at least directly mentioned in Holy Scripture as among these early missionaries, and nearly all the rest (with many accessory names) traditionally associated in one way or another with this great exodus and missionary effort occurring within a short time after the stoning of St. Stephen.

Let us put ourselves – so far as we can – in the place of these first disciples. 'Our Lord and Master has told us to "go and teach all nations," but before this He said, "Go rather to the lost sheep of the House of Israel." We have hitherto lived entirely in Palestine or have only wandered a little beyond its borders. In spite of the gifts of Pentecost we have no continuous gift of divers tongues;[2] and when forced by persecution to leave our country we must either turn to any scattered colonies of our people who will hear us, or to other nations or peoples with whose language and customs we are more or less familiar.

'Most of us have lived in Galilee, on the borders of Syro-Phoenicia. The Phoenicians have been our neighbours, and many of them àre our acquaintances and friends. Some of them have already seen our Lord and have believed in Him, and if they do not speak quite the same language as ourselves there is only a difference of dialect. They understand us and we can talk freely with them (*Mark* 7:26). Whether employed by them or working as merchants with them, we are already identified with their colonization and commerce. From the time of King Solomon, when the Hebrews and Phoenicians possessed a common navy, we have sailed the seas together. Wherever the Phoenician has gone the Hebrew has gone with him, and their colonies extend, as we know, along the borders of the Mediterranean Sea, embracing all the Mediterranean islands, and even extending through the "pillars of Hercules" into the great Atlantic.

'Large populations of our race have permanently settled in Africa, in Egypt and in the parts about Cyrene; while in Tarshish [or Spain] and even the countries beyond it, our sailors who traded and lived[3] there centuries ago have left colonies behind them, who undoubtedly still remember some of the language, traditions, and teaching of their forefathers.

'Most of these colonies of the Dispersion have never been quite forgotten by the Hebrews in Palestine. Accredited messengers from Jerusalem have been in the habit of visiting them at regular intervals, and it is not difficult to obtain quite recent and reliable information regarding their work and condition and welfare.[4]

'Here, then, are the "fields white unto harvest" spoken of by our Lord, ready for the reaping and waiting for the labourers.

'Others, more travelled and more full of pagan learning than ourselves, may hereafter preach the gospel in the great centres of Greece and Rome; we go, as Christ has bidden us, to our brethren and kinsfolk over-seas.

'Christ was with us on the lake of Galilee, and He will still be with us on the Great Sea, though we may not see Him.'[5]

Such would appear to have been the natural thoughts of the purely Hebrew disciples – the almost inevitable response they would give to the voices which were sounding in their ears – the voice of their Master and Lord bidding them go: the voice of persecution driving them before it; and, finally, the voice of all their scattered brethren and half-relations throughout the Phoenician colonies – in Cyprus, Crete and Sicily and Spain, calling – calling.

It is surely no accidental circumstance that the traditional Hebrew missions follow exactly the same course as that of Phoenician colonization, and that the traditional sites of these missions are found accordingly, first, at the Syro-Phoenician towns along the coast as far as Antioch and, secondly, at all the main Phoenician or Phoenician and Hebrew settlements – in Cyprus, in Sicily, in Crete, at Cyrene, in Sardinia and Spain, and finally at the so-called 'Cassiterides,' or Cornwall.

Lucius of Cyrene, whom many have identified with St. Luke, was certainly one of those who preached the Gospel at Antioch (*Acts* 13:1), and it is quite possible that Cleopas went with him, and that both may have been accompanied by the Blessed Virgin.

Associated with St. Luke was 'Simon called Niger,' who may well have been the same as Simon the Cyrenean, the father of Alexander and Rufus, who bore the cross of Jesus. The latter came from Africa, and if of mixed Jewish and African descent would naturally be called Niger on account of his colour.

Beside these (whom we already know in the Gospels) we read of Manaen, the foster-brother of Herod, who (in AD 39) was banished to Lyons, in Gaul; and in the old Aquitaine legends mention is made of St. Martial, 'son of Marcellus and Elizabeth,' and 'cousin of St. Stephen,' as preaching the Gospel at Antioch under St. Peter, and gaining there the special affection of two servants, who followed him afterwards in his travels to Rome and Gaul. One of these, having the curious name of 'Austroclinian,' or 'Aristoclinan,' is evidently referred to in the Book of the 'Acts of Barnabas,' supposed to have been written before AD 478:

> 'And on the following day we came to a certain village where Aristoclinan dwelt. He being a leper, had been cleansed in Antioch, whom also Paul and Barnabas sealed to be a bishop and sent to his village in Cyprus, because there were many Greeks there. And we were entertained by him in a cave in a mountain, and there we remained one day' (*Acts of Barnabas*, Ante Nicene Library, vol. xvi).

St. Euodius, too, and St. Ignatius, each of whom afterwards became Bishop of Antioch – St. Euodius first and St. Ignatius afterwards – may have journeyed there at the time of this first persecution.

St. Lazarus is traditionally associated with the earliest mission to Cyprus. He is honoured there as its first missionary priest, and the chief church at Larnaca is dedicated to his memory.

His supposed tomb is also shown there, but this is empty, and none of his relics have been found in the island, nor is there any local record of his death.

On the other hand, his successor, St. Barnabas, is stated to have suffered martyrdom at Salamis, on the east coast of the island; and during the reign of Justinian his grave is said to have been opened and his body found, with a copy of the Gospel of *Matthew* lying on his breast.[6]

The name of Phenice is open to two interpretations, and its exact meaning in the passage I have quoted is by no means certain. It may either refer to the old Phoenician district, 'the coasts of Tyre and Sidon' (though this in another portion of the *Acts* is called Phoenicia), or to the main seaport on the western side of Crete.

It is not of great importance, perhaps, to settle this point, as we know that men from Cyrene were preaching at Antioch, and Cyrene was at this time united to Crete in order to form the Roman province of 'the Cyrenaciae.'

In any case, the scattering of these disciples would necessarily give them such an experience of distant travel as would almost inevitably prepare the way for further enterprise and more distant journeys in later years.

In Crete the name of the Church of St. Paul and the ruins of the cathedral of St. Titus traditionally connect the island with the Apostolic Age, the Acts of the Apostles and the Epistle to Titus, but the names of the original missionaries or evangelists have been forgotten. Both Crete and Cyrene had a large Jewish population, and Cyrene was famous for its medical school and learning.

The importance of Crete lay in the fact that its seaports formed at this time the great resting-places or ports of call between east and west, being about equally distant from Rome and Marseilles on the west as from Alexandria, Jerusalem and Antioch on the east, and the establishment of a Christian Mission on the island could not fail to spread the knowledge of Christianity to Rome, and even beyond it. The tide of commerce, the tide of culture and learning, the passing and re-passing of military troops would all profoundly affect and be affected by the civilization of the Cretan seaports, and if we desire to form in our minds a correct impression of early Christianity it is well fully to recognize the part played by this advanced outpost of Christian Missions in the very earliest times.

Not, perhaps, that the island itself or its more permanent inhabitants counted for much. Like all countries and districts used mainly as ports of call, and therefore possessing a shifting population, Crete had a bad reputation. Some years later, when St. Paul was writing to Titus, he felt constrained to use towards the Cretans some of the severest language to be found in any of his Epistles. Notwithstanding this, however, the ports of Phenice and the Fair Havens were of just as much value to Christianity as to commerce, being for both the chief halfway shelters across the great sea, from which one could as easily ship to Massilia (Marseilles) as to Caesarea in Palestine.

The great merchants of Tyre and Sidon and of Jerusalem and Caesarea would have their vessels continually calling at these ports; and if, as many have supposed, and as the old Cornish legend has it (see Chap VIII), St. Joseph of Arimathea was one of these merchant princes who had interests in far countries, his own ships may have been trading to Crete, and even beyond it.

The endeavour to trace the beginning of the Christian Church at Rome forms an interesting study. We have evidence of Christian interest and Christian knowledge reaching back to the very earliest times, but it is hardly likely that the disciples and catechumens residing in the city were consolidated into a definite Church until some years later. Some Roman residents, as we are told in the *Acts of the Apostles,* had listened to St. Peter on the day of Pentecost in Jerusalem, and had been witnesses of the extraordinary effects attending the preaching of the Apostles (*Acts* 2:10). These, on their return, could not fail to talk to others of all that they had heard and seen; many would wish for fuller knowledge and teaching, and it is not unlikely that some of the older disciples would be asked to take up their residence in Rome and to minister to those who were already turning away from heathendom or Judaism and fixing their hope on Christ as their Saviour and Messiah.

Whether it was at the time of St. Stephen's martyrdom or even before this (as we shall see) that the fuller news of the Gospel was carried to Rome, it was evidently, I think, by the same band of workers, namely, Hebrews who were not of the number of the 'Twelve,' and yet Hebrews who had companied with the Lord Jesus during most of His ministry.[7]

In St. Paul's letter to the Romans, written before he himself visited Rome, but some twenty years after the time of which I am writing, when a large and important Church had been already formed there (as evinced by his numerous salutations), two names stand out conspicuously:

> 'Andronicus and Junia, my kinsmen and my fellow-prisoners, who are of note among the apostles, and who were in Christ before me.'

They were 'kinsmen,' therefore Hebrews, and almost necessarily Hebrews living under assumed names; for Andronicus and Junia are too distinctively non-Hebraic to have been the original names of Hebrew children. The names were probably rightly chosen by these disciples as less likely to attract hostile notice, as more familiar to the people among whom they were living and, perhaps, as not unlike, either in sound or suggestion, to the original Hebrew names first given to them. These kinsmen are also called Apostles by St. Paul, and not only so, but 'of note among the apostles.' This can hardly mean anything else than that they were noted disciples of Jesus during His earthly ministry.

The Greek word translated kinsmen ('συγγενεις') has no necessary reference to men as distinct from women, and may be applied equally to both sexes. The name 'Junia' has a distinctive feminine terminology; and though it is by no means necessary to take this as the proper name (a possible masculine alternative being Junias), it is the reading which has been accepted by most translators.[8]

Now, the only woman in the Gospels to whom such a description as that of St. Paul could apply, and whose Aramaic name bears sufficient resemblance to the Latin name in the Epistle, is Joanna, for which name there was at this date no perfect Latin equivalent. Joanna followed the Lord from Capernaum throughout the whole course of His ministry; she was present at the sepulchre with Mary Magdalene, and it is not so very improbable that she and her son (?)[9] may have been pioneers of Christian life and work in Rome. In any case, we have the fact recorded that noted disciples of our Lord, who were already disciples when St. Paul was converted, were working at Rome before St. Paul had visited the city. These must almost necessarily have been of those who were 'scattered abroad upon the persecution that arose about Stephen.'

In all these places – Antioch, Cyprus, the Cyrenaciae and Rome – the first evangelization was apparently accomplished by missionary disciples who were not of the 'number of the Twelve.' St. Peter and St. Paul took up their work, organized the believers into definite Churches, with Church discipline and government, and appointed bishops to rule over them. In this way St. Barnabas was appointed bishop of Cyprus and St. Titus first bishop of Crete. In all these cases, however, and probably in many others of which we are ignorant, the constructive work of the Apostles followed the evangelistic work of other disciples.

If we gather up all the information given us in the New Testament regarding these early missionary efforts and the circumstances attending them, certain conclusions may, I think, be fairly drawn, which, for clearness' sake, I will venture to tabulate.

1. Many of the earliest missionaries went westward to the Phoenician colonies. Most, if not all, of the Apostles remained for a considerable time in the East and chiefly at Jerusalem.

2. Among these early missionaries of Christ one would certainly expect to find, and one does find to some extent, those who were conspicuous

by their attachment to the Saviour in the Gospels.

3. The work done by these missionaries and their successors was primarily among the Jews and Phoenicians of the Mediterranean colonies, and then extended into all parts of the Roman Empire, so that St. Paul some years later (*c.* 64?) was able to speak of 'the truth of the gospel which is come to you as it is in all the world' (*Colossians* 1:5, 6).

4. St. Peter and St. Paul, who were essentially the chief Apostles of the West, took up and organized much of the work of the first enthusiasts and pioneers, in many cases appointing bishops and establishing settled Church order and government, in other cases leaving the natural extension of the Church to the future and to their successors.

5. The chief port from which these missions started was Caesarea, and the local head or 'organizing secretary,' from whom the missionaries went and to whom they returned, appears to have been St. Philip the Evangelist, who settled at Caesarea, and evidently helped the early Christians on their journeys.

So far we have kept almost entirely to New Testament authority – that of St. Paul and St. Luke; but there are traditions, monuments, and even histories, which may carry us further.

The *Recognitions of Clement*, purporting to have been originally written by him in the first century; the *Acts of Barnabas*, which has strong claims to be considered both genuine and reliable; the Life of St. Mary Magdalene and St. Martha, purporting to have been compiled from then existing documents, by Rabanus in the eighth century; and several traditions, Sicilian, Venetian, Provençal, Spanish, Cornish, British, or Welsh, English, and even Greek, contain references to the origin of early Western Christianity, which are at all events worthy of consideration, and have this one great feature in common: the reputed coming of Hebrew disciples of our Lord into the farthest regions of the West in the very earliest years of Christendom.

Now, it is worthy of note that this is very much more consonant with the earliest historical writings than is generally supposed. St. Paul, who was by no means a careless or extravagant or ignorant writer, speaks (as we have already seen) of 'the truth of the gospel which is come unto you as it is in all the world' (*Colossians* 1:5, 6), and doubtless meant what he was writing. He might, perhaps, use the expression 'all the world' as synonymous with the Roman Empire, but any definite part of this world would not be excluded by him.

Eusebius, the historian, writes of Tiberius Caesar as the Emperor under whom the name of Christ was spread throughout the world (bk. ii, c. ii); and Tertullian, in his writings (*c.* AD 200, see Appendix E) which contain the earliest definite references to Christianity in Spain and Germany and England, speaks of the 'farthest ends of Spain' – of 'the diverse nations of the Gauls' – and of the secret strongholds of the Britons 'inaccessible to the Romans,' as all being at this date won for Christ.

This is very much more in accordance with the theory of a much later growth.

Let us accordingly consider some of these legends or traditions which deal with the work of the first century of Christendom.

It will be noticed on reading the earlier chapters of the *Acts of the Apostles* that there is an almost unaccountable absence of the name of St. James the Greater from the company of his fellow-Apostles, St. Peter and St. John, and we read nothing of him until the brief account of his martyrdom when 'Herod the King . . . killed James the brother of John with the sword' (*Acts* 12:1, 2). This is said to have taken place in AD 44. Where was St. James, and what was he doing during the ten preceding years of unrecorded labour?

St. James waited in Jerusalem, as he had been directed, until the first day of Pentecost (*Acts* 1:3), but from this day until that of his death any notice of his life is wanting from the records of the Bible.

St. Peter and St. John were together at Jerusalem during the years immediately following, but nowhere do we read of the presence of St. James with them. This is remarkable, because he had been constantly with them before this. Sole sharer with them of the special revelation on the Mount of Transfiguration, sole sharer with them, again, of the final conversation in the Garden of Gethsemane, his absence from their company afterwards, and especially when 'Peter and John went up together into the Temple at the hour of prayer' (*Acts* 3:1), needs emphatically some explanation. The only possible conclusion is, that their constant companion in the older days must have been absent from Jerusalem.

Now, there are some very old traditions, reaching back to the earliest centuries, which, if accepted, thoroughly explain this phenomenal silence regarding one of the chief of the Apostles.

In these St. James is represented as a distant traveller in the West in the very earliest years after Christ, and as a missionary pioneer in Sardinia and in Spain.

These traditions about St. James are so old and so definite, however improbable they may appear to be, that I make no apology for reproducing their more prominent features. They represent the Apostle as coming from the East and preaching the Gospel both in Sardinia and in Spain; as then returning to Jerusalem for the keeping of the Passover Festival or Easter at Jerusalem, and as suffering martyrdom during this visit to the Church and to his friends in Palestine.

His body is reputed to have been taken care of and brought from Palestine to Spain by loving disciples, who buried him in Spanish ground among the people to whom he had first preached the Gospel of the

Kingdom.

A fact mentioned by contemporaneous historians – both Tacitus and Josephus – makes this mission antecedently more probable than it appears to be at first sight.

About AD 19 we are told by Tacitus (*Annals*, vol. ii, c. 85) that 4,000 youths, 'affected by the Jewish and Egyptian superstitions,' were transported from Italy to Sardinia. These are spoken of as '4,000 Jews' by Josephus (*Antiquities*, bk. xviii, cap. 3), and it is evident that their banishment and forcible enlistment (for they were used as soldiers in Sardinia) made a profound impression on the Jews in Palestine.

Some have supposed that these banished Jews were already believers in Christ or followers of the teaching of St. John the Baptist. This is hardly probable; but it is quite possible that many of them may have been old followers of Judas the Galilean (*Acts* 5:37), who had been living as prisoners in Rome during all the succeeding years. If so, they, or the families from which they came, would be personally known to 'James and John.' They would indeed be 'lost sheep of the House of Israel,' and would have a special and urgent claim on the sympathy of the great Apostle.

The active belief in the legend or tradition of the Spanish mission of St. James appears to date from about AD 820 when the body of the saint was 'discovered' by Theodosius, bishop of Tira. Around the reputed body of St. James there gradually grew the shrine, the cathedral, the city, and finally the pilgrimages of 'Santiago di Compostella.' The original cathedral was consecrated in AD 899, and this was destroyed by the Moors under El Mansui in 997. The later cathedral was founded in 1078 on the site of the one which had been destroyed. But long before the supposed discovery – or rediscovery – of the body of St. James, we have evidence that the essentials of the tradition were held by Spanish inhabitants and Spanish writers. From immemorial times, or at least from

AD 400, we find references to the tradition in old Spanish Offices. In the latter part of the next century or beginning of the seventh (about AD 600) there are three distinct references confirming the tradition of the preaching of St. James in Spain in the writings of Isidorus Hispalensis (vii, 390, 392 and 395; and v, 183), but this author writes of his body as having been buried in 'Marmarica' (Achaia). The tradition is again confirmed by St. Julian, who ruled the Church of Toledo in the seventh century (*Acta Sanctorum,* vol 33, p. 86), and by Freculphus, who wrote about AD 850 (bk. ii, cap. 4). The summing-up of the Bollandists in the *Acta Sanctorum* appears to be decidedly in favour of the thesis that the reputed Spanish mission of St. James is reliable and historical.

The next traditional mission claiming our attention is the mission to Sicily.

Only seven years after the crucifixion of our Lord, and therefore before the martyrdom of St. James, we find the traditional date of the introduction of Christianity into Sicily. St. Pancras and St. Martian are said to have been sent from Antioch by St. Peter. St. Pancras came to Taormina and is generally recognized as its first bishop. A statue erected to his memory in 1691 stands upon the beach at Taormina, and the accompanying inscription chronicles the tradition that he was first bishop of all Sicily and ordained by St. Peter in AD 40.

St. Martian is specially associated with Syracuse.

A large subterranean chamber beneath the Church of San Giovanni marks the scene of his preaching and his labours, and here, it is said, St. Paul stayed three days after his shipwreck in Malta on his way to Rome (*Acts* 28:12).

Here, too, is the burial-place of the earliest Christians. Mr. F. Marion Crawford writes of this: 'There is no city of the dead in all the world more solemn, more silent, or more suggestive of that peace which distinguishes Christian burial-places from all others. Corridor and chamber follow each other indefinitely, each vaulted hall surrounded by deep niches within which graves, deeper still, have been hollowed in the living rock. There are graves in the rocky floor, and to the right and left, and one above another in tiers to the spring of the solid vault; and we may go on and on, without end, mile after mile, through the unexplored silence. Some believe that the passages reach even to Catania, more than thirty miles away. There St. Martian lived and preached; and by the seashore, not far away, it is said he was put to death, not by heathens but by Jews, and that in the first place they laid him bound in a boat and put fire to it and pushed it from the shore, but that when they had seen that the fire had no power over him, they brought him to the beach again and strangled him' (*The Rulers of the South*, vol. i, pp. 357, 358).

Another writer (Capt. Smyth), who published an account of Sicily in 1824, speaks of primitive Christianity as having been already established in the island on the visit of St. Paul, and describes the Church of St. Martian as 'the earliest in Europe for Christian worship.' These accounts appear to have been taken from local traditions at the time of his visit (*Sicily and its Island*, London, John Murray, 1829).

It is worthy of note, too, that Chrestus, the bishop of Syracuse in 314, heads the list of signatures to the decisions of the Council of Arles (see Appendix G), apparently as bishop of the oldest Western see.

One of the oldest tales or narratives regarding the preaching of the Gospel in Rome is that contained in the important but somewhat neglected document called the 'Recognitions of Clement.'[10] Supposed by many to be a romance, but dating from the second century (for its antiquity is undoubted), it is yet quite possible that the foundation of it rests on a real account by St. Clement, who was contemporary with the Apostles, mentioned by St. Paul (*Philippians* 4:3), and afterwards bishop of Rome. At all events, we know positively that this was the opinion of

Rufinus, who translated the book in AD 410.

In it St. Clement tells of his first acquaintance with Christianity through the preaching of St. Barnabas in Rome. St. Barnabas is said to have been accompanied by others who had been personal witnesses of the miracles of our Saviour (Andronicus and Junia?). According to this account the mission of St. Barnabas to Rome must have taken place either before or shortly after the crucifixion, very possibly about the time of the conversion of Saul.

St. Clement is represented as following St. Barnabas to Caesarea and meeting there St. Peter, St. Zaccheus (the publican of the Gospels), St. Lazarus, St. Joseph, Nicodemus and others. The Holy Women are also mentioned incidentally. St. Peter and his fellow-disciples stay at Caesarea for the space of three months; the greater number of the men then accompany him in what appears to have been an historical journey from Caesarea to Antioch, wintering in Tripolis. Zaccheus is left as bishop of the Church at Caesarea, while Barnabas (presumably) goes on to his relatives in Jerusalem. At all events, he does not accompany the followers of St. Peter.

Supposing the narrative of Clement to be founded on fact, it may well have been at this time that the Church at Jerusalem sent St. Barnabas to Antioch and, if he went direct to his destination, St. Barnabas might have been teaching for nearly a year at Antioch before the arrival of St. Peter and his companions. The historical basis of the 'Recognitions' and 'Homilies' is certainly borne out by the *Acts of the Apostles*, by the writings of Eusebius and by tradition. The conflict of St. Peter and Simon Magus which bulks so largely in these books, the necessity for apostolic supervision at Antioch, the immediate departure of St. Barnabas, and the later leadership of St. Peter at Antioch, all follow and correspond in the different narratives (see Appendix B). The meeting of St. Peter with St. Paul at Antioch is also referred to incidentally in the *Epistle to the Galatians* (2:11).

The history of St. Mary and St. Martha, which has been preserved for us in the Magdalen College Library at Oxford, and which we shall consider in detail later on, appears to take up the history of some of these early disciples at a rather later stage. The Bethany family, St. Joseph of Arimathea and, according to some of the traditions, St. Zaccheus also, undertook a longer journey beyond Rome, as far as the neighbourhood of Massilia (the modern Marseilles). For the present it will suffice to note that this reputed mission appears to be only an extension, and a natural extension, of the great 'Propaganda' already begun by the authentic missions to Crete and Rome; that Salome, the mother of St. James, is said to have accompanied the mission; and that the time when these missions were undertaken, according both to history and tradition, appears to be fixed roughly by the martyrdom of St. Stephen and St. James, and therefore to be during the first ten years after the ascension of our Lord and between AD 34 and AD 44.[11]

Perhaps it may be well to consider the picture presented by these traditions and narratives as supplementing the New Testament history regarding the first ten years of Christendom. The earliest days after the first Pentecost are over. The day of power in Jerusalem, when 'fear came upon every soul,' has been succeeded by a period of criticism, of suspicion, and finally by a time of serious persecution. St. James the Greater is absent on a difficult and distant mission. St. Barnabas is preaching in Rome, and is accompanied by others who have been eye-witnesses of our Saviour's ministry and miracles (Joanna, her son, and others). St. Stephen has been martyred, and all the other residents of Jerusalem who have been publicly known as followers of Jesus have been hunted out of the city. Some of these, including St. Luke and Simon the Cyrenean, have journeyed through Syro-Phoenicia to Antioch, preaching as they go; others have fled to Caesarea where, for the present,

Roman toleration and the friendship of Cornelius are more powerful than Jewish hatred.

In Jerusalem itself most of the Apostles are still to be found residing in the house of St. Mark, upon the hill of Zion (though St. Peter is frequently absent on missionary journeys). With them, for a time, remains the Blessed Virgin.

Here are held the meetings for the breaking of bread and for special intercession, but all – from the beginning – have continued daily with one accord in the Temple; and although 'Peter and John' are well known as believers in the Christ, there is no very clear visible distinction between the devouter Jews and Christians.

At Caesarea we find (according to the 'Recognitions') St. Joseph of Arimathea, Nicodemus, St. Lazarus, St. Zaccheus, and the 'Holy Women' – probably St. Salome, the mother of St. James, St. Mary, the wife of Cleopas, St. Martha and St. Mary Magdalene. Such appears to have been, so far as we can gather, the earliest disposition of the disciples after the persecution which arose about St. Stephen.

A little later change takes place. St. Zaccheus is appointed bishop of Caesarea by St. Peter. St. Lazarus and St. Joseph follow the latter to Antioch, and St. Lazarus is sent by St. Peter to Cyprus. Other missionary priests or bishops are also sent abroad from the Church at Antioch and, notably, those of the mission to Sicily. With the establishment of a definite Church at Syracuse, the tentative efforts to form some centre of Christian teaching in Rome itself gather strength and permanence and, finally, with the returning of Clement, accompanied by St. Peter from Antioch, the Church at Rome is fully established. During all this time the Holy Women and St. Zaccheus appear to have remained at Caesarea, and these are joined by St. Philip the deacon who, after preaching in Samaria, takes up his residence at Caesarea.

Still, somewhat later, we may reasonably imagine St. Joseph as returning, and the whole of this little company (but especially St. Salome, the mother of St. James), eagerly expecting – and rejoicing – in the return of the Greater St. James.

And then comes the bitter sorrow, the bereavement, and the second persecution occasioned by or accompanying St. James's martyrdom.

Up to this point all I have imagined and described may be fairly inferred from the very oldest writings and traditions, the antiquity of which few, if any, are disposed to question.

Beyond this – and this is the weak point of the Western legends – there is for some four or five hundred years a marked hiatus or silence in the records of any history bearing on these disciples and their labours.

Then about AD 600 (as we shall see) we find references to St. Philip as having carried the message of the Gospel not only into Gaul, but to the shores beyond it, and some two or three centuries later (AD 800-1000 and later) we find various local traditions, and even histories, both in France and Britain, which treat of the after-life and labours in the West of some of the very disciples who (according to second or early third-century literature) lived at Caesarea after the Passion and Ascension of our Saviour – disciples who were of necessity associated with the work of St. Philip the Evangelist, and who are said to have been taught and prepared by St. Peter and St. Philip for such work as they are reputed to have afterwards undertaken.

There is evidently some relationship between these earlier and later histories which as yet no one has attempted to discover. Perhaps, if the intervening silence be not considered fatal to the claims of the later traditions, it may be accounted for by the fact the reputed mission does not profess to have been strictly apostolic, and that the Holy Women – rather than the men who accompanied them – are represented as its leaders.

Foremost among these is St. Mary Magdalene, one who for more than a thousand years now has been recognized and loved as belonging to the chief of the followers of Jesus Christ, but one who, at the beginning, was hardly, perhaps, considered worthy (save by Christ Himself) to receive the forgiveness, the love and the confidence of her Lord.

Have you ever thought of St. Mary Magdalene as an 'Apostle of Jesus'?

Those who had been named and known as Apostles of the Lord had been called to follow Him, and had been sent forth by Him to preach the Gospel of His Kingdom.

Like them she had been called and chosen, and followed Him through all His ministry. But had she no commission? What shall we say of those words which fell from the lips of Jesus on the resurrection morning? He appeared 'first to Mary Magdalene' and as she fell down before Him, worshipping, and held His feet, we read, 'Jesus saith unto her, Mary. She . . . saith unto Him, Rabboni. Jesus saith unto her; Touch Me not; for I am not yet ascended to My Father: but go to My brethren, and say unto them, I ascend unto My Father, and to your Father; and to my God, and your God.'

A personal message from the Lord Himself so full and so direct could never be exhausted by one 'telling,' and as the years went by, and the conception of the 'brethren of Jesus' widened, St. Mary, who had first carried the news of the resurrection to the eleven, would find her conception of the message itself increasing in meaning and in scope; and as St. Peter had already begun preaching Christ and the resurrection so, with a special claim, would St. Mary and her companions start upon their voyage; and, as it were, straight from the open sepulchre with the very words of the Blessed Saviour on her lips, in the way that even no one else could do, St. Mary would carry the great new message of Light and

Life – 'Christ and the Resurrection' – from the East to the West, from the Old World to the New.

Certainly there is nothing very unlikely or far-fetched in the belief that St. Mary and St. Martha, St. Zaccheus and St. Joseph may have been of those who travelled westward, 'preaching the Word.' The early persecutions came so soon after the crucifixion of our Saviour that very few besides those who had been personally identified in some way with His ministry would fall under the direct displeasure of the Jews, and who would incur this so certainly or, from their point of view, deserve it so richly as the family of Bethany, Joseph of Arimathea, Nicodemus, and the man 'born blind'?

These were all old residents of Jerusalem or its vicinity, and their position as adherents of the new faith would be far more noticeable than that of the Apostles, who were Galileans and comparatively unknown.

1. In the Gospel of *John* we read that 'the chief priests consulted that they might put Lazarus to death, because that by reason of him many of the Jews went away and believed on Jesus.' This would necessarily affect the whole of the disciples at Bethany (*John* 12:10, 11).

2. See Bishop Gore's *Epistle to the Ephesians*, p. 27.

3. 'For the king [Solomon] had at sea a navy of Tarshish with the navy of Hiram: once in three years came the navy of Tarshish bringing gold and silver, ivory and apes and peacocks' (I *Kings* 10:22).

According to an old legend, the Jews of Toledo in Spain addressed a letter to the Sanhedrin at Jerusalem declaring against the crucifixion of our Lord (see 'Spain,' *Jewish Encyclopaedia*). When the Moors first took Toledo, it is said to have been largely populated by Jews, to whom it was a place of refuge when Nebuchadnezzar sacked Jerusalem (Tradition).

'Tarshish . . . with silver, iron, tin, and lead, they traded in thy fairs' (*Ezekiel* 27:12).

4. The constitution and functions of these pre-Christian Apostles are thus described by Harnack:

1. They were consecrated persons of a very high rank.

2. They were sent out into the Diaspora to collect tribute for headquarters.

3. They brought encyclical letters with them, kept the Diaspora in touch with the centre and informed of the intentions of the latter (or of the patriarch); received orders relative to any dangerous movement and had to organize resistance to it.

4. They exercised certain powers of surveillance and discipline in the Diaspora; and

5. *On returning to their own country* they formed a sort of Council which aided the patriarch in supervising the interests of the Law (*Expansion of Christianity*, Moffat's translation, vol. i, p. 412).

5. Phoenician or Phoenician and Jewish settlements were found at this period, on all the coasts of the Mediterranean. Tarsus in Cilicia (the birthplace of St. Paul) was a Phoenician city, with Phoenician coinage and worship. In Cyprus the Phoenicians had established themselves for centuries; they had rebuilt the harbour at Citium (Larnaca) and thoroughly colonized the adjacent country. In Crete one of the chief ports, Phoenix (or Phenice) was named after them, and this and other of the Cretan seaports were used for the refitting and repairing of their fleets. In Sicily they had established colonies at Motya, Eryx, Panormus (Palermo) and Soloeis. In Africa a very great part of the sea border and much of the inland country was practically Phoenician or Phoenician and Hebrew. In Sardinia, 'Caralis' (or Cagliari, the present capital) and all the more open and level region of the south and south-west were occupied by Phoenician settlers, while in Spain they had numerous colonies, and at Gades (the modern Cadiz) had established a great centre of maritime traffic which is said to have included not only the coasts of Britain, but also those of North Germany and the Baltic (see Professor Rawlinson's *History of Phoenicia*, pp. 91-128).

The League formed by Judas Maccabeus (about 162 BC) between the Jews and Romans appears to have been prompted by the Jews residing in Spain and Gaul. Note that in the passages referring to this the Gauls are called 'Galatians' (Apocrypha, I *Maccabees* 8).

6. *Cyprus*, F. V. Lower. In the *Acts of Barnabas* we read of the copy of St. Matthew's writings which Barnabas carried with him.

What was the further history of the missionary journey of St. Barnabas and St. Mark when they went to Cyprus after parting with St. Paul? (*Acts* 15:39). The legends of St. Mark are strongly suggestive of a western course, but unconnected with the travels of St. Paul.

7. The growth of the Church in Rome, naturally unnoticed by the non-Christian writers, who regarded the sect as beneath contempt, and by the Christian historian

as it was unconnected with the work of any of the Apostles, was yet so rapid that the great persecution of AD 64 claimed very many victims in the city (*Life and Principate of Nero*, Henderson, p. 344).

8. St. Chrysostom writes: 'And indeed to be apostles at all is a great thing, but to be among those of note! Consider what great praise this is. Oh! how great is the devotion of this woman, that she should be counted worthy of the appellation of apostle!'

9. Note that 'Rufus' is mentioned before his mother in a later verse. The household of Chuza, as forming part of the greater household of Herod Antipas, would, if still living in Galilee, naturally accompany Herod on his second journey to Rome, in AD 39, and would probably remain in Rome after the banishment of Herod. If, as already suggested, Herod's steward originally came from Rome, the probability of the return of this household would be increased (p. 7).

10. Theological writers have treated the 'Recognitions' with scant courtesy, because it is said to be tainted with Ebionite errors and heresies. This, however, need not detract from its value as an historical document. 'Ebionite' or 'Jewish' Christianity dates from the very earliest times, and Josephus the historian is said to have been an Ebionite Christian. His testimony to the fact of the resurrection (*Antiquities*, 18), when considered side by side with the absence of any marked Christian enthusiasm in his writings, is very remarkable. Something similar to this is occasionally found in the 'Recognitions.'

11. Two other traditions of first century Christian missions, but belonging to a slightly later period, demand some attention as also bearing on Western Christianity.

The first is the tradition of 'St. Maternus,' and is connected with all the old country of the Treviri and Tungri beyond the Alps.

Here, and especially at Trier (or Trèves), the Romans had formed important colonies some fifty years before the coming of Christ; and although, as in Britain, there were frequent uprisings against the power of Rome, the Romans maintained their supremacy for two hundred years or more.

Nowhere so far north are the Roman remains and ruins so rich, so fine, and so remarkable as they are in Trèves today.

And the first Christian mission to Trèves is represented as partly Roman and partly Hebrew, as coming direct from Rome by the authority of St. Peter, and in the course or channel of Roman colonization.

In some of these points it differs entirely from those we have been considering. The tradition also has other points of very considerable interest. It runs as follows:

Three Saints — Eucharius, Valerius and Maternus — all of whom had been pupils of St. Peter at Rome, were sent by him to Trier to preach the gospel of Christ.

Eucharius was appointed as bishop, and Valerius and Maternus as his assistants. Maternus was of Hebrew birth, and came from the little town of Nain in Palestine, being 'the only son of his mother,' whom Christ had raised from the dead. But no special honour was at this time accorded him. He was the least of the three missionary disciples, one of the 'personal witnesses' who, as long as they lived, accompanied the other evangelists in most of their distant journeys.

But though ready to take the lowest place among his Greek and Roman companions, Maternus appears to have been most active in his apostolic labours. For while all three − Eucharius, Valerius and Maternus − are associated with the foundation of the church at Trier and Cologne (the scene of their chief labours at Trier being a little outside the present city, on the site of the old St. Matthiaskirche), Maternus alone is represented as pushing forward and reaching the farthest settlement of Tongres, where he is said to have built a little church which he dedicated to the Blessed Virgin − the first church beyond the Alps dedicated to her name and memory ('Ecclesia Tungrensis prima cis Alpes beatae Mariae Virgini consecrata').

Maternus is accordingly reckoned as the first bishop of Tongres.

The probability that the evangelization of this district was undertaken by Hebrews and Romans conjointly is somewhat increased by the further tradition that Servatius, the tenth bishop in descent from Maternus, was himself not only of Hebrew descent, but claimed to be directly related to the families of St. John the Baptist and the Blessed Virgin.

The tradition of Maternus is one of very great antiquity, and appears to be accepted by those who may be regarded as authorities on the history of Trier.

In the chronological table appended to the Triersche Geschichte, Eucharius, Valerius and Maternus are represented as living in the time of Nero; and St. Agritius, who certainly occupied the see in AD 314, is placed as twenty-fifth in descent from St. Eucharius.

The Relics of St. Maternus are said to rest in the 'Dom.' The tombs of St. Eucharius and St. Valerius still remain in the little crypt of the St. Matthiaskirche.

The second tradition is the old Venetian tradition of St. Mark. One of the very oldest mission centres to the north of Italy was the ancient Dalmatian city of Aquileia (II *Timothy* 4:10), the precursor of the later Venice; for when Aquileia was destroyed by Attila in 452 the inhabitants fled to the lagoons and founded there the earliest beginnings of the Queen of the Adriatic.

The tradition is that the first Church founded at Aquileia was visited by St. Mark, the historian of St. Peter and a fellow-worker with St. Paul, and that he gave to the church there a copy of the Gospel written by himself. This was one of the treasures of Aquileia so long as there was a cathedral there, and it has been said that the remains of the manuscript are still preserved in the treasury of St. Marco in Venice, but this appears to be doubtful.

'St. Mark, it is believed, stayed one or two years in Aquileia and then returned to Rome, going thence again to Alexandria, where martyrdom awaited him' (*Early Hist. of Venice*, Hodgson, p. 48).

CHAPTER IV

ST. PAUL AND CAESAREA

'Oft when the word is on me to deliver.
    Opens the heaven and the Lord is there;
Desert or throng, the city or the river
    Melt in a lucid Paradise of air.

Only like souls I see the folk there under
    Bound who should conquer: Slaves who should be Kings,
Hearing their one hope with an empty wonder,
    Sadly contended in a show of things.

Then with a rush the intolerable craving
    Shivers throughout me like a trumpet call.
Oh, to save these! To perish for their saving,
    Die for their life, be offered for them all.'
                    'St. Paul,' by F. W. H. Myers

The chief port of Palestine at the time of which I am writing was Caesarea. Built by Herod the Great on the coastline of the Great Sea, with a prodigal expenditure of labour and of wealth, having a temple dedicated to Caesar built on rising ground over against the mouth of the Haven, with amphitheatre, forum, baths, and many great houses or palaces built of white stone or marble, this great seaport rapidly attracted to itself a large and mixed and powerful population.

Greeks and Romans from across the Mediterranean lived here side

87

by side with the merchants of Palestine and Syria. 'A large mole ran out into the sea and afforded a secure harbour for shipping,' and vessels of all kinds were continually going to and returning from the chief Mediterranean ports.[1]

'Till Herod's day the plain of Sharon had been a broad tract of pasture, forest and tillage, with no history, but he raised it to the foremost place in the land. The want of a port to receive the commerce of the West had always been felt. The shore offered no natural harbour, but there was a rocky ledge at Strabo's Tower, and this Herod chose as the seat of his projected harbour. In twelve years a splendid city rose on the ledge and its neighbourhood, with broad quays, magnificent bazaars, spacious public buildings and courts, arched sailors' homes and long avenues of commodious streets. A double harbour had been constructed of about 200 yards each way, and also a pier over 130 yards in length, built of stones, 50 feet long, 18 broad and 9 thick. This great structure was raised out of water 20 fathoms deep, and was 200 feet wide, a wall standing on it, and several towers. It was adorned, moreover, with splendid pillars, and a terraced walk extended round the harbour.

'On an eminence, beside a temple of polished stone near the shore, rose a colossal statue of Augustus as Jupiter Olympus, visible far out at sea, and another of Rome, deified as Juno. A huge open-air theatre was built on the slopes of the hills, some miles north of the city, as well as an amphitheatre capable of containing 20,000 spectators. A circus, over 1,000 feet long, rose in the east of the city. The walls of the city enclosed 400 acres, but gardens and villas, it may be presumed, stretched far beyond them. Besides the theatre, a grand palace, afterwards the residence of the Roman governors, was erected for himself by Herod, and he had the wisdom to provide for the city a complete system of underground sewerage.

'To supply it with water two aqueducts were built: one stretching away, for over eight miles; to the great springs from the Carmel hills. The second aqueduct ran three miles north to the River Zerka.'[2]

Such was Caesarea Stratonis in the days of the earliest Christians.

Here life was larger and less circumscribed than at Jerusalem and though party feeling ran high, especially between the Jews and Greeks, the constant intercourse with the world beyond them produced a spirit of tolerance which was quite foreign to the inland Jew.

Here dwelt Cornelius, the centurion of the Italian band of whom we read in the *Acts of the Apostles*. Who was he? Was he simply some devout stranger to whom God gave the wonderful gift of the Holy Spirit? Or was he something more than this? If we read the account carefully the internal evidence of the narrative would lead us to conclude that he had some considerable knowledge of the Galilean ministry of our Lord, but was ignorant of much that had taken place beyond this. When troubled in mind he was directed to send for Peter (not '*one* Peter,' as we read in our Bibles, for the 'one' is an interpolation, but 'Peter,' as if the Apostle was not altogether unknown to him), and when St. Peter came, and told him of all that had happened, and especially of the crucifixion and resurrection, and of the commission to the Apostles to preach and to testify 'that Jesus was indeed He who was ordained of God to be both Saviour and Judge,' we are expressly told that St. Peter introduced his message in these words:

'The word which God sent unto the children of Israel, preaching peace by Jesus Christ. . . . That word *ye know*, which was published throughout all Judea, and began from Galilee, after the baptism which John preached; how God anointed Jesus of Nazareth with the Holy Ghost and with power: who went about doing good, and healing all that were oppressed of the devil; for God was with Him.'

How did Cornelius know this, and know this with a knowledge so perfect and direct that St. Peter recognizes it as needing no further teaching from himself, and so immediately goes on to tell Cornelius of the Passion of our Lord and His victory over death?

Was Cornelius associated in any way with that earlier ministry? One instinctively thinks of the centurion of Capernaum, and returning to the description of him in the Gospels, we remember that he had a servant who was dear to him (*Luke* 7:2), and whom our Saviour healed. We find it noted, too, that the elders of the Jews came to Jesus saying that the centurion was a worthy man, 'for he loveth our nation, and hath built us a synagogue.'

The description of Cornelius is curiously similar: 'Cornelius the centurion, a just man and one that feareth God and of good report among the entire nation of the Jews'; and after the angel had departed who spoke to Cornelius we find him calling on 'two of his household servants, and a devout soldier of them that waited on him continually.'

The removal of the centurion from Capernaum becomes more probable when we remember that Herod Antipas (in whose service he was) is said to have been deposed in AD 39, and it would be only natural that the Romans in taking over complete control of his province should make considerable changes among the subordinate officers (whether Romans or not) who had been associated with his rule.[3]

Again, who was it that appeared to Cornelius? We are told that 'an angel' called 'Cornelius,' but we find Cornelius answering, 'What is it, Lord?'

It seems quite possible that the centurion of Capernaum had been removed to Caesarea, and that our Lord Himself, remembering his faith, which was 'greater than any He had found in Israel,' came to Cornelius, and because, perhaps, of the resurrection-power which seemed inseparable from His glorified humanity, the miracles of Pentecost were renewed at the house of the centurion.

But Cornelius – although the chief Roman official who was a member of the Church at Caesarea – was by no means the only important Christian here. The chief pastor of the Church is generally supposed to have been St. Philip (the deacon) who, after preaching in Samaria, finally settled in Caesarea, and with his family of daughters entertained St. Paul, St. Luke and Trophimus, and others of the brethren as they touched at Caesarea on their journeys. We read of St. Philip as first preaching at Samaria and then teaching and baptizing the Ethiopian eunuch; so that we know him at once to have been a large-hearted man who did not feel himself in any way bound by the restrictions of Jewish customs but welcomed both Samaritans and negroes as equal sharers in the blessings of the Gospel. Traditionally, too, we find St. Philip mentioned in the old legend of Glastonbury as the authority who sent St. Joseph of Arimathea and his fellow-missionaries to be witnesses for Christ 'unto the uttermost parts of the earth'; and Isidorus Hispalensis, who wrote in the sixth or early part of the seventh century (having been born about AD 560 and dying in AD 636), refers to him as having first carried the news of the Gospel to the Samaritans, and as having preached Christ later to the Gauls and afterwards in Hierapolis of Phrygia, where he was crucified and is buried with his daughters (*Isidorus Hispalensis*, vol. vii, 392).[4]

In another place he writes 'St. Philip preached to the Gauls, and persuaded the neighbouring and savage tribes on the borders of the ocean to the light of knowledge and of faith' (vol. v, 184). And yet again (vol. vii, 395): 'St. Philip journeyed to the Gauls.'

So we find at Caesarea, Cornelius, his kinsmen and near friends 'his servants and one or more devout soldiers of his company,' St. Philip the deacon and his four daughters, and an increasing company of Christians constantly embarking or returning or waiting here during the course of their journeys. Those who went to Cyrene, Crete and Cyprus would go from Caesarea. Saul, on his first visit to Jerusalem after his conversion, was taken down to Caesarea by the 'brethren' and shipped from there to Tarsus (*Acts* 9:30). Those who were finally driven away from Jerusalem by the second great persecution, when Herod Agrippa killed 'James the brother of John with the sword' and cast St. Peter into prison, would naturally fly to Caesarea or beyond it; and this is the time, according to tradition, when St. Joseph of Arimathea, St. Mary Magdalene, St. Martha, St. Mary Cleopas, St. Mary Salome, St. Maximin, St. Parmenas, St. Restitutus and others escaped by the sea-coast westward.

The sudden journey of King Herod Agrippa from Jerusalem to Caesarea immediately after St. Peter had been delivered from prison (*Acts* 12:19) is consonant with this tradition, and rather suggestive of an attempt to intercept the fugitive Christians. Later on we find records of the repeated visits of St. Paul to Caesarea either when going to or returning from Jerusalem, and on the occasion of his last visit to Jerusalem we find him accompanied by many friends, certainly by St. Luke, Trophimus and Mnason (of Cyprus), and most probably by Sopater, Aristarchus, Secundus, Gaius, Timothy and Tychicus. We are also told of 'certain disciples of Caesarea' who not only welcomed and entertained the missionaries, but accompanied them on their way to Jerusalem.

It seems to me, if we look a little below the surface, that we find at Caesarea a centre of missionary life and work – the most important centre, perhaps, of Christianity after Capernaum and Jerusalem, in which St. Luke, the missionary historian, St. Philip, the deacon and Evangelist, St. Cornelius, the Roman centurion, St Zaccheus, the publican of the Gospels, St. Joseph of Arimathea, St Lazarus of Bethany, St. Barnabas, and very probably St. Cleopas, St. Mary, the wife of Cleopas, and the Holy Women of the Bethany household, took an important part.

What was the relation of St. Paul to these elder disciples who had been friends and companions and colleagues of St. Stephen?

St. Paul had listened to the last sermon of St. Stephen – is not the permanent record of it due to his memory? – had been 'consenting to his death,' and had heard, doubtless with a fine amazement, the martyr's dying prayer for those who were stoning him. At this time he would naturally imagine that the Christians (who were the especial objects of his persecution) would hate him for the active part he had taken in the martyrdom of St. Stephen, and we can well imagine his increasing wonder, his shame, his pained delight, to find on his conversion that the martyr's prayer was no isolated expression of ecstatic love, but that St. Stephen's nearest and dearest friends had also drunk of the martyr's spirit and were ready without any ungenerous reproaches specially to befriend him.

For was it not these – St. Philip, St. Luke, St. Barnabas, the other members of the Seventy, and the deacons, and *not* the Apostles – who believed in his word and took care of him in the time of his danger? Who obtained for him a passage in the ship from Caesarea to Tarsus when obliged to fly from Jerusalem, and with whom the new convert, Saul, found himself, even at this time, more in sympathy than with the bulk of the Church remaining at Jerusalem?

When writing of Emmaus I mentioned it as the possible meeting-place of the older and newer discipleship; for here, through St. Luke, who was living with St. Cleopas (and perhaps with the Blessed Virgin and St. John) the oldest disciples might very well have been brought into special intimacy with St. Paul during the early days after his conversion.

'Saul,' who was apparently directly related to St. Luke (*Romans* 16:21), who was brought up in Jerusalem and, according to some writers, was with St. Barnabas in the school of Gamaliel, would have the opportunity (for a time) of daily converse with all those who had

93

specially known our Saviour in the flesh and who had ministered to Him at His crucifixion and burial, and their personal knowledge of, and blessed companionship with, the Lord Jesus would prepare the way for it if, indeed, it did not rather suggest to St. Paul, his special mission to the Gentiles and his championship of their rights and liberties as independent of the Jewish law.

This fellowship and friendship which was formed or re-formed in Jerusalem between St. Luke, St. Barnabas and Saul was afterwards purposely renewed at Antioch, where all were associated together for the space of a year in preaching the Gospel.

Of the history of the immediately succeeding years but little is known beyond the records of St. Paul's travels, because the main historian of the period (St. Luke) accompanied St. Paul.

But it must not be supposed that there were not many other missionaries engaged in evangelistic work.

There were – as we have seen – many missionaries in the West, and especially in the neighbourhood of Rome and Sicily, while beside those at Caesarea, Cyrene, Cyprus and Antioch we find the saints of Damascus and Ephesus before the coming of St. Paul. We find, too, in Eusebius some record of a successful mission to Edessa undertaken by St. Thaddeus, of an episcopate established by St. Mark at Alexandria (bk. ii, cap. 16), and of a mission to the Far East by St. Bartholomew,[5] all in the very earliest years after Christ (*E.H.*, bk. i, cap. 3, 14, and bk. v, cap. 10). In Jerusalem itself, under the leadership of St. James the Less, the Church grew amazingly, not simply among the poor and oppressed or 'common people,' but also among the priests, for, as we read in *Acts* 6:7, 'a great multitude of the priests were obedient unto the faith.' These were full of Jewish feeling and tradition, and their spirit seems to have been largely shared by the bishop of the Church, St. James, the picture both of him and of the early Church at Jerusalem which we find depicted for us in the *Acts of the Apostles* fully bearing out this view and being confirmed by the writings of Hegesippus and Josephus. In all these writings two important points stand out very clearly: one, the extraordinary influence and respect inspired by St. James among a large number of the Jews; and the other, the peculiar position gradually assumed by the Jerusalem Church.

This was, curiously to us, perhaps, but very naturally to the devout Jews who belonged to it, a mixture of Judaism and Christianity – a '*via media*,' if one may call it so, in which although the Messiah had come, the types and worship pointing to His advent were valued all the more perhaps on account of this, and were in no sense cast aside.

Never abating his allegiance to Christ, nor forfeiting the esteem and friendship of the other Apostles, St. James and most of his followers remained 'Hebrew of the Hebrews,' attending the Temple services and living, as regards the Law, blameless. St. James was generally named 'The Just'; and so important and widespread did his influence become in Jerusalem, that when St. Paul returned from one of his long missionary journeys, as reported in the 21st chapter of the *Acts,* St. James was able to point to many thousands of Jews in Jerusalem who had become believers in Christ but retained all their interest in the Temple services. The exact words are: 'Thou seest, brother, how many thousands of Jews there are which believe, and they are all zealous of the Law.'

It was for this reason that he begged St. Paul to purify himself and to avoid occasions of offence. But offences necessarily came.

Imagine for one moment all the conflicting interests meeting in the Holy City. There were the orthodox Jews led by the families of Annas and Caiaphas, men who knew themselves to be mainly responsible for the crucifixion of our Saviour, and who would feel bound by this to maintain that He was an impostor. Mingling with them, devout, strict and blameless – if possible out-rivalling them in all religious ceremonial and observances – were the early Jewish Christians, men who held that Jesus is the Messiah, the Holy One, the very God Himself. Around both was the less religious contemporary Jewish world, critical of both but often confusing them, counting that every man blamelessly devout and zealous of the Law was worthy of equal honour and respect.

Again, outside these and more or less contemptuously indifferent are the Roman officials – men who, unless attracted by individual adherents of the new religion, endeavour to maintain an impartial attitude, to interfere but rarely and then to punish whatever parties or persons appeared to be responsible for public disturbances.

If we realize this, and keep it before us as we read the *Acts of the Apostles*, we shall, I think, find in it an atmosphere or setting largely explanatory of the scenes described as taking place within Jerusalem. How increasingly bitter would be the feeling of the orthodox Jews! Forced to associate and to worship day by day with those who brought continually to their mind the remembrance of what might be the most awful crime of which man could be guilty, powerless to get rid of them, unable to find any valid pretext for turning them out of the Temple – finding that they were increasing in number and in influence – discovering that the new belief was spreading in the most unlooked-for quarters – that the very family and household of the High Priest was itself infected – father divided against son, and brother against brother – the quiet Theophilus becoming the friend and disciple of St. Luke and the teacher Gamaliel (as we read in the 'Recognitions') secretly befriending the Christians – all this must have been as gall and wormwood to the Jews who had paid for the betrayal of our Saviour, had incited the populace to cry, 'Crucify Him!' and had then condemned Him to the cross.

It must be acknowledged, too, that much of the practice of the early Christians would tend to excite curiosity, suspicion, and even perhaps alarm. The early morning Eucharists, the secret meetings, the orderly establishment of settled Church government and discipline, the headship of St. James – the departure of the Apostles on their missionary journeys accompanied, as they often were, by several friends to see them off upon their mission – the occasional influx of Gentile strangers from abroad – all these would irresistibly suggest the idea of some far-reaching conspiracy subversive of the national custom and religion of the Jews.

And therefore, although (for several years apparently) we read, 'The Churches had rest throughout all Judea and Galilee and Samaria, and were edified; and walking in the fear of the Lord, and in the comfort of the Holy Ghost, were multiplied'; yet in Jerusalem itself, as time went on, the quietness of their persecutors was rather that of a smouldering fire ready at any gust of wind to burst into an active flame.

How the wind arose and the flame at last was kindled we are told in the *Acts of the Apostles*. Strangers in distant towns and countries, Greeks and Romans – who had become disciples of Christ – began, I suppose, to feel a longing to visit the scenes of our Saviour's Passion – a longing which has been felt by thousands of loving hearts for all the centuries since. And so, when St. Paul came back from Ephesus to Jerusalem on this very occasion when St. James was anxious lest trouble should arise, he and St. Luke brought with them several disciples, two of whom are particularly mentioned; one pilgrim from Cyprus named Mnason, and another named Trophimus, who had come all the way from Ephesus with St. Paul, accompanying him backwards and forwards between Asia Minor and Greece and probably assisting him in his work. The latter was the unwitting occasion of very great disturbances in Jerusalem, and became the chief or exciting cause of a religious persecution more lasting than any which had preceded it. All the closing chapters of the *Acts of the Apostles* are full of storm and controversy, occasioned apparently by this visit of Trophimus.

97

The chief priests pretended that St. Paul had taken him into the Temple and so profaned it. They incited the people to kill St. Paul, and so great was the uproar and excitement in Jerusalem, that the Romans had to protect the Apostle by force.

Claudius Lysias, the captain of the Roman Guard, with a company of soldiers and centurions, had to rescue him from the fury of the mob, and later on, when a plot was formed by over forty of the Jews to assassinate St. Paul, he was sent, with a special escort of four hundred and seventy men, to Felix the governor at Caesarea.

It is in connection with this disturbance that some of the most dramatic incidents of St. Paul's life took place. At one time, just after his rescue by the Roman soldiers, we see him dragged away from the Jews into the shelter of the fortress of Antonia, and on the stairway leading to the entrance, craving permission from the captain to speak to his accusers. There, standing on the stairway, the massive portals of the fortress framing him as in a picture, surrounded by the Roman soldiers in uniform tunics with shining helmets and lances held at rest, like a small forest of spears, around their prisoner, the excited mob of Jewish worshippers, fresh from the Temple service, crowding closely below, St. Paul stands and tells the history of his life, and makes a good confession of the faith till, drowned by the clamour of the multitude, his voice can be heard no more, and we see the Roman guard draw him quickly within the fortress gate and close the doors.

Again, a few nights later, we catch a further glimpse of St. Paul, the centre of a powerful guard of soldiers, horsemen and spearmen, setting out on the strange night journey to Caesarea. The dark streets of Jerusalem are full of unwonted noise and commotion. The square in front of the fortress is thronged with horsemen and foot-soldiers. Late arrivals come galloping up in haste, and the noise of the horses' hoofs, the champing of the bits, and the calling of the men, wake the sleepers in the adjoining houses. Doors and casements are thrown open, heads peer out inquiring the cause of the uproar. Gruff voices answer. Torches are lighted and one sees the whole of the square packed with soldiers. The centurions take command, and almost immediately the scene is full of orderly and dramatic interest. At the short, sharp word of command the troops form into rank and draw up in front of the prison. The guard is summoned and the gates cautiously opened. The order is handed to the warder, and shortly afterwards the doors are flung wide open and St. Paul is brought out. He is given a horse, and chained to two horsemen, one on either side. Again the sharp, clear words of command ring out into the night. The doors of the fortress fall-to, and the long cavalcade of foot-soldiers, spearmen and cavalry pass down the dim streets of the city, out by the Jaffa Gate, and so down the hill towards the distant sea-coast.

In this way St. Paul leaves Jerusalem, and probably (so far as we know) for the last time. He is carried captive to Caesarea and kept a prisoner there for two years. Appealing from the tribunal at Caesarea he is finally sent on from Caesarea to Rome, and with the history of this journey, in which he was accompanied by St. Luke, the *Acts of the Apostles* closes.

What happened during these two years at Caesarea or, rather, what is likely to have happened? For much must be conjectural. The friends who had come with St. Paul to Palestine, and who had been with him through so many dangers, would not forsake him in adversity. St. Luke, we know, remained with him, and during these two years probably finished writing his Gospel and began the *Acts of the Apostles*. Trophimus, who had been the innocent cause of St. Paul's imprisonment, would feel doubly bound to do what was possible for his comfort, and Aristarchus appears to have been so carried away by his enthusiasm, or so identified with St. Paul in word and act, as to come under the same condemnation and to share his imprisonment.

Timothy, Tychicus, Gaius, Secundus and Mnason, if they could not remain through all the weary months of waiting, would at all events be present during the earlier part of the imprisonment, until the call of duty or St. Paul's commands forbad them to stay longer. The nephew of St. Paul, too, who discovered the plot to kill him, and disclosed it to the chief captain, Claudius Lysias, would probably find Caesarea a safer place to live in than Jerusalem, and the unnamed disciples who had accompanied St. Paul from Caesarea to Jerusalem would naturally return home when St. Paul was brought back a prisoner.

What did imprisonment mean as applied to St. Paul? He had committed no offence recognized by Roman law; and the governor, Felix, was favourably disposed towards him, and evidently interested in religious controversy. We are told (*Acts* 24:23), 'he commanded the centurion to keep Paul, and to let him have liberty, and that he should forbid none of his acquaintance to minister or come to him,' so that for a large portion of this time St. Paul, Aristarchus, Trophimus and St. Luke would not only have free communication with one another but with all who chose to visit them.

St. Philip, the first great missionary pioneer and friend of St. Stephen, would often be in their company and, protected perhaps by the friendship of Cornelius, the news brought from distant countries by the ships which entered the harbour, or the arrival of some of 'the brethren' from Ephesus or Cyprus or Greece or Rome or Cyrene, would bring fresh interest and spirit into the days of waiting. Nothing perhaps answered so nearly to the newspapers of modern times as the cultivated memories and narratives of the sailors and news-carriers of those days who journeyed from port to port across the Mediterranean; and it was in this way, but by special messengers, that the chief news of the scattered Churches was carried to the ears and knowledge of the Apostles.

At the beginning of St. Paul's detention at Caesarea, when he was brought before Felix, and at the close of his stay, when he appeared before Festus and King Agrippa, both Caesarea and Jerusalem would be profoundly moved by his trial and by the necessary preparations for the hearing of his case. But the chief feature of all the intervening time seems to have been the formation (if we may call it so) of a great standing missionary committee or council, in which the work of the oldest Hebrew missionaries under St. Philip, the mission to the Gentiles under St. Peter and St. Paul and, later still, the work of their Greek and Roman disciples – all – would be considered in the light of the great commission, 'Go ye, therefore and teach all nations.' What interesting histories St. Paul, St. Timothy, Trophimus and Tychicus would give of their travels and labours! And as St. Luke sat and occasionally wrote at St. Paul's dictation, eager faces would press in on the conclave and questions be asked which only long and repeated explanations could thoroughly satisfy.

Those who were gathered together would be especially interested in the history of that foreign tribe of the Galatians who, like themselves, were beset with troubling questions as to whether Jewish ritual was either necessary or advisable for Gentile Christians.

The city of Tarsus, from which St. Paul came and where he had lived for many years, was on the borders of this province, and St. Timothy and Gaius of Derbe (a town in Lycaonia, which was the southern part of Galatia) had been travelling and working with St. Paul and Trophimus immediately before St. Paul's imprisonment. Indeed, it is quite possible that both of these remained with St. Paul during the whole, or a large part, of his forced confinement in Caesarea.

So that the people of the Galatians, among whom were St. Paul's earliest converts and dearest friends, would often be in the mind and on the lips of St. Paul and those who were associated with him during his stay in Caesarea. The country from which they originally came or, at all events, the more southern part of it, 'Provincia Gallica,' would be known to all on the Mediterranean coast as one of the oldest and richest of the Roman dependencies overseas; and whether the family of Bethany had already gone there, or the land was still waiting for the news of the Gospel, there is very considerable reason to believe that both country and people were much in the mind and heart of the Apostle.

That this is no mere conjecture is evident from the writings of St. Paul himself. Shortly before he came on this last visit to Jerusalem he had been writing to the Church at Rome and describing his plans for the future, the chief feature of which was a long journey from Jerusalem, via Rome, into Spain. In this proposed journey he would almost necessarily pass through Marseilles and all the large towns near the sea-coast between Rome and Spain, confirming and strengthening the Church at Rome and all the scattered Churches or bands of catechumens to be found upon his route.

So that the mind of St. Paul must have been already occupied with the needs of the Massilians, the Galatae and the Iberians long before his imprisonment; and this occupation with their necessities could only be increased by enforced seclusion, when he had more leisure to consider and compare the relative requirements of the various parts of the Roman Empire, and especially those in which the Gospel of Christ had hardly yet obtained a footing. And as the months went by, and no prospect appeared of the release of the Apostle, the question would naturally and inevitably arise as to who could possibly supply his place. Who was there, however imperfectly trained, who would take this Western journey instead of St. Paul, and report to him on the condition and necessities of the scattered bands of Christians already appearing in the distant parts of the Empire?

Mixed up with legends, which may or may not have some true foundation we may yet find in certain old histories of the Bethany family and St. Joseph, and in the traditions of the old Provençal Churches, some real historical clue to the answer of this question.

Let us consider them first.

1. 'When Nero succeeded Claudius in AD 54 the "Province of Judaea" (consisting of Judaea proper, Samaria, Galilee and Judaea beyond Jordan) was governed by a procurator, appointed at pleasure by the Emperor, and he controlled a small Roman garrison, never exceeding, in ordinary times, three thousand men in number. The seat and headquarters of Roman administration were fixed at the city of Caesarea, on the sea-coast, north-west of Jerusalem, and some sixty miles by road from that city. In Jerusalem itself was a small Roman garrison, and the procurator occasionally visited the city. For general supervision and military interference in case of emergency Judaea, like every other "second class" province, depended on a neighbouring governor of high rank with legionaries at his disposal. In this case the legate of Syria was charged with this as one among his numerous and engrossing duties. The procurator in AD 54 was one Antonius Felix, He had been appointed two years previously by Claudius, and Nero left him undisturbed in his office. Felix's wife was Drusilla. She was sister to the only king now left in the neighbourhood, namely Herod Agrippa II – the "Agrippa" of the *Acts of the Apostles*. To him Claudius had, in AD 52, given the tetrarchy of Balanea Trachonitis ("all the country in the neighbourhood of the sea of Galilee"), and Nero on his accession added to his dominions four Galilean cities on the Lake, Tiberias and Taricheae on the western shore, Julias in Gaulonitis and another. A Jew by birth, he was none the less a firm friend of the Romans, and constantly assisted the procurator with his presence and advice, and, when it came to fighting, with his small army' (Henderson's *Life and Principate of Nero*, pp. 362, 363).

2. Geikie, *The Holy Land and the Bible*.

3. The estimated date of St. Peter's visit to Caesarea is given in our Bibles as AD 41.

4. Messrs. Haddan and Stubbs write of this as referring to St. Philip the Apostle; but (although there is a great confusion in all the old writings between the Apostle and evangelist) there can be no doubt that Isidorus was referring to St. Philip who was 'one of the seven deacons,' for he expressly says so.

See also, Eusebius *Eccles. Hist.*, ii, 25: 'And after this there were four prophetesses, daughters of Philip, at Hierapolis in Asia. Their tomb is there, and that, too, of their father.'

5. There is also a very old tradition (supported by evidence from the second and third centuries) that St. Thomas preached the gospel in India. 'It is believed that the Apostle landed at Cranganore in AD 52, and that he founded seven Churches, which remain to this day as monuments of his missionary labours. Placing the infant Church in charge of elders appointed from the converted Brahmin families of Pakolomattarm Sankarapuri, Kalli and Kaliankal, the Apostle went to the opposite coast and died a martyr at Mylapore' (E. M. Philip in 'An Indian National Church,' *Church Times*, January 1, 1904).

King Alfred is said to have sent presents or alms to the Christians in India (of the churches founded by St. Thomas). These were taken by Sieghelm, bishop of Sherbourne, in the year 883. On his return he brought back jewels and spices (Anglo-Saxon Chronicle and William of Malmesbury).

6. We even have evidence of many British Christians making pilgrimages to the Holy Land in AD 386. See letter from Paula and Eustochium 'ad Marcellam' (Palestine Pilgrims Text Society, vol. i). 'The Briton separated from our world, if he has made any progress in religion, leaves the setting sun and seeks a place known to him only by fame and the narrative of the Scriptures.'

CHAPTER V

THE STORY OF RABANUS

'I saw a vision of a woman, where
    Night and new morning strive for domination;
Incomparably pale and almost fair
    And sad beyond expression.

Her eyes were like some fire-enshrining gem,
    Were stately like the stars and yet were tender;
Her figure charmed me like a windy stem
    Quivering and drooped and slender.

I stood upon the outer barren ground,
    She stood on inner ground that budded flowers;
While circling in their never-slackening round
    Danced by the mystic hours.

But every flower was lifted on a thorn,
    And every thorn shot upright from its sands
To gall her feet; hoarse laughter pealed in scorn
    With cruel clapping hands.

She bled and wept, yet did not shrink; her strength
    Was strung up until daybreak of delight;
She measured measureless sorrow toward its length,
    And breadth, and depth, and height.

Then marked I how a chain sustained her form –
A chain of living links not made nor riven:
It stretched sheer up through lightning, wind and storm,
And anchored fast in heaven.'

C. Rossetti, from 'House to Home'

I n the Magdalen College Library at Oxford there is a remarkable old manuscript Life of St. Mary Magdalene.[1]

This manuscript, which professes to be the copy of an original Life of St. Mary Magdalene compiled by Rabanus Maurus, Archbishop of Mayence, who was born in 776 and died in 856, is supposed by a former librarian to date from the earlier part of the fifteenth century, before the foundation of the College, which was in the middle of the century.[2]

No history is known of the manuscript. It is very neatly written on parchment and is prettily illuminated in colours and gold. The writing and illumination is very similar to that of the manuscript copy of the Tertius Opus of Roger Bacon in the Bodleian, and this is generally considered to date from the end of the fourteenth or beginning of the fifteenth century.

The title is in red at the top of each page, and was probably inserted or added after the text had been completed, for it has left an occasional impression on the opposing leaf. The handwriting, however, of both title and text exactly corresponds and cannot be distinguished. Moreover, at one part of the chief illumination at the beginning of the manuscript some of the blue colouring of the initial letter 'D' has left a similar impression on the opposing fly-leaf of the bound volume, so that the impressions may be simply the effect of damp and pressure.

That this copy of the Life of St. Mary (presumably by Rabanus, and the only copy known) is written by a professional scribe is abundantly evident by the careful 'illumination,' by various errors of copying, and by the fact that immediately at the close of the work the writer goes on to transcribe a homily of Origen on St. Mary Magdalene. The bound volume contains six manuscripts, and the binding probably dates from the sixteenth century or rather later (?).

The original work of which this is a copy was undoubtedly written either by Rabanus himself, or its author must have made considerable use of the Homilies of Rabanus, for the general style and composition of the work (as M. Faillon has well shown) closely follows that of its reputed author.

The book has been recognized as a work of Rabanus in the past[3], and appears as such in the well-known list or catalogue of William Cave (*Scriptorum Ecclesiasticorum Historia Literaria*, vol. ii, p. 38 fol., Oxford, 1740-1743).

I am inclined to think that the manuscript is altogether too important, and the indications of the authorship of Rabanus too frequent and too marked, for the work to be a forgery; and if originally written by Rabanus Maurus we can certainly trust his statement in the 'Prologus' that it was compiled by him from then existing records and manuscripts of still older date.[4]

By the kindness of the College authorities and of the librarian, I am able to reproduce here the first page of the manuscript, and (through the publication of the deciphered text in the work of Faillon) to add a detailed account of its contents, translating some of the more interesting paragraphs or chapters in full.

The work, which is a Life not only of St. Mary Magdalene, but also of her sister St. Martha, is divided into fifty chapters and preceded by a Prologus or 'Preface' (which may be read from the original text in the accompanying reproduction). The 'Prologus' runs as follows:

The contemplative life of the most blessed Mary Magdalene, named with the highest reverence as the sweetest chosen of Christ, and by Christ greatly beloved, and the active life of her glorious sister, the minister of Christ, St. Martha, and the friendship and resurrection with which our Lord honoured their venerable brother Lazarus, do not stand on some tradition of modern times recently found, but on the authentic testimony of the four Evangelists, and the Catholic Church throughout the whole world devoutly believes and esteems these facts as they have been preached from the very beginning of our Faith.

A belief so justified by the Divine oracles has therefore no need of human advertisement.

'Who hath ears to hear let him hear what the Spirit saith unto the Churches' by the mouth of the blessed Evangelist, St. John, concerning the great love, the many associations and sweet companionship which took place between the Son of the Glorious Virgin and His friends Martha and Mary and Lazarus.

For, as it is written, 'I love them that love Me,' so St. John writes, 'Now, the Lord Jesus loved Martha and her sister Mary and Lazarus.' This is the testimony of John the disciple, who loved Jesus more than the rest of the disciples. It is the testimony of the Apostle who at the Last Supper reclined on the breast of Jesus. It is the testimony of the Evangelist to whom Christ on the cross committed the care and keeping of His Virgin Mother.

O! happy saints, to whom the Holy Gospel gives such great glory, such pre-eminence, such testimony!

In order that the facts may be set forth more thoroughly I have thought it wise to write in one narrative the Divine accounts of the evangelists, and then to add faithfully the events affecting these friends of our Saviour which took place after His ascension according as our fathers have told us and according to the accounts they have left for us in their writings.

And to pursue our work more easily and to avoid repetition we will endeavour at once shortly to set forth what the ancient histories tell us of the origin, birth, education and talents of Martha, Mary and Lazarus, to the praise of God our Saviour and to the honour and glory of His friends.

The 1st chapter accordingly opens with a short history of the family of Bethany:

In the territory of Jerusalem, on the Mount of Olives, at fifteen stadia to the east of the Holy City, is situated the little town of Bethany, the country of Mary Magdalene, of Lazarus and of Martha. Here was born the blessed Martha, the venerable hostess of our Lord.

Her mother, whose name was Eucharia, was descended from the royal family of the House of Israel. Her father, Theophilus, was a Syrian prince and governor of the maritime country.

St. Martha had a sister of great beauty named Mary and a young brother called Lazarus, All these were noted for their fine character and intelligence, and for their knowledge of the language of the Hebrews, in which they had been well instructed.

In the 2nd chapter we are further told that they possessed a rich patrimony of lands, of money, and of slaves, that a great part of the city of Jerusalem (beside the village of Bethany) belonged to them, and that they also had lands at Magdala (on the left side of the Lake of Galilee), and at another Bethany (or Bethabara), the scene of the preaching of St. John the Baptist.

The three lived together, and Martha as the eldest of the family had the administration of their property. As the younger sister grew up she moved from Bethany and took up her residence at Magdala, either on her own property there, or as the wife or mistress of one of the rich inhabitants who dwelt on the borders of the lake.

There, for a time, she lived a life of sin, in conscious disobedience to the command of God and to the wishes of her family until aroused by the preaching of our Lord and pardoned by Him in the house of Simon the Pharisee.

The latter is said to have been related to St. Martha 'by the ties of blood and of friendship.' (If this means that Martha, who is described as being much older than the other children, was only half-sister to them and specially related to Simon, it is interesting to note that Mary, in coming to his house to see the Saviour, was also at the same time, in a certain sense returning home.)

From the 5th to the 9th chapter we read of the first anointing and conversion of St. Mary, the account closely following the narrative in the Gospels.

In the 9th chapter we read of the women who followed our Lord as He went about with the twelve Apostles declaring the coming of the Kingdom of God, of Joanna, of Susannah, and of Mary Magdalene. Some of the miracles belonging to this portion of our Lord's history are related in detail, and notably that of the Phoenician woman who was cured of her haemorrhage by touching His garment. We are told that she was of Caesarea Philippi, and that her name was Martha. An account is also given of the statue erected in honour of this miracle at Caesarea Philippi; the account of this being very similar to that given by Eusebius the historian.

In the 10th chapter we are told that it was at Magdala, at the estate of Mary Magdalene, where Martha and Mary Magdalene entertained our Lord and His disciples as recorded by St. Luke (10:38).

In the company of the Saviour were the twelve Apostles, the seventy disciples and a large following of illustrious women, so that it was natural that St. Martha, as the elder sister and chief hostess, should have been somewhat worried with the preparation for so large a gathering. In this chapter we are introduced to Marcella, the servant or stewardess of the house who, together with St. Martha, Joanna and Susannah, waited on the guests.

At this time our Saviour often came to Magdala to the house of St. Mary and St. Martha and lodged there, and when He was gone on any distant journey, and they could not accompany Him, refreshments and other necessities were sent from the sisters to Him, either by the hands of the servants of the house or by Judas Iscariot, who had charge of the money and provisions.

From the narrative it appears to have been at this house at Magdala that Jesus was teaching the multitude when His mother and brethren came seeking Him (as recorded in the Gospel of *Luke* 11:27), and it was Marcella, 'a woman of great devotion and faith' who exclaimed: 'Blessed is the womb that bore Thee, and the paps which Thou hast sucked.'

At times our Saviour is said to have frequently used the other residences of Martha and Mary as His resting-places – Bethany near Jerusalem and the other Bethany on the Jordan; and it was at this second Bethany in Galilee that our Lord was staying when news was brought of the illness of Lazarus at the Bethany near Jerusalem.

The next chapters (from the 14th to the 16th) deal with the resurrection of Lazarus, closely following the Bible story. The 16th chapter finishes with an interesting homily on the analogous loosing of a man from the death of sin, declaring that if a man truly repents of his sins and yet is prevented from having recourse to the usual channel of confession and (priestly) absolution ('*confidenter pronuntio*'), 'I confidently pronounce that if the confession is not wilfully neglected but prevented by necessity, the Sovereign Priest finishes what the mortal one cannot finish, and God holds as done that which the sinner would truly do but is unable to perform.'

Both the matter and the method of this passage appear to be very consonant with its reputed authorship, while no one reading the narrative in the original could imagine that it was an interpolation.

The 11th chapter brings us to the Sabbath before the Passion, when our Lord, who had been staying in a town called Ephrem, came to Bethany near Jerusalem and attended the feast in the house of Simon the leper. This and the following chapter deal mainly with the second anointing of St. Mary. On this (Saturday) evening He is said to have slept at Bethany. On the following day (on Palm Sunday) occurred the triumphal procession to Jerusalem, but no one offered our Saviour a lodging in the city. Accordingly (as we are told also in the Gospels), He and all the twelve Apostles returned to Bethany, obtaining with Martha and Mary and Lazarus the hospitality which was denied them in Jerusalem.

The following day (Monday) He is said to have cursed the barren fig-tree as He went into Jerusalem. All this day He spent teaching within the Temple precincts returning to Bethany in the evening.

The next day (Tuesday) He again spent in Jerusalem. His Apostles were with Him and noticed the withered fig-tree as they passed. Again our Lord slept at Bethany, returning to the Temple at Jerusalem early in the morning (Wednesday) and speaking there to His Apostles regarding the end of the world and all that must be accomplished. It is said to have been at the close of this day that He said, 'Ye know that after two days is the feast of the Passover and the true Lamb, the Son of man, shall be delivered to be crucified.'

After this saying He left the Temple and returned to Bethany sleeping for the last time at the house of Lazarus, of Martha and of Mary.

All the earlier part of the next day (Thursday) He is said to have spent at Bethany, taking leave of His hosts, however, before the evening. As evening drew near He went into Jerusalem to the house of the upper chamber (on the Hill of Zion), where the Passover had been prepared for Himself and His Apostles.

The 20th and 21st chapters contain an account of the Passion and crucifixion of our Lord, in strict accordance with, and closely following, the record in Holy Scripture.

In the 22nd chapter, containing an account of the embalming and burial by Joseph of Arimathea and Nicodemus, a detailed description is given of the mausoleum and sepulchre of St. Joseph, which he had made for his own body. St. Joseph is called '*nobilis decurion*,' which probably means that he had an officer's position in the Judean or Roman army, and accounts for his friendship, or rather acquaintance, with Pilate.

The sepulchre is described as consisting of two chambers, an outer room (afterwards the 'Chapel of the Angel'), which was of sufficient height so that 'a man with his hand raised could scarcely touch the roofing of it,' and an inner chamber, where the body of the Saviour was laid. In both the entrance is said to have faced eastwards, and the body of the Lord is said to have been placed in a recess to the north side of the second or inner chamber, His feet directed to the east, His head to the west, and His left side touching (or lying against) the rock wall of the tomb.

Mary Magdalene and her companions are depicted as weeping in the Judgment Hall on the way to Calvary, as suffering acutest agony at the crucifixion, as waiting at the tomb, and then, in the little time remaining before the Sabbath, hurrying to purchase balms and spices for that third anointing of the Holy Body, which appears to have been rendered unnecessary or impossible by the great resurrection. Mary Magdalene, Mary Cleopas, Mary Salome, Joanna and Susannah are mentioned as carrying the spices on the resurrection morning.

The chapters from the 24th to the 30th are occupied with an account of the resurrection from the various descriptions of the Evangelists, special references being made to the appearance of the angels. Mary Magdalene is noticed as the only visitor to the tomb who saw the two angels, and as the first to see her risen Lord. Her commission from Him to the holy Apostles is fully recognized and enforced, and this portion of the Life closes with a review of the chief incidents which marked the piety and love of St. Mary Magdalene for her Saviour, and the reward which she received.

In the 31st chapter an account is given of the ascension of our Lord.

Forty days after His resurrection, desiring once more to be visibly present with His disciples, we are told that our Saviour appeared to them as they sat at meat and partook of the final meal with them. The company is said to have included the Blessed Virgin, all the eleven Apostles, Mary Magdalene, Martha, Lazarus, Mary Cleopas, Salome, Joanna and Susannah. All appear to have received at this time the commission to preach the Gospel – first in Jerusalem, then in Judea and Samaria, and then to all the world, and our Lord was accompanied not only by these, but by a great multitude of disciples as He led them forth as far as Bethany – there, in the presence of about one hundred and twenty persons, He said, 'Behold I am with you always, even to the end of the ages,' and, lifting up His hands, He blessed them, and was seen of all to arise up into the heavens, a luminous cloud receiving Him out of their sight.

With Him also are said to have ascended the thousands of holy souls who had been waiting since the beginning of the world, and those who (as we are told in Holy Scripture) 'came out of their graves after His resurrection, and went into the Holy City and appeared unto many' (*Matthew* 27:53), and were witnesses of our Lord's resurrection-life.

The 34th chapter contains the narrative of the day of Pentecost and the descent of the Holy Ghost. It also tells of the life of the early Church, and of the honour and esteem in which St. Mary Magdalene and the holy women, with whom she had been so much associated, were held by the Apostles. In doing this, reference is made to the dispute recorded in *Acts* 6:1, as arising from some jealousy of the preference accorded to these by the holy Apostles. It was for this reason (in the first place) that the seven deacons were appointed – Stephen and Philip, Parmenas and Timon, Prochorus, Nicanor and Nicholas.

This and the succeeding chapter narrate how Lazarus, Martha and Mary sold their properties in Jerusalem, Magdala and the Bethanies, the house at Bethany near Jerusalem alone being preserved, and brought the amount to St. Peter as chief of the Apostles.

St. Mary Magdalene is represented as especially devoted to the service and care of the Blessed Virgin and, because of this, is said to have rejoiced with her in the vision and ministry of angels who were sent from time to time for the succour and consolation of the Virgin Mother.

The house at Bethany near Jerusalem, where the Saviour had so often slept or watched through the long summer nights, appears to have been retained by the Apostles as a house of prayer, and was subsequently consecrated, Lazarus being appointed priest or bishop of the Church there. When, however, the persecution of the Jews arose Lazarus left Bethany for Cyprus, and there preached the Kingdom of God, becoming the first Christian bishop in Cyprus.

The 36th chapter is as follows:

After the death of Stephen, the first martyr, Saul was called from heaven to the Faith, but was not named Paul until twelve years later. Those who were dispersed abroad with St. Philip and the other companions of St. Stephen went everywhere preaching the Kingdom of

God. They came finally to Antioch, where a great Church of disciples was gathered together. There the name of 'Christian' took its origin; there the patriarchal seat was established by the blessed Peter, and there afterwards he ordained Euodius as bishop, when he returned to Jerusalem to the rest of the Apostles. These all, according to the Saviour's command, continued for the space of twelve years preaching only to the twelve tribes of the Hebrews.

In the thirteenth year after the ascension (AD 47), James, the brother of John, was killed by the sword; Peter was cast into prison; and Saul, called to the Apostleship of the Gentiles by the Holy Spirit, departed on his mission. At this time he took the name of Paul.

The following year (the fourteenth after the ascension, AD 48) the following division was made of the Apostles:

Thomas and Bartholomew were allotted to the care of the east.
Simon and Matthew to the south.
Philip and Thaddaeus to the north.
Matthew and James to the centre of the world ('*Medium mundi*').
John and Andrew to the provinces of the Mediterranean, and Peter and Paul to the kingdoms of the West.

At the same time Paul came to Jerusalem to see Peter, both giving and receiving from James and John and Peter due recognition of their union in the apostolate. He then departed with Barnabas to preach the Gospel in Syria and Illyricum.

St. Peter chose from among the eldest and best of the disciples of Christ certain preachers of the Gospel for those regions of the West which he could not himself visit; for the regions of the Gauls, in which there were seventeen provinces, a similar number of priests, and for the Spanish provinces, of which there were seven, a similar number of teachers.

Of these twenty-four older disciples Maximinus was the first and foremost. He was one of the seventy disciples of our Lord and Saviour, illustrious both by his power of miracles and of teaching, and chief of the Christians next to the Apostles.

Mary Magdalene, who was united by the ties of love to the religion and holiness of this disciple, determined not to be separated from his company or conversation wherever it should please God to call him.

As ten of the Apostles had already departed, however great the attachment of the disciples for the Apostles, it was impossible for them to remain together after the hate of the Jews had aroused the persecution against the Church, after Herod had cut off the head of St. James, had cast St. Peter into prison, and had chased the Christians out of his borders.

At the going of the disciples the noble matrons and widows, who had ministered to them in Jerusalem and the East, accompanied them. Among these was St. Martha, whose brother Lazarus was already bishop of Cyprus; Marcella, the stewardess and follower of Martha; St. Parmenas, the deacon, full of faith and of the grace of God, who was also of the number of His disciples.

It was to his care that St. Martha committed herself in Christ, even as St. Mary had already committed herself to the care of St. Maximin.

By an admirable counsel of Divine providence these took their way to the regions of the West; God willing that not alone through the Gospel the praise of the blessed Magdalene and her sister should be known in all the world, but that as the East had until then been favoured by the example of their holy conversation, so the coasts of the West should be made famous by their presence, and sanctified by the deposit of their most holy relics.

Chapter 37

Therefore the chief, St. Maximinus, the blessed Parmenas, the Archdeacon; Trophimus and Eutropius, bishops, and the rest of the leaders in this Christian warfare, together with the God-renowned Mary Magdalene and her sister, the most blessed Martha, departed by way of the sea.

Leaving the shores of Asia and favoured by an east wind, they went round about, down the Tyrrhenian Sea, between Europe and Africa, leaving the city of Rome and all the land of Italy to the right. Then, happily turning their course to the right, they came near to the city of Marseilles, in the Viennoise province of the Gauls, where the River Rhone is received by the sea. There, having called upon God, the great King of all the world, they parted; each company going to the province where the Holy Spirit had directed them; presently preaching everywhere, 'the Lord working with them, confirming the word with signs following.'

The chief, St. Maximinus, went to Aix (Aquensem), the capital of the second Narbonnaise – where, too, Mary Magdalene finished the course of her wanderings.

Paul to Narbonne ('Narbonam'), the capital of the first province of the Narbonnaise.

Austregisilus to Bourges ('Bituricam'), the capital of the first province of Aquitaine.

Hirenaeus to Lyons ('Lugdunum'), the capital of the first Lugdunoise.

Gratian to Tours ('Turonem'), the capital of the third Lugdunoise.

Sabinus and Potentianus to Sens ('Senonas'), the capital of the fourth Lugdunoise.

118

Valerius to Trèves ('Treverim'), the capital of the first Belgic province.

Feroncius to Besançon ('Bisuntium'), the capital of the greatest province of the Sequanae.

Eutropius to Saintes ('Sanctonas'), a city of the second Aquitaine.

Trophimus to Arles ('Arelatem'), now capital of the Viennoise province.

These ten provinces of the Gauls believed through the preaching of these ten disciples.

Other teachers preached – not in the remaining seven provinces, but in seven provincial towns:

Eutropius at Orange ('Aurasicum').

Frontinus at Perigeux ('Petrogoras').

Georgius at Veliacum.

Julianus at Mans ('Cenomanum').

Martialis at Limoges ('Lemovicas').

Saturninus at Toulouse ('Tolosam'), where he was thrown down from the capitol for the faith of Christ.

Parmenas at Avignon ('Avenicorum').

With St. Parmenas went the venerable servant of our Lord and Saviour, St. Martha, and Marcella, her servant, Epaphras and Sosthenes, Germanus, Euchodia and Syntex.

In addition these are the names of those who were sent by the Apostles into Spain – Torquatus, Thesiphum, Secundus, Indalecius, Coecilius, Esicius and Euphrasius. These united the seven provinces of Spain to the Christian Faith.[5]

Chapter 38

St. Maximin, having gone to Aix, began to sow the good seed of the heavenly doctrine in the hearts of the Gentiles, giving himself, night and day, to preaching, prayer and fasting, so that he might bring the unbelievers of that country to the knowledge and service of God.

Soon the preaching of the Gospel produced a new harvest of the faith, and the blessed Maximinus at the head of his Church at Aix, shone forth by the many and Divine excellences of his miracles.

With him, and in the same Church, St. Mary Magdalene, the special friend of the Saviour, gave herself to contemplation; for since she had chosen, with so much wisdom, the better part which she found at the feet of her Lord, this, as He had promised, was never taken from her.

But, full of anxiety for the salvation of the souls for whose sake she had come Westward to the very ends of the earth, she often desisted from the joys of contemplation, in order to preach to unbelievers or to confirm the Christians in their faith. 'Out of the abundance of the heart the mouth speaketh,' and this made her preaching a true Divine meditation. She herself was ever an example to sinners of genuine conversion – to penitents of the certain hope of forgiveness – to the faithful of loving sympathy, and to all Christian people a proof of the Divine compassion.

She would point to her eyes as those which had washed with her tears the feet of her Saviour, and had seen Him first when He rose from the dead – to her hair which had wiped His sacred feet – to her lips which had kissed them, not only during His life here, but even after His death and resurrection – to her hands which had touched them and anointed them.

But why should I further recount here these things? As Jesus Himself has said: 'Verily, I say unto you, wherever this gospel shall be preached throughout the whole world, this also which she hath done shall be spoken of for a memorial of her' (*Mark* 24:9).

Chapter 39

St. Martha also, with her companions, preached the Gospel of the Saviour to the people in the cities of Avignon and Arles, and among the towns and villages which were on the borders of the Rhone in the province of Vienne. She chiefly bore testimony to all that she had seen touching the person of our Lord – to what she had heard or learnt from His lips when publicly teaching – to what He had disclosed concerning heavenly powers – joining these with wonders (or miracles) of her own. First had been given to her, when necessity demanded, by prayer or by the sign of the Holy Cross, to cleanse the lepers, to cure the paralytics, to quicken the dead, to heal the blind, the deaf, the dumb, the lame, and all who were in any way diseased.

Similar powers were granted to St. Mary who performed miracles with an inexpressible graciousness when these were needed either to establish the truth of her words or to incite the faith of her hearers.

Both St. Mary and St. Martha possessed a noble beauty, an honourable bearing and a ready grace of language that was captivating. Rarely or never did any one come away from their preaching incredulous or without tears. Their very look appeared to be able to inflame others with the love of Christ or to fill them with true contrition.

They were abstemious in food and drink and discreet in their clothing; Mary, indeed, providing herself with too little food and clothing after losing the corporeal presence of the Lord of salvation. The matrons, however, who lived with her and had a great affection for her, provided sufficiently for her necessities.

From this arose (in all probability) the apocryphal account that she was daily lifted into the air by angels and refreshed by them with celestial food. Understood in a mystical sense this is not altogether incredible (but not otherwise). Further, the account that, after the ascension of the Saviour, she fled into the desert of Arabia, and there lived unknown and without clothing in a cave, where, being visited by some priest, she demanded from him his vestment, 'these and other similar particulars are altogether false, and made up from fictitious fables regarding the acts of the penitent of Egypt.'

In the 40th chapter we find an account of the dragon – a species of crocodile – which at that time was found on the banks of the Rhone near Tarascon, and greatly alarmed the people.

These are represented as saying that if the Messiah preached by St. Martha had such infinite power, why could it not be shown in the destruction of this beast?

Martha replied, 'Everything is possible to those who believe,' and leading a company of those who were brave enough to follow her she went to the lair of the beast and, making the sign of the cross, tied the neck of the animal with her girdle. She then permitted the people to destroy it.

The 41st chapter deals with the life of St. Martha at Tarascon, and runs as follows:

All venomous reptiles being thus expelled by the power of God from Tarascon, St. Martha chose it as her dwelling, and changed what had been formerly a hateful and noxious place into one that was both beautiful to the eye and lovely.

She made here an oratory, which she studied to enrich with virtues and good deeds rather than with dainty and useless ornaments. Here she lived alone for seven years, her food during this time being edible roots, green herbs and fruits. Yet to refresh herself with food more than once in the day she considered as wrong for herself, but not as wrong for her friends and neighbours. For considering that this daily fast without charity would only be a suffering for herself and a burden to those who stayed with her, she was ever mindful of her old hospitality.

The poor were always with her, and to these she gave largely of whatever she had for herself, always making those who were destitute be part at her table and, while reserving herbs only for herself, giving these (poor) meats for their necessities with tender solicitude, and that gentleness which was habitual with her. She did this with the greater eagerness and desire . . . remembering how He, whom she had so often received in the old days when He was on earth and who then suffered from hunger and thirst, now had no need of these temporal aids, but still in His poor desired to be refreshed and comforted.

And the handmaid of Christ remembered how He had said to them: 'Inasmuch as ye have done it to the least of these My brethren, ye have done it unto Me.' Therefore, as she had formerly served the Head of the Church, so now she applied herself to the service of its members, showing to all the same love and kindness.

And because God loveth a cheerful giver, so He took care that like an inexhaustible fountain, the stores in her cellars, although daily emptied by her generosity, should never be exhausted; for the faithful, seeing her delight in giving, contributed so much the more; and without any care of her own, she was always able to give abundantly.

Her clothing was rough. During seven years she simply wore two garments (*saccus* and *cilicium*) gathered together by a (knotted) girdle of horsehair. Her feet were naked, and she wore on her head a white cap of camel's hair. Branches of trees and vine-leaves over which was placed a coverlet served her as a bed, while her pillow was a stone.

Her spirit, surrendered from everything to God and (often) continuing all night in prayer, was lost in Him, and He whom in time past in His humility she had seen in her own house, she now adored upon her knees as reigning in heaven.

Frequently she went into the neighbouring towns and villages, preaching to the people the faith of the Saviour, returning to her solitude with the news of many fresh companies added to the Faith.

The 42nd chapter deals with the raising to life again of a young man who had been drowned when swimming across the Rhone to hear the preaching of St. Martha.

The 43rd gives an account of the consecration of the house of St. Martha as a church:

The bishop, Maximinus, the protector of St. Magdalene and director of her life, came from his province of the second Narbonnaise to Tarascon, in order to see St. Martha, the servant of Jesus Christ.

With similar intention, on the same day and at the same hour, came Trophimus, bishop of Arles, and Eutropius, the priest of Orange, none expecting the arrival of the others, but all coming together by the inspiration of God, who disposes all things delightfully.

The sainted heroine received them with honour, entertained them liberally and insisted on their stay and, on the sixteenth day of the kalends of January (which is the seventeenth day of the month of Casleu, called December among the Latins), they dedicated to our Lord and Saviour as a church the house of the most blessed Martha – a house already rendered sacred by her deeds and virtues and conversation.

And after the consecration, when the priests sat at meat, she listened to them with great affection. Now there was a multitude of people gathered together, who sat at meat also, and there was a deficiency of wine. The hostess of the Saviour, therefore, ordered them to draw water in the name of Jesus Christ, and to serve it abundantly to all. And when the priests had tasted it they found that the water had been changed into the best wine. They, therefore, ordered that this day should be henceforth observed reverentially, both as the day of dedication of the church and as the day when the water was converted into wine.

Chapter 44

The bishops, having said farewell to the blessed servant of Jesus Christ, and commending themselves to her holy merits and prayers, gave and received each other's benediction, and then departed, each to his own place.

In parting with St. Maximinus

St. Martha sent her salutations to her venerable sister, Mary Magdalene . . . begging her to come and visit her before she died.

When St. Mary Magdalene heard this from St. Maximinus, she returned the salutation of her sister, promising what she asked, if not in this life, then after she was dead.

Whence it is to be believed that the Saints of God remember their loved ones after death, sometimes then fulfilling the promises made while they were living.

Now, at this time a persecution arose in Aquitaine among the Gentiles, and a great number of Christians were thrust into exile. Among these, Frontinus, bishop of Perigeux, and Georgius, of Veliacum, fled together to the blessed Martha at Tarascon. She, with her usual charity, kindly received them, showed them every generosity, and honourably studied to retain them with her, until they were permitted to return to their own dioceses.

When they were just ready to depart, St. Martha said, 'O bishop of Perigueux, you must know that next year I shall leave this mortal body. I beseech, if it please you, that you will come to bury me.' To which the bishop replied, 'I will come, O daughter, if God permits it, and I am still alive.'

The priests then returned to their homes, and the blessed Martha calling her own people around her, foretold to them that the day of her death was to take place after one year from this date. She then lay down on her couch of branches, and was consumed by fever through the whole of that year, 'as gold is tried in the furnace.'

Chapter 45

In the meantime the blessed Mary Magdalene, rapt in heavenly contemplation, guarded faithfully that better part which she had chosen; . . . and when the time drew near that the earthly tabernacle of her most holy spirit should be dissolved, and she was ready to enter into those heavenly courts for which she longed, so that she might be more fully united to her Lord, the Son of God, her Lord and Saviour Himself appeared to her. For truly she saw Jesus Christ Himself, the object of her desires who, attended by a multitude of angels, called her to the glory of His celestial kingdom, gently and compassionately saying, 'Come, My chosen, and place thyself on My throne, for the King desireth thy presence. . . . He to whom thou didst minister when He was on the earth among men shall receive thee to eternal life among choirs of angels, praising and excelling, world without end.'

This special friend of her Lord and Apostle of the Saviour then passed away on the eleventh day before the kalends of August, attended by rejoicing angels, being made partners with them of heavenly powers, and worthy (with them) to see the King of Ages in His beauty, and to rejoice in the glory of His eternal light.

The blessed Maximinus placed her most holy body, preserved with diverse aromatics, in a wonderful sepulchre, and then, over her blessed remains, erected a church of noble architecture. Her tomb is shown of white (or shining) marble (alabaster?), and bears upon it the carved representation of the anointing in the house of Simon, where St. Mary found the pardon of her sins, and also the service she rendered to her Lord when she brought spices to His sepulchre.

Chapter 46

While these things were taking place near Aix, the metropolis of the ecclesiastical province of the Narbonnaise, at the same hour near Tarascon, in the province of Vienne, the servant of the Lord, St. Martha, being detained in bed by the fever, suddenly saw a choir of angels bearing the soul of her sister Mary Magdalene to heaven. Calling together those who attended her, she related to them what she had seen, asking them to rejoice with her and saying, 'O! most happy sister, what is this that you have done? Why have you not visited me as you promised? And are you rejoicing without me in the embrace of the Lord Jesus whom we have loved and who has so loved us? But I shall follow where you are going. In the meantime rejoice in that eternal life to which you have gone. But be not forgetful of her who remembers you.'

The sainted heroine, comforted by this vision, more than ever desired to be dissolved and to be with Christ, scarcely bearing any longer to remain in the flesh, but desiring to be with her sister and the angels she had seen. Knowing that her departure would not be long delayed, she continually admonished, instructed and strengthened the Christians around her. So it came to pass that the report spread that the servant of God was dying, and a great multitude of the faithful came together; and determining to stay with her until she was buried, they made tents in the neighbouring woods, and fires were lighted in all directions.

Chapter 47

On the evening of the seventh day following St. Martha commanded her attendants to light seven candles and three lamps. And about the middle of the night those who were watching were oppressed by a deep slumber and slept. And behold there came a vehement rushing wind and put out all the candles and lamps. Which when St. Martha saw she made the sign of the cross and prayed that she might be preserved from the

127

snares of the evil ones. Then, calling her attendants she prayed them to rekindle the lights. This they ran to do, but while they were gone suddenly a heavenly light shone all around, and in that light appeared Mary Magdalene, the Apostle of Christ our Lord and Saviour, holding in her right hand a burning torch, which presently by its heavenly radiance re-lit the seven candles and the lamps that had been put out. Then, approaching the bed of her sister, she said, 'Hail, sainted sister!' And when St. Martha had returned her salutation she continued, 'Behold, I have come to visit you while still living in the body as the blessed Maximinus asked me, and here is your loving Lord and Saviour who calls you from this vale of miseries. So also He appeared to me, before my passing, and brought me to the palace of His glory. Come, then, and do not tarry.' Saying this, she hastened with joy to make way for her Lord, who came near to Martha, and with most gentle aspect said to her, 'I am here to whom a short time since thou didst minister devotedly with all thy powers, to whom thou didst give the most grateful hospitality, to whom after My Passion thou didst many good deeds in My members and before whom, prostrating thyself, thou didst affirm, "I believe that Thou art the Christ, the Son of the living God, who should come into the world." Come, then, my hostess, come from your exile and receive your crown.'

Martha, hearing these words, attempted to rise and to follow the Saviour incontinently, but He said, 'Wait awhile, for I go to prepare a place for you, and will again return and receive you to Myself, that where I am there you may also be.'

Having said this He disappeared, and her sister St. Mary was no longer seen, but the light which appeared with them continued to shine. At the same time the watchers returned and were astonished to see the lights which had been put out shining with unusual brilliancy.

Chapter 48

When the day was come St. Martha commanded her attendants to place her out of doors. Quickly as the time passed, it seemed slow to her, and the morning appeared to have the length of a thousand years. A rough couch of straw was laid down under a spreading tree, and covered with a linen pall on which the figure of the cross was made with cinders. When the sun arose the servant of Christ was carried out and placed upon the cinders and, according to her wish, an image of the crucified Saviour was set up before her. There she rested for a space, and then looking at the multitude of Christians around her, she begged them in their prayers to entreat for her speedy release, and as they broke into weeping she turned her eyes to heaven and said: 'O my Lord and Saviour, wherefore is this waiting? When shall I come and appear before Thy face. Since Thou didst speak to me at the dawning of the day my soul hath failed me; . . . confound me not, O Lord, in my desire. O my God, make no long tarrying.'

So meditating she came in the spirit to consider how Christ had expired upon the cross at the ninth hour (as she had herself formerly witnessed), and bethinking her of the book of the Passion of Christ, written in Hebrew, which she brought with her from Jerusalem, she called St. Parmenas to her, gave him the book, and prayed him to read it to her that so the tedium of her expectation might be lightened.

On hearing him read in her own language of the Saviour's sufferings – of which she had been a witness – she burst into tears of compassion and began to weep, and forgetting for a time her own departure, she fixed her whole attention on the passion of her Lord. When the recital came to the passage where Christ, committing His Spirit into the hands of the Father, 'gave up the ghost,' she gave a deep sigh, and directly expired.

St. Martha thus slept in the Lord on the fourth day before the kalends of August, the eighth day after the death of her sister, St. Mary Magdalene, or the sixth day of the week, at the ninth hour of the day, and in the sixty-fifth year of her age. Her body being laid out and enfolded with due honour, was carried into the church of St. Martha by the friends who came with her from the East, and who, to that day, had remained with her. These were St. Parmenas, Germanus and Sosthenes, and Epaphras, who had been the companion of St. Trophimus, bishop of Arles; Marcella her servant, and Euchodia and Syntex.

These seven devoted three days to St. Martha's funeral rites, together with a multitude of people who came from all parts, and who until the third day kept watch around the holy body, praising God and making general illuminations by lighting candles in the church, lamps in the houses, and open fires in the neighbouring forest.

Chapter 49

On the Sabbath day a tomb was prepared for the body of St. Martha in the church which had been consecrated, and on the day which is called the Lord's Day, at the third hour of the day, all came together in order to worthily bury the holy body of St. Martha. This was on the eve of the kalends of August.

At the same hour, at Petragoricus (Perigueux), a city of Aquitaine, St. Frontinus,[6] the priest, being about to celebrate Mass, had fallen asleep in his chair when Christ appeared and said to him: 'Come, My son, do what thou didst promise and assist at the burying of Martha, My hostess.' And immediately in the twinkling of an eye both our Lord and St. Frontinus appeared in the church at Tarascon holding books in their hands and standing, Christ at the head, and St. Frontinus at the foot of the body of St. Martha, and they alone placed it in the grave, to the wonder of those who were present. When the burial service was finished they departed.

Some of those who had attended the servant of the Saviour returned to the East – viz., Epaphras, Marcella, and Syntyche, who is buried in Philippi, and of whom the Apostle writes: Parmenas, full of faith and of the grace of God, who was found worthy of the martyr's crown, and Germanus and Euchodia. These afterwards, with St. Clement and others, helped the blessed Apostles in their work 'whose names are written in the book of life' (*Philippians* 4:2, 3).

Since the day of the death of St. Martha miracles without number have taken place in her church, health and soundness being restored to the blind, the deaf, the dumb, the lame, paralytics and persons suffering from fever, from leprosy and from possession of devils. Clovis, King of the Francs and Teutons, the first who bore the profession of the Christian faith, moved by the multitude and greatness of the miracles performed at the shrine of St. Martha, came to Tarascon, and as soon as he had touched the tomb of the saint was delivered from a grave disease of the kidney, which had caused him severe suffering. In grateful record of this great deliverance King Clovis gave to God three measures of lands around the church of St. Martha reaching to the farther side of the Rhone, with the towns, villages and woods situate upon them, sealing the deed with his ring. All this property the (church of the) sainted heroine possesses to this day. Robbery, pillage, sacrilege and false witness were frightfully and immediately punished here by the direct judgment of God and to the praise of the Lord Christ.

Chapter 50

Hitherto it has sufficed to narrate the religious life and precious death of St. Martha the venerable servant of the Son of God, and this has now been done. The wonderful things done after her death, through her intercession and owing to her influence, as well as the account of the holy life and passion of her brother the blessed Lazarus bishop and martyr, these are reserved for a new volume. We shall here only briefly refer to the miracles that were done through (the intercession of) Mary Magdalene, the chosen of God, and only lightly glance at the death of the holy priest St. Maximinus.

Knowing that the time was near when he should be taken away from this world and receive the reward of his labours – as it had been revealed to him by the Holy Spirit – St. Maximinus ordered a place to be prepared for his burial in the church which we have already spoken of as having been built (with cunning workmanship) over the most holy body of the blessed Mary Magdalene. And he desired that his sarcophagus should be placed close to that of St. Mary, the chosen of God.

So, after he was dead, the holy body of St. Maximinus was thus honourably deposited by the faithful, and both St. Mary and St. Maximinus make beautiful the place of their burial, and by their intercession obtain miracles here for those who pray that they may gain health of soul and body.

This place has since become so sacred that no king or prince, or anyone else, however endued with power or wealth, can enter into the church here in order to ask for a blessing, except he shall have first put down his arms and set aside all animal desires and angry passions, so that, at length, he may enter in with all humility and devotion. And no woman of any condition, however high her rank or position, has had the boldness to presume to enter into this most holy temple.

This monastery-church is called the Abbey of St. Maximinus. It is situated in the county of Aix, and is greatly endowed with riches and honours. And it was on the sixth of the ides of June that the blessed priest St. Maximinus received his heavenly crown.

1. At the time that Rabanus was writing, fantastic miracle tales were circulating throughout the Churches of the Continent. Some of these are unpleasant to Protestant readers, but we consider that the local history contained in these quotations from Rabanus is of such importance as to make the publication of them of value. (Ed.)

2. 'Mr. Madan, of the Bodleian, is inclined to think it is not later than 1450, and would, I think, be inclined to put it rather earlier than the second quarter of the fifteenth century – from 1400 to 1425, rather than from 1425 to 1450' (letter from the Revd. H. A. Wilson).

3. It is quoted by John de Cella (?) in the earlier part of the Chronicles of *Matthew of Paris* (about 1190).

4. A recent writer (Mr. Gaskoin, in *Alcuin, his Life and Work*, London, 1904) says of the work of Rabanus Maurus: 'The writings of the Fathers on which (his) commentaries were based, were literally produced, the share of the compiler in the composition being designedly and almost ostentatiously reduced to the smallest possible proportions.'

5. It will be noticed that these names of the early missionaries, though apparently directly referring to the 'seventeen' and the 'seven' of a previous page, are mentioned rather as the first priest-bishops than as necessarily coming together with St. Mary and St. Martha.

The name 'Hirenaeus' associated with Lyons appears to point to the great Irenaeus, who was not bishop of Lyons until about AD 179. This must, therefore, be a marked anachronism unless it refers to another and earlier Hirenaeus who may have preceded Pothinus in the bishopric. That this may not be impossible appears from a passage of Gregory of Tours (*Hist. Franc.*, bk. i. cap. 22), who speaks of the great persecution of AD 177 as following the time of Irenaeus, but he, like many more of the old writers, appears to be hopelessly at fault in the matter of dates (See also Appendix D where Irenaeus writes of his predecessors.)

6. A 'Fronto' is mentioned as a missionary Christian from Ephesus in the Epistle of St. Ignatius to the Ephesians (chap. i, 7), 'Crocus, Aresimus, Burrhus, Euplus and Fronto' being mentioned together as meeting St. Ignatius on his journey as a prisoner to Rome. Is there any relationship between this disciple and St. Front of Perigueux?

CHAPTER VI

THE TRADITIONS OF THE THREE MARIES AND THEIR COMPANIONS

'How pure at heart and sound in head,
  With what divine affections bold
Should be the man whose thought would hold
  An hour's communion with the dead!

In vain shalt thou, or any, call
  The spirits from their golden day,
Except, like them, thou too canst say,
  My spirit is at peace with all.

They haunt the silence of the breast,
  Imaginations calm and fair,
The memory like a cloudless air,
  The conscience as a sea of rest.

But when the heart is full of din,
  And doubt beside the portal waits,
They can but listen at the gates,
  And hear the household jar within.'

Tennyson, 'In Memoriam,' xciv

No words are needed, I think, to point out or recommend the many interesting features of this Life of St. Mary and St. Martha.

There are undoubtedly mistakes and inaccuracies in it, but the evident good faith of the author, his reverence and respect for the authorities at his command, his real devoutness and his determination not to be misled by what is plainly spurious – all testify to a transparent honesty, carefulness and goodness that can hardly be questioned.

This is the only ascertained copy of the *Life of Rabanus*, but some other six or seven old manuscript lives of St. Mary Magdalene are still extant. Some of these are probably older than the *Life of Rabanus,* and all bear out the main details of the Provençal mission.

The oldest is in the form of a hymn which appears to belong to the seventh century, and is published by M. l'Abbé Narbey in the supplement to the *Acta Sanctorum.*

In this we read of the departure of St. Mary Magdalene and St. Maximinus from Palestine after the martyrdom of St. Stephen, of their arrival at Marseilles, their missionary labours, their death and burial at Aix; the whole corresponding to the history of Rabanus, but containing nothing beyond the bare details here recorded.

The next in point of date appear to be two old manuscript Lives preserved in the Paris libraries dating from the tenth century (Faillon) or from the eleventh to the thirteenth century (Duchesne). If the original *Life of Rabanus* was compiled by its reputed author, these manuscripts are copies of a pre-existing 'Life,' for portions of these histories have been incorporated word for word in the *Life of Rabanus.* For this reason Faillon traces the original of these manuscripts to the sixth century, but any date before the time of Rabanus would be consistent with the supposed authorship of the Oxford manuscript.

Next to these in date of composition, but not perhaps in date of manuscript (but all are copies) is the *Life of Rabanus* in the Magdalen College Library.[1] Then we have the MS. Laud 108 of the Bodleian (thirteenth century?) and several later manuscripts, of which the *Buchedd Mair Vadlen* and *Buchedd Martha*, in the Hafod Collection at Cardiff (1604), and the fragment in the Llwfyr Gwyn Rhydderch of the Hengwrt MS., are the more important in British libraries.

In addition to these, too, we have the devotional romance of the Life of St. Mary Magdalene by an unknown Italian writer of the fourteenth century, recently translated into English by Valentine Hawtrey and published by Mr. John Lane at the Bodley Head. In this, though the writer confines himself to the period of the Gospels, and professedly fills his pages with imagined interviews and conversations, it is noticeable that the setting of his story is taken either from the *Life of Rabanus* or from some corresponding Life, for the parentage of Martha and Mary, their possessions at Bethany and Magdala, and the residence with them of Marcella, or 'Martilla,' are given almost exactly as in the record of Rabanus.

In examining these various Lives one important feature must strike every observer. All the older manuscripts, which profess, too, to be copies of histories more ancient still, contain very little or no account of any miraculous events; the oldest of all simply recording the coming of St. Mary Magdalene, St. Martha, St. Lazarus and St. Maximin to Provence, and giving the plainest details of their life and death. The *Life of Rabanus* is much fuller but contains very little that is miraculous. The later Lives, on the other hand are full of miraculous, wild and unbelievable additions.

Corresponding to the main narrative contained in these Lives we find local traditions, local monuments and relics, and local liturgies preserving, in some way or another, the same essential features.

These local traditions and monuments may be said to start from the little old town and church of Les Saintes Maries in the Camargue, the supposed scene of the landing of the first Hebrew missionaries. Here we find a church of the eighth or ninth century, enshrining the reputed relics of St. Mary Salome and St. Mary Cleopas; possessing, too, architectural features corresponding to the tradition, and a yearly pilgrimage in honour of the 'Holy Maries' and of their reputed handmaid 'Sara.'

Again, at Marseilles we find the local tradition mainly concerned with the life and labours of St. Lazarus, its reputed first missionary-priest or bishop, the local monument connected with this being a grotto or cave in the crypt of the old church of St. Victor.

Farther on, at Aix, at St. Maximin and La Sainte Baume, we find local traditions, monuments and relics relating to the apostolate of St. Mary Magdalene, St. Maximin and Sidonius or Chelidonius; the chief relic, the head of St. Mary Magdalene, being preserved in a small crypt in the great church of St. Maximin. At Arles we find innumerable traces of St. Trophimus. At Tarascon – rightly or wrongly – the whole town is devoted to the memory of St. Martha, and the fine church of St. Martha not only enshrines her supposed relics, but forms an architectural monument to commemorate and perpetuate the main details of the Provençal tradition. Up the Rhone Valley, farther on still, we find the rock village of St. Restitut devoted to the shrine and memory of the 'man born blind,' and a long way to the West, in old Aquitaine, we find (at Rocamadour) reputed traces of St. Zaccheus and St. Joseph of Arimathea. These I shall refer to later on.

Perhaps the best local account of the whole Provençal tradition as it lives today in the scattered homesteads of the Camargue, and in the brains and hearts of all the people in the adjacent country, is the narrative given by the poet Mistral in his *Mireio,* published in 1859.

According to this:

After the first persecution, when St. James was slain by the sword, those who had followed him were thrust into a boat, without oars or sails, on the coast of Palestine somewhere near to Mount Carmel, and so got rid of. In the boat were:

St. Mary, wife of Cleopas.
St. Salome (often called St. Mary Salome also).
St. Mary Magdalene.
St. Martha, and with the two latter was their maid Marcella.

These were accompanied by the following men:

Lazarus.
Joseph of Arimathea.
Trophimus.
Maximin.
Cleon.
Eutropius.
Sidonius (Restitutus, 'the man born blind').
Martial, and
Saturninus.

As the boat was drifting out, Sarah, the handmaid of St. Salome and St. Mary Cleopas, cast herself into the sea to join her mistresses, and by the help of Salome was brought into the boat. After beating about for several days, the boat drifted to the coast of Provence, and following the Rhone, arrived at Arles, which was converted to Christianity mainly through the blessing of God on the preaching of Trophimus.

St. Martha and Marcella went to Tarascon and Avignon.

Martial to Limoges.

Saturninus to Toulouse.

Eutropius to Orange.

St. Lazarus to Marseilles.

St. Maximin and Sidonius to Aix and 'St. Maximin.'

St. Mary Magdalene to St. Baume.

St. Joseph is stated to have gone farther and to have crossed the sea to Britain.

St. Mary Salome, St. Mary Cleopas, and Sarah their maid, stopped near the sea coast in the Camargue and died there, the church and little town of the 'Three Maries' enshrining their relics and perpetuating their memories.

An old cantique or song, the age of which it is impossible to determine, gives much the same account. One of the verses runs as follows:

'Entrez, Sara, dans la nacelle

Lazare, Marthe et Maximin,

Cleon, Trophime, Saturninus

Les trois Maries et Marcelle

Eutrope et Martial, Sidonie avec Joseph

Vous perirez dans le nef.'

Another version of the same legend is met with in Spain, as far south as Ciudad Rodrigo. According to this, Mary Salome, Mary Cleopas, Mary Magdalene (the sister of Lazarus), Lazarus, Maximin, Chelidonius, Marcella and Joseph of Arimathea, came to Aquitaine Gaul, and there preached the Holy Gospel of the Lord Jesus, 'as the histories of the Gauls and the local traditions plainly teach.' St. Mary brought the martyred body of St. James into Spain, and died at Civitatensum (Ciudad Rodrigo), a city of Lusitania, on April 10th (*Acta Sanctorum Apr.*, vol. i, p. 814).

There appears also to be an old Hebrew tradition that the earliest Jewish settlers of Arles 'came in a boat which had been deserted by its captain' (see *Jewish Encyclopaedia* under 'Arles').

Before considering more particularly the claims of these local traditions on our respect and consideration, I would like to draw some attention to their mutual consistency. They contain no rival contradictory elements, as they might well possess if they were simply the product of the local imagination of the romancers of contending towns. For a short time, it is true, the town of Vezelai disputed with St. Maximin the possession of the true relics of St. Mary Magdalene, much as the town of Ciudad Rodrigo appears to have disputed with Provence over the body of St. Mary, but these disputes, though finally decided in favour of St. Maximin and Les Saintes Maries, were purely subsidiary questions, and did not involve in any way (beyond confirming it) the belief in the essential truth of the old tradition.

There is no doubt that this tradition, much as it is given in the *Life of Rabanus*, was accepted by the whole Latin Church for over a thousand years. For proof of this we have only to turn to the Breviary at St. Martha's Day, July 29th. There we find a lection for the second nocturne which tells how Mary, Martha and Lazarus, with their servant Marcella, and Maximin, one of the seventy-two disciples, were seized by the Jews, placed in a boat without sails or oars, and carried safely to the port of Marseilles. Moved by this remarkable fact, the people of the neighbouring lands were speedily converted to Christianity; Lazarus became bishop of Marseilles, Maximinus of Aix, Mary lived and died an anchoress on a high mountain of those parts, while Martha founded a convent of women, died on the fourth day before the kalends of August, and was buried with great honour at Tarascon.

Again, not only the Latin Church, but we ourselves to a certain extent accept this history. In all our Prayer Books the 22nd of July is honoured as St. Mary Magdalene's day, and it is on one or more of these histories, I suppose, that we depend for our date of her death.

And this consensus of belief is proved by many historical buildings and by references in ancient literature.

The ninth-century fortress church of the Holy Maries in the Camargue – the great church of St. Maximin (1295-1410), which enshrines the body of St. Mary, and the cave of Ste. Baume, remembered as her residence and shelter – the oratory and cathedral at Arles (1152), which commemorates St. Trophimus – the Church of St. Martha at Tarascon (1187-1192), and the crypt of the old Abbey of St. Victor at Marseilles, dating from the fourth century, which forms a lasting memorial to St. Lazarus, all bear witness to the faith and devotion of those who built them.

Other interesting references showing current beliefs occur in old French and English and ecclesiastical literature. One is in the Life of St. Louis (Louis IX), by the Sire de Joinville. He narrates how he and St. Louis, returning from the Crusade (in 1254), made a short detour in order to visit Aix, St. Maximin, and Ste. Baume. He writes:

'After this, the king set out from Hières and came to the city of Aix, in Provence, in honour of the blessed Magdalene, who is interred a short day's journey off. We visited the place of Le Basme, which is a deep cave in a rock, wherein it is said the holy Magdalene resided for a long time at a hermitage' (Col. Johnes' Trans.).

Another reference is from the *Otia Imperialia*, a book written by Gervais de Tilbury, 'Maréchal' of the kingdom of Arles in 1212, and dedicated to Otho IV.

He writes as follows regarding the old church of Les Saintes Maries in the Camargue:

'There, on the sea-coast, one sees the first of Continental churches which was founded in honour of the most blessed mother of our Lord, and consecrated by many of the seventy-two disciples who were driven from Judea and exposed to the sea in an oarless boat: Maximin of Aix, Lazarus of Marseilles, the brother of Martha and Mary, Eutrope of Orange, George of Velay, Saturninus of Toulouse, Martial of Limoges, in the presence of Martha, Mary Magdalene and many others.

'Under the altar of this church, formed by them of earth, and covered by a slab of Paros marble, containing an inscription, six heads of certain holy saints, according to a very old tradition, have been placed in the form of a square.

'The other members of these bodies are enclosed in their tombs, and of these it is stated that two belong to the two Maries who, the first day after the Sabbath, came carrying spices, to see the tomb of the Saviour.'[2]

Another reference is from the annals of our own Roger de Hovedon (730-1200). In his third volume dealing with events which happened between 1170 and 1192, he gives a good description of Marseilles, and writes:

'Marseilles is an episcopal city under the dominion of the King of Arragon. Here are the relics of St. Lazarus, the brother of St. Mary Magdalene and Martha, who held the bishopric here for seven years after Jesus had restored him from the dead' (*Roger de*

Hovedon, edited by W. Stubbs, Longmans, 1868, vol. iii, p. 51).

Another is from old Church literature. In 1040 in the bull of Benedict IX (relative to the establishment of the Abbey of St. Victor, at Marseilles, after the expulsion of the Saracens), we find the history of the foundation of the Abbey of St. Victor in the time of the Emperor Antonine, of its building by St. Cassien, and of its enshrining the sufferings and relics of St. Victor, his companions, Hermes and Adrian, and 'St. Lazarus, who was restored from the dead by Jesus Christ.'

Yet another is from the old history of the kingdom of Arles, where it is stated that William Gerard, son of Otho, King of Italy, and Marquis of Provence, came to Arles about the year 935, when his father was at Marseilles, and went from there as a pilgrim to the cave where Magdalene lived and died, returning thanks there for the protection which he had received.[3]

About AD 800 (or slightly later) we have evidence not only of the writing of the Life of St. Mary and St. Martha by Rabanus (the copy of which in the Magdalen Library we have already considered), but also of a contemporary Life of St. Lazarus (now lost), written or edited by him, and evidently directly associated in his mind with the history of the two sisters, St. Mary and St. Martha.

In this book (of the Life of St. Mary and St. Martha) we read of the cure of Clovis after a pilgrimage to the tomb of St. Martha, at Tarascon, and of his (consequent) gift to the church of St. Martha. Now, this gift is confirmed by repeated evidence, down to the letters patent of Louis XI in 1482 (still extant), so that, through the *Life of Rabanus*, we have historical evidence of belief which takes us back to AD 500, this being approximately the date of the cure and gift of Clovis.

And if we add to these considerations the old liturgies and local service books of the Rhone Valley Churches and the attested records of the relics preserved by them, it seems impossible to find any Christian date when the people of Marseilles and Arles and Aix and Tarascon did not believe that the Bethany family had lived and taught and died among them.[4]

Few people, perhaps, recognize all that was involved in Roman conquest or protection and Roman colonization at the time when Roman power was at its zenith.

In almost every part of accessible Europe, Asia, or Africa – in Judea, in Northern Africa, in Italy and Sicily, in Spain, in Provincia Gallica, and even in Britain – the traveller was more or less 'at home.' He found very much the same institutions, regulations and government in all places, for the wonderful remains of Roman buildings found everywhere, testify to the fact that the Roman occupation and residence was in no way limited to the military camp, but that in every city protected by her, Roman influence pervaded the whole of its life and customs, and every necessary adjunct to an advanced civilization was to be found in full activity in all the countries which owed allegiance to her rule. Even language was a far simpler problem then than at any time before or since. The Latin language would carry the traveller almost everywhere and sufficed for the necessities of life, while he who was conversant with Greek also had 'the *entrée*' to all the cultivation and intellectual life of the then known world.

Particularly do these considerations apply to all that district which is now known as the South of France. This was under Roman protection, and was called Provincia, or 'the Provinces.' Very much as in later years America was colonized by England, and afterwards became the favourite emigration ground of generation after generation of Englishmen, until the England beyond the sea became greater than the little Mother Country of Great Britain and Ireland, so, on a much smaller scale,

Provence became the favourite emigration ground of Rome, and generation after generation of Romans traded here, lived here, made their fortunes here, and died here – and costly palaces and temples, amphitheatres, baths and aqueducts vied with and sometimes excelled similar creations in Rome. The Maison Carrée, the Pont du Gard, the Arena, the Baths and Tour Magne at Nîmes; the palace of Constantine, the Arena, the ruins of the theatre, and the old pagan cemetery at Arles; the monument at St. Rémy, the theatre at Orange, the baths at Aix, and the triumphal arches at Carpentras and Orange, most of which are still standing, remain as evidence of the extent of the Roman occupation and of the remarkable strength and beauty of their architectural creations.

Five nations met here – the Galatae or original possessors of the adjacent continent, the Phoenicans[5] who had first colonized the sea-coast, the Greeks who had followed them and had lived here for centuries, then the Romans who protected the civilized population from the invasions of the barbarians, and finally the Jews, who had probably accompanied the Phoenicians for centuries in their trading expeditions, and to some extent had colonized the seaports.[6] Each nation brought elements of strength and vitality, and the result appears to have been a civilization stronger and more powerful, perhaps, than that of Rome itself.

The great port of Massilia, the modern Marseilles, by means of which most of the intercourse between Provence and the rest of the civilized world was carried on, was quite an old city in the early days of Christianity. Founded by the Greeks some six centuries before the birth of our Lord, it had steadily increased in size and in importance as the commerce of the world had widened. Pytheas sailed from Marseilles when he made his first voyage to British waters in 350 BC, and consequently at this early date, Marseilles must have been a maritime centre of very considerable importance.

A most interesting account both of Marseilles and of the adjacent country is given by Strabo (bk. iv, cap. 1). This description appears to have been written some time before the birth of our Lord, and cannot therefore depict a more advanced civilization than that which was existing when the first disciples brought tidings of the Gospel from Jerusalem to Gaul. Strabo writes:

'Marseilles, founded by the Phocaeans, is built in a stony region. Its harbour lies beneath a rock which is shaped like a theatre, and looks towards the south. It is well surrounded with walls, as well as the whole city, which is of considerable size. Within the citadel are placed the "Ephesium" and the temple of the Delphian Apollo. The "Ephesium" is the temple consecrated to Diana of Ephesus. All the Colonies sent out from Marseilles hold this goddess in peculiar reverence, preserving both the shape of her image and also every rite observed in the metropolis.

"The Massilians live under a well-regulated aristocracy. They have a council, composed of six hundred persons, called Timuchi, who enjoy this dignity of life. Fifteen of these preside over the council and have the management of current affairs; these fifteen are in their turn presided over by three of their number, in whom rests the principal authority; and these again by one.

'No one can become a Timuchus who has not children, and who has not been a citizen for three generations. The country abounds in olives and vines, but on account of its ruggedness the wheat is poor; consequently the people trust more to resources of the sea than of the land, and avail themselves fully of their excellent position for commerce.

'The people of Marseilles possess dry-docks and armouries. Formerly they had an abundance of vessels, arms and machines both for the purpose of navigation and for besieging towns; by means of which they defended themselves against the barbarians and likewise obtained the alliance of the Romans, to whom they rendered many important services, the Romans in their turn assisting in their aggrandisement. Sextius, who defeated the Salyes, founded not far from Marseilles a city which was named after him and the hot water found there (Aquae Sextiae, now Aix). Here he established a Roman garrison and drove from the sea coast which leads from Marseilles to Italy, the barbarians whom the Massilians were not able to entirely keep back. The land which the barbarians abandoned he presented to the Massilians, and in their city are laid up heaps of booty taken in naval engagements against those who disputed the sea unjustly. Formerly they enjoyed singular good fortune as well in other matters as also in their amity with the Romans, but since the war of Pompey against Caesar, in which they sided with the vanquished party, their prosperity has in some measure decayed. Nevertheless some traces of their ancient industries may still be seen among the inhabitants, especially the making of engines of war and ship-building. Now that the surrounding barbarians under the dominion of the Romans are daily becoming more civilized, and leave the occupation of war for business of towns and agriculture, there is no longer the same attention paid to these objects by the people of Marseilles. The aspect of the city at the present day is a proof of this. All who profess to be men of taste turn to the study of elocution and philosophy. The city for some time back has become quite a school for the barbarians, and has communicated to the Galatae such a taste for Greek literature that they even draw contracts on the Greek model. Further, at the present day it so entices the noblest of the Romans that those desirous of studying resort thither in preference to Athens. These, the Galatae observing, and being at leisure on account of peace, readily devote themselves to similar pursuits, and that not merely individuals but the public generally; professors of the arts and sciences, and likewise of medicine being employed not only by private persons but by towns for common instruction.'

Further on Strabo writes of Arelate on the Rhone (Arles), as a city and emporium of considerable traffic; of Avenio (Avignon), of Arausio (Orange), of Vienne, the metropolis of the Allobroges, and of Lugdunum (Lyons), a city of the Segusii.

On the other side of the Rhone he describes Narbonne and Nemausus (Nîmes). Of the latter he writes:

'Though far inferior to Narbonne both as to its commerce and the number of foreigners attracted thither, it surpasses that city in the number of its citizens, for it has under its dominion four-and-twenty villages, all well inhabited and by the same people, who pay tribute. It likewise enjoys the rights of the Latin towns, so that in Nemausus you meet with Roman citizens who have obtained the honours of the Aedile and Quaestorship, wherefore this nation is not subject to the orders issued by the quaestors from Rome. The city is situated on the road from Iberia to Italy; this road is very good in the summer, but muddy and overflowed by the rivers during winter and spring. Some of the rivers are crossed in ferry-boats and others by means of bridges constructed either of wood or stone. Nemausus (Nîmes) is about a hundred stadia distant from the Rhone, situated opposite to the small town of Tarascon, and about seven hundred and twenty stadia from Narbonne.'

This description by an almost contemporaneous writer puts before us a graphic picture of the civilization of Marseilles and of the Rhone valley during (and before) the earthly lifetime of our Lord.

We recognize at once that this was no barbarous country, no unknown district, but a rich and prosperous land, especially associated on the one hand with Rome, and on the other with Ephesus, a country to which the earliest Christian missionaries would naturally turn as ready and waiting for the message God had sent them to deliver.

Then, as now, the country beyond the sea-border would be a land of olive gardens and vineyards, not unlike that of Palestine at its best, and the husbandry needed in both countries would be practically identical. In the larger towns, and especially in Marseilles, we should have found a freedom, breadth and brilliancy, cosmopolitan rather than national, which could hardly be met with elsewhere, which would freely give and receive the latest currency of thought and be specially 'grateful' to the missionary and the Jew.

At this epoch Ephesus, Athens, Rome and Massilia were the four greatest cities of civilization; the four greatest centres not only of commerce but of learning, and Massilia was by no means the least important of the four. Specially connected by race and religion with the older civilization and learning of the East, it yet stood in the very van of Western progress, and drank daily of the strength and vitality of Roman spirit and power which ebbed and flowed as in a ceaseless stream through the very heart of it.

Great ways or roads passed through Marseilles to the west and north, the great western road leading through Narbonne into Spain, and the great northern road leading through Arles, Vienne and Lyons, towards the northern parts of Gaul and across the sea to Britain. Both of these were constantly used by Roman soldiery and civilians. About the very time of which I am writing the Emperor Claudius had himself gone through Marseilles to Boulogne and across to Great Britain as far as

Colchester, returning by the same route in triumph to Rome. This was followed by a continuous stream of troops going to and returning from Britain, for the war with the British was prosecuted with vigour throughout the reigns of Claudius and Nero. If there had been no purposed missionary effort here during the first Christian century it is almost impossible to believe that the southern part of Provence, at least, could have escaped the accidental knowledge of Christianity from Christian visitors, soldiers or civilians. For all the time, within easy distance of Marseilles both by land and sea, Rome was becoming a great centre of Christian life and influence. Several years before the traditional journey of the Bethany family, certain citizens of Rome had heard St. Peter's sermon on the day of Pentecost (*Acts* 2:10). From that day (if not before it) the Church had been growing in Rome until, at a somewhat similar period *after* the traditional journey, St. Paul, though a comparative stranger who had never been to Rome, was able to count among his Christian acquaintances there the following list of disciples:

Aquila and Priscilla, who had been temporarily banished from Rome by Claudius Caesar, and had worked with St. Paul at Corinth.
Epaenetus (of the household of Stephanas?) (I *Corinthians* 1:16).
Mary.
Andronicus and Junia (Joanna?). (Andronicus afterwards bishop in Spain.)
Amplias.
Urbane.
Stachys.
Apelles (the same as Apollos?).
The household of Aristobulus (Aristobulus himself being absent in Britain?).
The household of Narcissus.

Herodion.

Tryphena and Tryphosa.

Persis.

Rufus (son of Simon the Cyrenean?) and his mother (who had befriended St. Paul at Antioch). [7]

Asyncritus.

Phlegon.

Hermas (writer of the 'Shepherd'?).

Patrobas.

Hermes.

Philologus.

Julia.

Neraeus and his sister.

Olympas 'and all the saints with them.'

So that all the known antecedent history, which may be regarded as a background or setting for the Provençal traditions, seems to be in harmony with the main outlines of the story. Time, place and characters have all been perfectly chosen, and if the whole be a romance, even the various sections of the romance, as we shall see, support each other and combine to form a series of tableaux or a great mystery play, which may well startle us by its vivid reality and intense human interest.

I am aware that the value of these traditions has been disputed by many French critics; by Launoy and Tillemont in the past, and more recently by the Abbé Duchesne. Into all the details of this controversy I cannot now enter. The arguments, for and against, are fully discussed by Faillon in his great work (*Monuments Inédits*) and also by the Bollandists in the *Acta Sanctorum*.

One of the main points of objection is founded on the writings of

Gregory of Tours, the oldest French historian who, although mentioning Pothinus and Irenaeus as earlier bishops of Lyons, makes no mention of any definite mission earlier than the middle of the third century, when (as he states) 'under the consulship of Decius seven bishops were ordained and sent into Gaul to preach the faith: These are the bishops which were sent: Gatien to Tours, Trophimus to Arles, Paul to Narbonne, Saturnin to Toulouse, Denis to Paris, Austremoine to Auvergne and Martial to Limoges' (St. Greg. Turon., *Hist. Franc.*, lib. i, cap. 27, 28).

This historian is well known to have been frequently mistaken in matters of fact and date, and this very passage is utterly discredited and proved to have been mistaken by the history of the Church at Arles. At the very time of which St. Gregory is writing (AD 250) or only a few years later, in an undoubted and historical letter of St. Cyprian to Pope Stephen (No. 68), we have evidence that the Church of Arles, which was then presided over by its bishop Marcianus, had lapsed into heresy, and that for some years previously many of the Christians had been allowed to die without the proper ministrations of the clergy. St. Cyprian suggests to the Pope that he should call upon his 'fellow bishops in Gaul' no longer to suffer the forward and proud Marcianus. (See Appendix F.)

This is not the history of any newly formed Church, but the history of an old Church possessing authority over many other old Churches, and one in which the original faith had grown feeble, the bishop of this date having himself become heretical. Trophimus is known to have been long antecedent to Marcianus.

Any idea, too, that Southern France was evangelized by a mission from Rome so late as the third century, is altogether inconsistent with the life and labours and writings of the great Irenaeus in the latter part of the second century, and with the history of the Church before his coming. It is also inconsistent with what we find in the records of the synods and councils of the early Church (Mansi).

About AD 167 we find the letter of Pope Anicetus, *Ad Galliae Episcopos*, to the bishops of Gaul, showing that already there were several Gallican bishops and that some necessity had arisen for directing them regarding the duties of archbishops and metropolitans (vol. i, p. 683); about AD 179 the letters of Pope Eleutherius, *Ad Galliae Provincias*, and *Ad Lucium, Britanniae Regem* (pp. 695, 698); about AD 190 two Synods of Lyons under St. Irenaeus, the one attended by twelve bishops and the other by thirteen (pp. 723-726), and in AD 197 the holding of the Gallic Council (p. 715). The dates of some of the letters may be mistaken, as (for example) the supposed ones of Pius I to Justus, bishop of Vienne (pp. 677, 678) but there can hardly be much doubt as to the dates of the Synods and Council. Moreover, the holding of a Council of the Churches of Gaul under Irenaeus regarding the keeping of the Passover is definitely recorded by Eusebius[8] (bk. v, c. 23).

Duchesne, who has compiled, or is compiling, a history of the old French Episcopal sees, appears to attach prime importance to the general difficulty or impossibility of directly tracing the Episcopal succession up to the apostolic age. A practical acquaintance with original missionary work, even in the most recent times would, however, show the unreasonableness of expecting such a history.

Even now, when a mission is sent out fully equipped to a heathen country, there is often but little or no need for direct Episcopal or apostolic functions until after three generations; for nearly a century of work is necessary before it is possible for Christian converts to be admitted to the ranks of the diaconate and priesthood. Then (when the full dignity and value of the episcopate is recognized) is more probably the date from which the record of bishops begins. To take an illustration familiar to most English Churchmen of today – the Universities' Mission to Central Africa. The knowledge of Christianity was brought to this district by Livingstone, in the eyes of the Church a layman. The actual work of the mission was begun by Bishop Mackenzie[9] in a part of Africa which was afterwards abandoned, and it was not until his death that the present and more permanent sphere of labour was mapped out and worked.

In future ages if the history of this mission depended solely on native historians there can hardly be a doubt that the names of Livingstone and Mackenzie would be shadowy and traditional only, the first date of the mission probably coinciding with the foundation of the cathedral at Zanzibar.

The history of the earliest missionary enterprises must have been very similar to this. Of all the traditional company who came to Provence it is very uncertain whether any possessed Episcopal powers. Some were doubtless authorized by the Apostles to celebrate the Divine mysteries, but the first company who left the shores of Palestine for Gaul may well have started on the mission – like those who went to Antioch – with no direct apostolical authority other than that which Christ Himself had given to Mary Magdalene.

So that one could neither expect the immediate foundation of bishoprics on the arrival of missionaries from the East, nor could we reasonably expect, in this age, a connected account of the various steps and labours which led up to the formation of a see.

One of the chief documents, or rather, perhaps, *the* chief document of the early Church of France (recognized as authentic by all writers), is the famous second century letter from the Churches of Lyons and Vienne to the Churches of Asia and Phrygia,[10] a portion of which has been accidently preserved to us by Eusebius. In it we are introduced to a great company of Christians and martyrs:

Pothinus, their bishop, more than ninety years of age.

Sanctus, the deacon.
Vetius Epagathus, a man of eminent standing.
Maturus, a new convert.
Attalus, a pillar of the Church.
Alexander, a physician.
Alcibiades.
Ponticus, a boy of fifteen.
The mistress of Blandina.
Blandina.
Biblias, and
Irenaeus, then presbyter of the Church at Lyons.

These are especially mentioned. Beside these we are told of many others – of numbers who died in prison, of those 'who appeared to have the Roman citizenship and were beheaded,' and of those who were 'worthy to fill up the numbers of the martyrs and were seized from day to day, so that all the zealous members of the two Churches were collected.'

This letter,[11] rightly considered one of the most precious documents of the early Church, begins as follows: 'From the servants of Christ dwelling at Vienne and Lyons in Gaul, to those brethren in Asia and Phrygia having the same faith and hope with us, peace and grace and glory from God the Father and Jesus Christ our Lord.'

This was written in the year AD 177; it gives a graphic account of the martyrdom of a large number of the Christians belonging to both Churches, and is exceedingly valuable as describing the position, the constitution and the life of two Churches in the upper part of the Valley of the Rhone within less than a hundred years after apostolic times. It gives us, however, no account of the missionary labours of those Christians who first came to this district and who may have preceded

Pothinus as the teachers or priests of the first disciples.

It does, however, show conclusively that Lugdunum or Lyons was the seat of a flourishing Church and episcopate in the latter half of the second century, and that this Church was presumably (from his name) presided over by a Greek bishop. Moreover, on his death, in 177, he was succeeded by another Greek bishop, the great Irenaeus, whose writings are well known. It also shows that these Churches of Lyons and Vienne – before the time of Irenaeus – had such special associations with the Churches of Asia that their most important news and messages were sent direct to Asia as well as to Rome, the necessary inference being that these Churches had themselves been founded by some Greek mission from Asia shortly after, if not during the time of the Apostles.

Lyons is almost in the centre of France. If one acknowledges no precedent teaching on the road to such a central city – and this is what the Revd. W. Palmer in his *Origines Liturgicae* and what Duchesne in his *Fastes Episcopaux*[12] appear to contend for – it seems to me we are brought to a conclusion so contrary to common sense as to be practically unbelievable. The road to Lyons was through Marseilles, and Aix, and Arles, and Avignon, and Tarascon, and Vienne; and that early Christian missionaries should have passed through all this populous and civilized district, founding two Churches at Lyons and Vienne, which a hundred years afterwards became two of the most renowned in Christendom, yet leaving no trace of their journey – no Churches on their line of march – attempting nothing at Marseilles, which we have seen rivalled Rome and Athens in learning, is a thing quite unbelievable.

Further, one of the most important acts of the early Church was the Council of Arles in 314, which was attended, among others by three English bishops.[13] If the Church of Lyons had been older than Arles it is not likely that Arles would have been preferred before her and we should not find, as we do later on, Arles contending for her primacy among the

Provençal Churches, and (about AD 450) on the ground that St. Trophimus had been appointed chief pastor or bishop by the Apostle Peter.

At this time there had been considerable rivalry and conflict between the sees of Arles and Vienne, both claiming the right of metropolitan and the power of appointing bishops. In 445 Pope Leo took away from Hilary or Arles the right of metropolitan and the jurisdiction he claimed over the province of Vienne; but Ravennius, Hilary's successor, still claimed the ancient right, and appointed a bishop to Vaison. The bishop of Vienne complained of this, and sent deputies to Rome to lay his complaint before the Pope. This called forth the letter of nineteen bishops 'who had formerly been under the primacy of Arles,' and who wrote to the Pope as follows:

'Everyone in Gaul knows, and the holy Roman Church is not ignorant that Arles was the first city in Gaul which received for its bishop St. Trophimus, who was sent by the Apostle St. Peter, and that from this stream of the Faith, derived from an apostolic source, religion has spread little by little, and that other towns received bishops before that of Vienne, which claims the primacy today with so little shame. Our predecessors have always honoured the Church of Arles as their mother and, according to tradition, have always sent to her to ask for bishops, we and our predecessors having been ordained by the bishop of Arles.'[14]

I am bound to say that having studied the district and its monuments, as well as the history of the subject, I am at least forced to the conclusion that Christianity came to Provence quite early in the apostolic age, that it was impossible for Marseilles to remain long ignorant of a new religion that was flourishing in Ephesus and Rome, and that the knowledge would necessarily come first to Marseilles and next to Aix[15] and Arles, and then to Vienne, and it was not probably until after this it came to Lyons. I think I may go beyond this and add that St. Trophimus (Trophimus of the *Acts*, the friend of St. Paul), whether assisted by others or not, was almost certainly the chief successful missionary of Provence in the apostolic age.

If we turn, too, to the signatures appended to the decisions of the Council of Arles in 314 (a full list of which is given in Appendix G), we see that the earlier signatures have all the appearance of being written in the order of priority of see, and the names of the Viennoise bishops are in the following order:

> Orose of Marseilles.
> Martin of Arles.
> Verus of Vienne.

While the remains of Christian first century refuges or buildings, such as the cave of St. Lazarus in the Crypt of St. Victor at Marseilles; the oratory of St. Trophimus at les Aliscamps and his rock dwelling at Montmajour; the cave shelter of St. Mary Magdalene at La Sainte Baume – whether directly connected with the Saints whose names are immemorially associated with them or not – all bear evidence of the very earliest Christian settlements to be found perhaps in any country.

Some further reference may be needed to St. Lazarus and to Restitutus – the man born blind of St. John's Gospel (*John* 9). There was at one time (as we are told by Rabanus) a Life of St. Lazarus very analogous to that of St. Mary and St. Martha, but no complete copy of it is existing, some fragments only of his Life (which were formerly incorporated in the Office for St. Lazarus' Day at Marseilles and Autun) having been preserved.

These appear to have been taken from a Life which was written by the monks of the Abbey at Bethany, a church and monastery having been erected at Bethany before the ravages of the Saracens, to guard the tomb from which our Lord was said to have raised St. Lazarus.

The extracts, according to Faillon (*Monuments Inédits*, vol. ii, p. 114, etc.), read as follows:

'Tradition states that St. Lazarus, after the ascension of Jesus Christ, remained for a time in the company of the Apostles, with whom he took charge of the Church which was at Jerusalem. After this he went to the Island of Cyprus in order to escape from the persecution which arose (about Stephen).

'Having filled there for several years the office of a missionary priest, he entered into a ship, and traversing the sea, by the grace of God arrived at Marseilles, the most celebrated town of Provence. Here, exercising the functions of his priesthood he served God, to whom he had entirely consecrated his life in righteousness and true holiness. He preached the word of Life to those who had not yet received it, and gained many converts to Jesus Christ. . . . We, who occupy his old house at Bethany – that is to say, his former tomb – and perform our religious duties at the place of his first interment, humbly pray to Jesus Christ by the merit of St. Lazarus, our patron and His own especial friend, that He would deign to lead us by His goodness, so that we may rejoice in His help during this present life and be associated with Him in the joys of eternal life hereafter.'

The church and monastery here referred to appear to have flourished from about AD 400 to AD 870, when they were visited by a monk named Bernard. Not long after both were destroyed by the Saracens.

With regard to Restitutus – the man, or boy, born blind – we are told, according to the Provençal tradition, that he accompanied the Bethany family to Provence, but of his after life, so far as I have been able to gather, we appear to have two different and irreconcilable traditions. The one is that he was the same as Chelidonius or Sidonius, that he accompanied St. Maximin, and after his death took charge of the Church at Aix. The other identifies his history with the little village of St. Restitut and the more important old town of St. Paul Trois Châteaux (the Roman colony of 'Augusta Tricastinorum'), of which he is said to have been the first bishop or priest.

The Church of 'St. Restitut' is said to have formerly contained his relics. 'Its west bay, which has the appearance of a tower, is surmounted by a cupola and contains two storeys. In its lower storey (is) the tomb of St. Restitut' (Hare).[16]

1. The essentials of this are also found in the first volume of the Chronicles of *Matthew of Paris,* probably dating from 1190 or before this.

2. 'Illic ad littus maris est prima omnium Ecclesiarum citramarinarum in honorem beatissimae Dei genetrics fundata ac a discipulis a Judaea pulsis et in rate sine remigio dismissis per mare, Maximinio Aquense, Lazaro Massiliense evangelico fratre Marthae et Mariae, Eutropia Aurasicense, Geogio Vellaicense, Saturnino Tolosano, Martiali Lemovicense ex lxxii. discipulis consecrata, adstantibus Martha et Magdalena cum aliis multis' (Leibnitz, *Scriptores rerem Brunswicensium,* p. 914, quoted by Duchesne, *Fastes Episcopaux,* vol. i, p. 329). See also Faillon *Monuments Inédits,* vol. i, p. 1278 *et seq.*

3. 'His rebus peractis Wuillermus (Gerardus filius Othonis) dismisso exercitu, Arelatum proficiscitur: hinc cum rex abesset (in enim erat Massiliae) in itinere antrum, in quo diva Magdalena paenitentiam egit, et animum efflavit (ut fert ejus historia), visere statuit, ibique summas Deo gratias agere, ob res prospere gestas' (Faillon, *Monuments Inédits,* vol. i, p. 805).

4. The idea advanced by Baring-Gould, Cook and others, that all this body of religious tradition and belief has arisen solely as a legendary outcome of the wars of Marius, one hundred years before the Christian era, I regard as quite inadequate

and untenable. There may be some confusion of the two traditions in the neighbourhood of Tarascon, but I cannot recognize anything more than this. Apart from other considerations, what have Trophimus, Sergius Paulus, Zaccheus and Joseph of Arimathaea to do with the Marius traditions?

5. The Phoenicians plied a busy trade along these coasts. Their language has left traces in the Provençal dialects, and images have been found at Marseilles of Melkarth and Melita—the Baal and Ashtoreth of the Bible. There has even been found a tariff for sacrifices in the temple of Baal (Caird's *Cities of Provence*).

6. Rabbi Akiba, who flourished in the first century, makes mention of his visit to France. 'No Jewish Rabbi would then have travelled to any country unless inhabited by his co-religionists' (Margoliouth, *Land of my Fathers*, London, 1850).

7. The strongest case seems to emanate from those works which associate Rufus with Rufus Pudens, the young Roman nobleman who was known to have been a Christian, and was married to the British Princess Claudia. He is believed to have served in the Roman Army in Britain. Claudia's name was Gladys, daughter of King Caractacus, whose speech before the Roman Senate is recorded by Tacitus. Their home in Rome was called the Palatium Brittanicum. Here they lived with their two daughters, St. Pudentiana and St. Prassides, and the present Church of St. Pudentiana has been erected on the foundations of this early home. With them lived Gladys' brother Linus, who became the first Bishop of Rome, and whose name is also recorded as the first Bishop in St. Peter's. The poet Martial mentions them in several of his epigrammes, which are quoted by Miss Gladys Taylor in her book *Our Neglected Heritage*. Readers are also referred to *The Drama of the Lost Disciples*, both obtainable from The Covenant Publishing Company.

8. See Appendix D.

It is much to be regretted that so many French critics (with an astonishing want of candour) refer to this discredited statement of St. Gregory as if it were worthy of credence.

9. The party consisted of the Bishop, Miss A. Mackenzie, the Revds. Proctor and Scudamore, Messrs. Horace Waller, S. A. Gamble, and Alfred Adams. Miss Mackenzie is perhaps chiefly known for some twelve years of subsequent work in England.

10. Note that St. Isidorus (AD 600) states that St. Philip preached the gospel to the Gauls and afterwards at Hierapolis in Phrygia, where he suffered martyrdom.

11. Appendix C.

12. Duchesne even labours to prove that the 'Churches of Lyons and Vienne,' in the letter of the martyrs, refers really to only one Church, and that of Lyons, forgetting or ignoring that in the very text of the letter the expression occurs. See also the scholarly criticism of Harnack in his *Expansion of Christianity*, vol. ii,

'The members of the two Churches,' See Appendix. ('εκ των δύο Εκλησών.') pp. 81-85. The reference to the 'Origines' is in vol. i, pp. 149-153.

13. Eborius of York, Restitutus of London and Adelphius of Caerleon.

14. *Patrologia Latina*, vol. liv, pp. 880, 881. See Appendix J.

15. It is remarkable that French archaeology appears to recognize an inscription preserved at *Marseilles* and a sarcophagus found at Gayole in the territory of *Aix*, as the two oldest authentic Christian monuments to be found in France (Leblant, cited by Duchesne *Fastes Episcopaux*, vol. i, p. 74).

16. See chap. 'On Pilgrimage.'

CHAPTER VII

ST. TROPHIMUS AND ARLES

'Let no man think that sudden in a minute
   All is accomplished and the work is done:
Though with thine earliest dawn thou shouldst begin it
   Scarce were it ended in thy setting sun.

Oh, the regret, the struggle, and the failing!
   Oh, the days desolate and useless years!
Vows in the night so fierce and unavailing!
   Stings of my shame and passion of my tears!

How have I knelt with arms of my aspiring
   Lifted all night in irresponsive air,
Dazed and amazed with overmuch desiring,
   Blank with the utter agony of prayer!'
                              'St. Paul,' by F. W. H. Myers

Many years ago, when I first read the legends of the country-side in the writings of Mistral, of Augustus J. C. Hare and of Père Lacordaire, and in years since then, when I traced them for myself at Marseilles, at St. Maximin and at Arles, I very naturally concluded that if there had been any 'Coming of the Saints' at all to Provence, they had come together.

But as I began to read the *Life of Rabanus*, the other Lives of St. Mary Magdalene preserved in Paris, and to reconsider the Lives of St.

Trophimus and St. Lazarus as we find them in the New Testament and in tradition, I began to doubt whether this was possible.

The information of the coming of St. Mary Magdalene and St. Martha with St. Maximin (one of the seventy disciples) is so definitely associated with the martyrdom of St. James the Greater, and again (in Rabanus) with the fourteenth year after our Lord's ascension, that if we accept the details of the Life as at all historical we are forced to the conclusion that these came first to Provence, that they were afterwards joined by St. Lazarus, and that St. Trophimus probably followed them some years later still.

If so, there might very well be exceptional difficulties in the original mission on account both of nationality and language (all the members of it apparently being Hebrews), but there would not necessarily be any real difficulty in the journey.

We are told in Rabanus that the Bethany family inherited an extensive and rich patrimony, possessing considerable property not only at Bethany but also at Magdala and in Jerusalem, and that in common with many of the other early disciples they sold this and laid the proceeds at the Apostles' feet.

St. Maximin, if indeed he was the young man who came to Jesus and 'who had great possessions,' and if he was now bent on the giving of himself, might reasonably count the expenses of this journey as part of the 'giving to the poor' denoted by his Lord's command, while St. Joseph of Arimathea, if (as many of the older traditions state) he accompanied them, was still a rich man, and all the necessities of the journey would probably be provided for before leaving Palestine.

So apart from the perils of the sea journey, which might well account for the tradition of the dismantled vessel – the Gulf of Lyons being, as every sailor knows, a rough and treacherous sea – the main difficulties of the mission would be encountered after the sea journey was over.

Alien in race, in custom, and to a very large extent in language (Aramaic being very different from Massilian Greek), it would be mainly by personal life and example that such teachers could hope for any influence; and progress would necessarily at first be slow.

Granting this, the silence in the *Acts of the Apostles* respecting these personal friends of our Saviour is easily explained. Long before all the later events recorded in the Book of the *Acts*, they would have been working on or near the sea coast in the neighbourhood of Marseilles; fighting an uphill fight, hiding in rocks and caves, perhaps only able to assemble for worship in some cave by stealth, and only rarely finding an opportunity of communication with their friends in Palestine.

But, whatever we may think of the traditional history of the early Hebrew missionaries – of St. Mary and St. Maximin, of their reputed journey from the Camargue across the Rhone towards Aix and La Ste. Baume and of the apostolate of St. Lazarus at Marseilles[1] there is a later missionary effort which we have still to consider – the fruits of which cannot be well gainsaid. This was Greek rather than Hebrew, and connected with the labours of St. Paul. It is confirmed by much circumstantial evidence, and apparently resulted in a chain of successful missions all along the Rhone Valley, from which were developed the two great Churches of Lyons and Vienne in the succeeding century.

Let us go back and again consider its probable beginning.

As St. Paul journeyed to Jerusalem to confer with the other Apostles on the occasion of his last fateful visit, he took with him Trophimus the Greek from Ephesus and one Mnason of Cyprus. If there had been any news at Cyprus of the departure of St. Lazarus and Sergius Paulus for the West, he would necessarily hear of it and be anxious to establish their work on a permanent basis. What was in the mind of St. Paul during the final journey to Jerusalem it is not difficult to imagine, for he himself has

165

given us an important clue in his *Epistle to the Romans*. His fixed intention, he tells us, was in his next missionary journey to go to Rome, where he had many friends, co-workers and relatives, and then to go on from Rome to Spain.

He explains to the Romans that he was going up to Jerusalem carrying with him contributions from the Churches of Macedonia and Achaia for the poor of Jerusalem, and that after he had performed this mission he would come via Rome into Spain (*Romans* 15:24-28).

But what was meant by Spain or Iberia in the days of St. Paul? Strabo writes: 'Formerly the name of Iberia was given to the whole country between the Rhone and the Isthmus formed by the two Galatic gulfs; whereas now they make the Pyrenees its boundary and call it indifferently Iberia or Hispania; others have restricted Iberia to the country on this side of the Ebro (that is, between the Ebro and the Pyrenees).'

It is accordingly evident that the names of Iberia and Spain had a restricted as well as a more extended meaning – that it was especially applied to the north-eastern part of the country bordering on and connected with Massilian civilization, and that it was sometimes held to include the country north of the Pyrenees as far as the Rhone Valley. In fact, we find that the Massilians founded or held a whole series of towns on the sea border from Spain to Italy. In Spain we find Hemeroscopium (Denia or Artemis) with a temple to Diana of Ephesus on the promontory, Emporium (Ampurias) and Rhodope; while on the eastern side of Marseilles we find Tauraentium (Taurenti), Olbia (Eoube), Antipolis (Antibes) and Nicoea (Nice). 'All of these were Massilian towns essentially Greek, all worshipping the great Diana of Ephesus, and all practising the Grecian mode of sacrifice.'

And there was a good road connecting all this country with Rome – so good that Strabo writes, 'Historians report that Caesar came from

Rome to Obulco (Porcuna, not far from Cordova), and to his army there within the space of twenty-seven days when about to fight the battle of Munda' (against Pompey). From all of this we may reasonably infer that the projected journey of St. Paul from Rome into Spain would include all the main Massilian towns and pass through Nîmes and Narbonne to the south. Indeed, if Spain be regarded rather as the limit than the centre of the journey, its essential purpose would be not so much what we now know as Spain itself, but Marseilles and the lower portion of the Rhone Valley.[2]

And how St. Paul was bent upon this journey one may judge from his double reference to it. 'When therefore I have performed this, and have sealed to them this fruit, I will come by you into Spain and I am sure, that when I come unto you, I shall come in the fulness of the blessing of the Gospel of Christ' (*Romans* 15:28, 29).

And then came St. Paul's last journey to Jerusalem and his imprisonment.

There is a curious old manuscript (Faillon, vol. ii, p. 575) of the tenth century (No. 5,537 in the old Royal Library of Paris) which begins: 'Concerning the seven men sent by St. Peter as preachers into Gaul in the time of Nero'; and the names given are 'Trophimus, Paul, Marcial, Austremonus, Graecian, Saturinus and Valerien.' In the text it is stated that these were sent by St. Peter under Claudius ('Sub Claudio'). Possibly some official permission was needed, which was obtained before the death of Claudius Caesar in AD 54, but it does not appear that any of those named came until the time of Nero, and this would bring us close to the usually accepted date of St. Paul's imprisonment.

It is probably always wise to take any list of names, such as this – or the larger list figuring in the 'Life of Rabanus' – *cum grano salis*, for all the older writers had a certain contempt for accurate chronology and often jumbled together the names of important men living in very different ages; but with regard to one or two names – Trophimus and Paul[3] – we know the age in which they lived and we know the circumstances under which Trophimus, at least, would be likely to make the journey which tradition has assigned to him. He stands out conspicuously among the rest. We know more about him, and as we read of him, and as we hear of him, history and tradition together make for us fleeting but definite pictures of a personality and character which cannot well be other than that of a living saint and a most interesting mind.

Born, I suppose, at Ephesus (for he is called an Ephesian) (*Acts* 21:29), brought up in the worship of the great Diana, learned in all the wisdom and philosophy of the Greeks, he was probably already weary of the religion of his own people and 'seeking after God, if haply he might find Him,' when Christianity, or Christ Himself, came to him; for some have held that he met our Lord in Palestine, being one of the Ephesians who had been disciples of St. John the Baptist (*Acts* 19:3[4] and *John* 12:20).

Living at Ephesus until the mission of St. Paul, and visiting Ephesus in later years, he became not only an intimate friend and follower of St. Paul but, in all probability, was also known to St. John and to the Blessed Virgin, for his first church or oratory is said to have been dedicated to the 'still living Mother of our Lord.'

Somewhat poetical and visionary (as we shall see), not strong and self-reliant like St. Paul, he would find in the loving heart of St. John a sympathy, a breadth of understanding and a depth of affection to which the Greek in him would immediately respond.

He would directly understand and appreciate the wonderful opening of the Gospel of *John*; and, if there be any truth in the tradition regarding the Hebrew mission of the Bethany family and St. Restitutus, Trophimus himself, as a direct carrier of messages and perhaps documents between

Provincia Gallica and Ephesus, might be responsible for, and explain, the presence of those narratives which, with their minutiae of detail, are among the great critical difficulties of the Gospel of *John*. The account of the visit of Nicodemus, the long account of the illness and burial and resurrection of Lazarus, the extraordinary full description of the man who was born blind, and his miraculous healing, containing details that apparently could only be known to the chief persons concerned become at once easy to understand if we imagine these very persons sending their own narratives to Ephesus for insertion in the latest Gospel.

The great Irenaeus, who succeeded Pothinus as bishop of Lyons in 177, writes that 'John the disciple of our Lord, the same that lay upon His bosom, published this Gospel while he was yet at Ephesus in Asia' (Eusebius, E.H., bk. v, c. 7); and it is at least very remarkable that nearly all the characters chosen by St. John for special mention should be those traditionally associated with Trophimus and the Rhone Valley.

Tall, fine, of commanding presence, I think (for the coming of Trophimus was immediately noticed by the people of Jerusalem), the sweetness and light of his culture and affection manifest in face and bearing, he would form a marked contrast to St. Paul and would probably admire in St. Paul what was perhaps naturally lacking in himself, and find a healthy stimulus in that energy, enthusiasm, unceasing labour and courage which were distinguishing features of the character of St. Paul.

Standing by him and possibly restraining him, during the time of riot at Ephesus – for he was very likely one of the 'chief of Asia' who were friends of St. Paul (*Acts* 19:31); working with him in Macedonia and Greece; enduring persecution with him and arranging methods of escape; sailing with some of his companions (but without St. Paul) to Assos; waiting until the Apostle should elude his pursuing enemies and join them; sailing together again down the Aegean by Mitylene, Chios, Samos, Trogyllium and Miletus, and again straight across the

169

Mediterranean from Patara to Tyre – what experiences would be crowded into these months of active work, of pressing danger, and of quiet rest – what opportunities of learning from St. Paul and of developing the true missionary spirit and life!

Do you remember the repeated leave-takings on this memorable journey? Both St. Paul and all who were about him appear to have had an ill-defined premonition or dread of coming evil, of death or imprisonment or parting. At Miletus, the elders of the Church at Ephesus came down to greet St. Paul and Trophimus and Tychicus, and after St. Paul had spoken and prayed with them, all wept and fell upon his neck and kissed him. 'Sorrowing most of all for the words that he spake that they should see his face no more . . . and they accompanied him unto the ship.'

Again at Tyre, after a seven days' mission, when St. Paul and his companions were leaving, the Christians came out of the city with their wives and children; and finding, I suppose, a quiet place in some vineyard or stone quarry leading to the sea, they all knelt down; and in the open air, by the side of the Mediterranean, they prayed and took their leave of one another, many to the very last anticipating danger and beseeching St. Paul to stay.

In such scenes was St. Trophimus taught and trained and strengthened for the trouble and the work which was before him. For serious trouble came to him, as we know, at Jerusalem. To feel that he was the cause, the innocent cause, but still the cause of St. Paul's persecution, his possible murder and his imprisonment – to know that those who so loved St. Paul, who depended on his guidance, and others who were waiting for his ministry, might be bereft forever of his care – *and through him* – to watch through anxious days and sleepless nights while the Jewish mob was clamouring for the life of the Apostle – to be conscious that he could do nothing to help or to appease, and to be forced day after day to do nothing but pray – to carry his weight of cares and burden of pleading all the day long and to carry it alone – for a time at least to be shut out from any companionship with his friend and master – this was indeed a second and a deeper training in which St. Trophimus had to lean on no earthly help, but on Christ alone, the Man of Sorrows and acquainted with grief, Whose will was best.

In such a time of suffering and comparative friendlessness (for even St. Paul's friends could hardly forbear, one thinks, to look somewhat askance at the Greek who had brought this trouble upon them), the imprisonment at Caesarea, and especially the later permission to see St. Paul again, would come as a welcome relief, and as the future grew clearer and the prospect widened and the possibility of St. Paul's reaching Rome, but only as a prisoner, took substance and shape, one almost inevitable course for Trophimus to take would be recognized, I think, both by him and St. Paul, that he should go the longer journey towards Spain *for St. Paul, and in his stead.*

And when we find a traditional account of his doing this, and of his founding the Church at Arelate or Arles, a tradition held strongly and contended for so early as AD 450, and when we find such a tradition explanatory not only of the events leading up to this, but also of the events succeeding – of the historical Greek influence on early Gallican Christianity; and again of the curious historical relationship between the Churches of Gaul and Asia in the second century, then, although we may not regard the coming of St. Trophimus to be a matter of strict history, it approaches very closely to this, and the probability of the story grows as we consider his life and times, and search for that living link which must inevitably connect the earliest Church in Palestine with the wonderful Church of martyrs in AD 177 at Lyons.

Whatever may have been done by the Hebrews who are said to have preceded St. Trophimus, but little progress, I think, would have been made among the cultivated Greek or Greco-Roman population until St. Trophimus came to Provence. With his coming possibilities of influence would immediately increase.

I picture him as quite 'at home' in Marseilles. He would find the same dominant religion as that of his native city Ephesus. Standing, I suppose, somewhere near the site of the present Moorish-looking cathedral, with its domes and cupolas, he would see the Ephesium, sacred to the worship of Diana, and he would probably bring letters of introduction from his friends at Ephesus to some of the Timuchi of Marseilles, and from the Apostles St. Paul, St. Peter and St. James, to those who had preceded him.

As an Ephesian from Ephesus he would, I think, be accorded special honour by the Massilians who, in religion at least, were an offshoot from their acknowledged centre of religious life and enthusiasm at Ephesus, and anything that St. Trophimus might have to say would be listened to with attention and respect.

There would be no difficulty of language. Most of the population were Greek; and full, as we have seen, of Greek interest in new customs and new learning. Many of them would have already heard of the new religion which had caused such disturbances at Ephesus, and would inquire of St. Trophimus, as one understanding the subject and one who had been present, what was the reason and meaning and claims of this newer learning? And then, I imagine, St. Trophimus, a Greek among Greeks, who had watched and listened and worked with St. Paul at Ephesus, at Athens and at Corinth, who would know exactly how to interest his audience without giving unnecessary offence, might begin to speak to his hearers of the nearness of heaven and of the increasing revelation of God to man through all the ages; of the Word of God by whom all things were made, and in whom was life – of the Light of Life – the Light of all who choose to seek, the Light of the world.

And as his audience gathered and increased and pressed closer, before they realized all that it involved, they would be listening with breathless interest as he told them, *not* of an image which came down from heaven (as that of the great Diana was supposed to have done) but of the Son of God who came down from heaven to seek and save that which was lost – how He came to His own, and His own received Him not – how He was coming now to everyone who opened his heart to that coming and 'as many as received Him to them gave He power to become sons of God, even to them that believe in His name.'

And then, perhaps, St. Trophimus might cease and give place to one of his companions who would be able to speak of more personal visible knowledge of Jesus, of the words He spoke to them, of His life and Passion, death and resurrection; of His final blessing and the message which He gave through them to all the world. In fact, when one realizes the practical value of this union of Greek and Hebrew in missionary effort, it seems to give an assurance of certainty to what we are told of St. Mary's teaching.

'These are the hands that anointed my Lord.'

'It was my lips that kissed His feet.'

'It was I whom He pardoned, the chief of sinners for whom He had compassion and forgiveness' (*Life of Rabanus*).[5]

It is not very easy to understand the various districts, and to some extent governments, existing in what is now the South of France at this epoch.

The Massilians, as we have already seen, held Marseilles and irregular patches of coastline and towns all along the sea border. They were under the protection of Rome and lived in amity with Rome, but had their own government and appear to have managed their own affairs, as Strabo has described.

Above this was Provincia or the Narbonnaise, extending from immediately above Marseilles as far as Vienne. This seems to have been the peculiarly Roman district, under direct Roman Government and colonized by Rome. It belonged to Rome long before the rest of Gaul was conquered, and during all this time of conquest, and for a very long time afterwards, was known as Provincia Gallica, while the rest of the continent above it was known as Gaul (or Gallia). Just over the border (in Gallia, therefore, and not in Provincia Gallica) was Lugdunum or Lyons, the capital of the Segusii, but at this time under Roman government or supervision.[6]

Probably here a measure of self-government was permitted by the Romans to the Segusii whom they had conquered, so that in this south of France we find in the first and second centuries three notable districts and governments – the Massilian in Marseilles, the Romans in the district north of this as far as Vienne, and in Lugdunum 'or Lyons of the Gauls' as it was often called, a modified local government with Roman occupation and control.

To this middle district, 'Provincial Gallica,' which was Roman almost as much as Rome was, we are told St. Trophimus came. St. Maximin was already established at the old capital of Aix, and St. Trophimus came to Arles.

If you go to Arles today you will be able to form some conception of the city to which he came, for some of the old Roman buildings are still standing, notably the arena, which easily holds some 25,000 people. St. Trophimus is known there as the first bishop of the city. Some stones, said to be of the first century church or oratory built by him, are shown to you as still standing, and the later cathedral (originally dedicated to St. Stephen the first martyr) was rededicated to the memory of St. Trophimus when his body was removed here in 1152. The cathedral is

1. Ruins of the synagogue at Capernaum, at the head of the Sea of Galilee, a place associated with the beginning of Christ's ministry

2. An aerial view of Jerusalem, looking approximately north-westward, with the Judaean mountains in the distance

3. The Golden Gate, Jerusalem. In its present form, probably built by Justinian (AD 527-565). It is said that it was through the former Golden Gate on this site that Jesus entered in triumph into Jerusalem. The gate is now filled, in part because the ground level has risen on the other side of the gate

4. Santiago Cathedral, Spain

5. The Cathedral, Marseilles, built near the site of the 'Ephesium,' a temple of Diana

6. The Church of St. Victor, Marseilles, built over the supposed 'Cave of St. Lazarus'

7. The Hill of Fourvière, Lyons, with the Church of Notre Dame de Fourvière on the summit

8. Abbey of Montmajour (near Arles)

9. The Village and Sanctuaries of Rocamadour

10. The first page of the Manuscript of Rabanus. The page is headed 'Rabanus de Vita Marie Magd'

11a. The site of the supposed grave of Zacchaeus

11b. Interior of the Church of St. Paul Serge (Sergius Paulus) at Narbonne

11c. The entrance to the Church of Restitutus (St. Restitut)

12. Cloisters of the Church of St. Trophime, Arles

13. The old 'Pagan and Christian' Cemetery of Les Aliscamps at Arles

14a. The interior of the Grotto and Cave of St. Mary Magdalene (1901)

14b. The Church of Les Saintes Maries where the relics of St. Mary Cleopas and St. Mary Salome are said to have been preserved

14c. The Crypt and Shrine of St. Martha at Tarascon

15a. St. Michael's Mount, Cornwall. Probably the 'Ictis' of Diodorus Siculus

15b. The old Roman gate of Trèves (Trier) – the Porta Nigra, or Black Gate

16. The ruins of the Abbey Church, Glastonbury, with the Chapel of St. Joseph in the distance

still called the cathedral of St. Trophime, and the tomb of St. Trophimus forms a font or baptistery on the left side of the nave as you enter it.[7]

The local history of St. Trophimus is that he came from the East – was of Greek nationality and the personal friend of St. Peter and St. Paul. St. Paul is reported to have visited him on one of his missionary journeys, and the house (or site of the house) in which they met is pointed out to you and known as 'La maison des Saints.'

But the great glory of Arles in which St. Trophimus participates (for his connection with it has left an ineffaceable impress of his own on all its beauty) is the vast Pagan or Pagan and Christian cemetery of 'les Aliscamps.' For acres upon acres the earth is honeycombed with graves. As you look today[8] at the railway cutting which runs right through the old burial-ground you see many graves laid open by the spade and pickaxe revealing the sarcophagi within, and yet in spite of this and of the profanation of so much of the holy place by railway, workshops, high-road and canal, as you enter the long avenue of trees and see many of the old monuments still standing, it is quite possible to understand and to feel something of that earlier beauty and sacred association which made it for so many centuries the favourite resting-place of Christians.

For here one of the sweetest and best of all old Christian legends – the legend of the Genouillade, a legend that may yet carry a useful lesson to many Churchmen of today – came into being, and the mind which fashioned it or the eyes which saw the vision in 'les Aliscamps' belonged to St. Trophimus.

Les Aliscamps, or the Elysian fields, had been already a Pagan cemetery long before St. Trophimus came to Arles. You can still see the old Roman sarcophagi both of this period and of later times, many carved with loving inscriptions, and with the usual invocation to the gods (D.M.), showing the Pagan belief of those who buried them; and when St. Trophimus came and gathered round him early Christian converts, it

175

soon became an important matter to decide whether these should be buried among their relatives and friends in the old Pagan cemetery or seek for some special and distinctive place of burial. It was not an easy question to decide, for no people perhaps thought so much of the sacredness of the lifeless clay which had once been a temple of the Holy Spirit, and no people sacrificed more to secure for this a Christian, safe and quiet resting-place than did the very earliest Christians.

And, as St. Trophimus paced the cemetery through the summer night considering what it was right and best to do, we are told that a light shone in the darkness and Christ Himself appeared to him. Kneeling among the tombs, as if identifying Himself with those whose bodies were resting underneath the soil, the Saviour was seen to raise His hands and to solemnly bless the Pagan burial-place.

Henceforth no doubt was felt as to the reality of this heavenly consecration. On the spot where our Saviour knelt St. Trophimus erected an altar, and from that time 'les Aliscamps' became the coveted burial-place of all Christians.

Whether this is the record of an actual vision or the poetical way in which the Greek described to Greeks the light which God had given him, there can be no doubt of the result. Christian tombs lie side by side with Pagan, and tradition tells us that so eager were many Christians for burial here that – something like the body of Elaine, which was sent down the river to the court of King Arthur in the Arthurian legends – bodies of saints from distant countries came floating down the Rhone in funeral barges, seeking for reception in the holy ground which Christ had consecrated.

The altar chapel of the Genouillade, or kneeling Saviour, now stands hard by the Marseilles road at some distance from the preserved part of the cemetery, while in the latter we find the ruins of the Church of St.

Honorat (built on the site of the Pagan temple of Jupiter), with the oratory of St. Trophimus leading from it. This, when originally built by St. Trophimus, is said to have been dedicated by him to the Virgin Mother of our Lord, who at that time was still living at Ephesus. The chapel is said to have borne the following inscription:

'Sacellum dedicatum
Dei parae ad huc viventi.'[9]

St. Trophimus is reported to have died at Arles on November 28th, AD 94, and after a temporary occupation of the See by St. Denis he was succeeded by Regulus.

The succession after Regulus is uncertain. Owing to a short series of careless, and finally heretical, bishops, the names of these have been purposely omitted from the records of the See. The chief of these bishops was the 'proud and forward Marcianus' (see Appendix F), who was probably deposed towards the latter end of the third century, and was succeeded by Marinus.

Four miles from Arles, at Montmajeur, is still shown the hermitage of St. Trophimus – a series of four little chambers near the chapel of St. Pierre. This sufficed him for his daily needs, and catechumens and penitents are supposed to have come here for instruction and counsel.

First there is a cell, or chamber of waiting, and as you enter this two early Christian graves are seen, cut in the solid rock. Beyond this are two small chambers called the confessional of St. Trophime – the one for the priest and the other for the kneeling penitent. Beyond this, again, there is a large chamber or cave in which St. Trophimus is said to have lived for ten years, the tradition being that this was the scene of his earliest labour, that here he converted a colony of Moors who had established

177

themselves at Montmajeur, and that afterwards he removed to Arles.

In the living chamber there are traces of an extremely old private stairway and exit.

It is perhaps worthy of remark that this chamber or cave, and also the traditional representations of St. Trophime, are perfectly consistent with the picture I have drawn of him as a man of fine stature and of noble bearing.

Such are the main glimpses of the life of St. Trophimus given us by tradition after he parted from St. Paul at Caesarea. They met again two or three times, I think – once, perhaps (according to tradition) in Arles itself, and once, certainly, at Miletum, when Trophimus, as nearly every missionary does, was either returning home for a temporary visit or going back to work – most likely when going back to Arles from Ephesus, where he had been to meet St. Paul, to see his friends, and to interest the Ephesian Christians in his mission.[10] That he succeeded in doing this appears to be evident from the fact that the Churches of Gaul and Asia retained a lively interest in each other's welfare, and the only rival for the tomb of St. Mary Magdalene is Ephesus, where a namesake of the real St. Mary is said to have suffered martyrdom.

The reasons for not accepting the account of this martyrdom and burial as referring to the true St. Mary Magdalene are well given by Faillon (vol. i, p. 369).

Further details regarding the (second) meeting with St. Paul and all that followed this may be gathered from the *Second Epistle to Timothy*, which was written from Rome when St. Paul had been 'brought before Nero a second time.'

Let us consider what St. Paul had been doing while Trophimus was working at Arles. He had had a long and adventurous journey to Rome – well described for us in the *Acts of the Apostles* – and after this had lived in Rome for at least two years, 'dwelling in his own hired house, receiving all who came unto him, preaching the Kingdom of God, and teaching those things which concern the Lord Jesus with all confidence, no man forbidding him' (*Acts* 28:30, 31). During this time Aristarchus and Epaphras had been his fellow-prisoners, St. Luke and St. Mark his voluntary companions, Demas – until the great persecution came – one of his trusted friends, and Onesimus (the servant or slave(?) of Philemon) his special attendant. After this time he had in all probability been formally tried and acquitted, and was once more a free man, able to leave Rome and to journey where he pleased.

Such a great deliverance, such a happy ending of all the troubles and anxieties of the past five years, would naturally call for some celebration – some special Eucharistic gathering.

What would be more natural than that the thoughts of St. Paul should turn to St. Timothy, his dearly beloved disciple and friend – his own 'son in the faith'? And what more natural again than that other disciple and friend, St. Trophimus, who was the friend of both, and who had been the innocent cause of St. Paul's imprisonment, should wish to join them in their happy meeting? We have very good reason to believe that St. Paul and St. Mark set out from Rome for Ephesus, and that most of the old companions of St. Paul arranged to meet him there.[11]

Timothy, who had been appointed bishop of the Church at Ephesus, was already residing there.

Trophimus, as we believe, came home from Gaul, arranging his visit so as to be present with St. Paul at Ephesus; Aquila and Priscilla either accompanied St. Paul or preceded him, having again had to leave their residence in Rome; and Erastus the Chamberlain came from Corinth to take part in the rejoicing and reunion.

Whether Aristarchus, who had accompanied St. Paul on his first journey to Rome, and had been his fellow-prisoner through all the time of waiting, was set free at the same time as the Apostle and returned to Ephesus with him, we are not told, but three at least of the old company who, five years previously, had worked and taught and suffered and waited and journeyed together – Timothy, Trophimus and Paul – would meet in Ephesus and be able to tell one another of fresh fields won for Christ and to praise God for all the light that had come out of darkness and the glory out of suffering.

And then the happy conference and fellowship was again rather hurriedly and rudely disturbed. The cause of this was, most likely, the news of the great Neronean persecution in Rome, for St. Paul is suddenly called back, and the occasion seems urgent and dangerous. He will not take St. Mark, but leaves him with St. Timothy. Erastus, St. Trophimus and St. Paul leave Ephesus together, St. Trophimus probably intending to journey all the way to Rome in company with St. Paul, and then to take the great north road alone from Rome to Arles. But sudden sickness or the anticipation of serious dangers involved by the returning journey appear to have been too great for St. Trophimus to bear. They have scarcely left Ephesus when St. Trophimus is taken ill – so ill that he is obliged to be left at Miletus, and St. Paul and Erastus go on without him. When they reach Corinth Erastus remains there and the rest of the journey (from Corinth to Rome) is taken by St. Paul alone.

On arriving there the shadows seem to close around him. At first he is occupied with the care of the Churches. He sends Crescens to Gaul, probably to supply the place of St. Trophimus – who must now be absent for several months – and Titus to Dalmatia. Both probably start together, going in company as far as the north of Italy and then separating, Titus going to the East and Crescens to the West.[12]

The little company of Christians in Rome – all that have been left after the recent persecution – are still further harassed by trials, defections and other losses.

St. Paul is taken prisoner a second time soon after his return, and this time has sad forebodings of the future. He says, 'I am ready to be offered, and the time of my departure is at hand.' St. Tychicus he sends to Ephesus to supply the place of St Timothy, at the same time pathetically begging St. Timothy and St. Mark to come to him that he may see St. Timothy before he dies. He evidently feels his loneliness: 'Demas hath forsaken me, having loved this present world – only Luke is with me.' Even the reunion at Ephesus appears to have been spoilt by the maliciousness of Alexander, and the too short time of freedom is succeeded by the settled presage of approaching martyrdom.

Yet, through the whole chapter, I think, there lies an undercurrent of remembrance of the old happy, vigorous days before his imprisonment, when Tychicus, Trophimus, Timothy and St. Paul lived and worked together; of the days of the Ephesus riots; of nights and days upon the blue Aegean, when Christ was very near to them; and of many times of sweet companionship in seasons of peril and of parting when, as on the coast at Tyre, the loving words and deeds of the disciples had made a very Paradise of danger.

Was there a third and final meeting between St. Paul and St. Trophimus? In spite of the local tradition of his death, did St. Trophimus ever return to Arles?

In the writings of Hippolytus we come across one pregnant sentence regarding him: 'Trophimus, who was martyred along with Paul.'

So that we have some grounds for believing that as soon as St. Trophimus was better, he did not (as he might have done) evade the danger of the journey through Rome. If his courage had failed him. at the outset of the journey, he hastened to rejoin St. Paul, stayed with him and shared with him the sufferings and the darkness of the final days, and (possibly) hand-in-hand with him obtained the martyr's crown.

The following are some of the chief dates as given in history, in the chronicles of 'Matthew of Paris':

Archelaus banished to Vienne in Gaul . . .	AD	6
Pilate banished to Vienne in Gaul	"	38
Herod Antipas banished to Lyons in Gaul . .	"	39
St. Peter comes to Rome	"	41
St. Mark preaches in Aquileia and writes his Gospel	"	42
Martyrdom of St. James the Greater . . .	"	43
Invasion of Britain by Claudius	"	44
Coming of St. Mary and St. Martha to Provence .	"	47
Coming of St. Trophimus to Arles	"	57 (?)
Ordination of Linus and Cletus by St. Peter . .	"	59
Death of Mary Magdalene	"	63
Martyrdom of St. Peter and St. Paul . . .	"	66
Death of St. John	"	95

1. In some legends, the pro-consul Sergius Paulus is said to have accompanied Lazarus from Cyprus, and to have been afterwards known as St. Paul of Narbonne. The present cathedral of Narbonne is dedicated to St. Serge. The church of St. Paul Serge (Sergius Paulus) in Narbonne is an old Church in an old neighbourhood, and so crowded and encroached upon the adjacent houses that its exterior can hardly be seen advantageously from any position. It is apparently kept up by the State, for the words 'Liberté, Egalité et Fraternité' are conspicuously fixed over each entrance.

The relics of St. Paul Serge are preserved in a special chapel behind the high altar on the south side of the chancel or east end of the church.

2. The inference that the road journey from Rome into Spain was contemplated by St. Paul is certainly strengthened by the following passage in his letter:

'Whensoever I take my journey into Spain, I will come to you; for I trust to see you in my journey, *and to be brought on my way thitherward by you*' (*Romans* 15:24).

3. Sergius Paulus (?).

4. He is numbered among the 'Seventy' by Hippolytus.

5. Compare the beginning of the First Epistle of *John*.

6. In 125 BC the Massilians called in the aid of the Romans against the Ligurian inhabitants of the surrounding country, and the Romans soon made themselves masters of the territory which afterwards formed the provinces of Languedoc, Dauphiné and Provence. The new province, of which the capital was Aquae Sextiae (Aix), was called Provencia Gallica until the total conquest of Gaul, when the name of the district was changed to Gallia Narboniensis or the Narbonnaise (*Encycl. Brit.*, Provence).

7. His body was subsequently moved to Autun.

8. Recent enlargements of the railway cuttings and station have destroyed many of the graves which used to lie open for inspection.

9. The third historical Council of Arles in 453 is said to have been held in the Church of St. Marie Majeure. Did this Church take the place of the original oratory? To the south of this are found the remains of the chapel of St. Madeleine, dating from the Roman period.

10. The return to some definite Council of the Church for the purpose of reporting what he had done and the condition of the Christians under his care, is almost a necessary consequence of his suggested commission by St. Paul; it is also in strict accordance with the precedents afforded by the pre-Christian Apostolate (of which St. Paul, as Saul, had been probably a member). See note 4 on p. 82 and also *Acts* 4:2.

11. 'It is . . . likely that (St. Paul) revisited Asia Minor, and coming back too soon to Rome, perished in the persecution of AD 64' (*Life and Principate of Nero*, by Bernard Henderson, M.A., Methuen & Co., p. 346).

12. I know that in most of our Bibles the passage is written 'Crescens to Galatia,' but in the Codex Sinaiticus the word is 'Gallia' (see Revised Version), and both Gaul and the province of Galatia were equally called Galatia in the time of St. Paul, while the coupling with Dalmatia is very much more consonant with this reading than with the usual interpretation. In addition to this, too, both Eusebius and Epiphanius very definitely state that Crescens was sent to Gaul, and in the list of the seventy Apostles drawn up by Dorotheus, Crescens is enumerated as bishop of Chalcedon in Gaul; in that drawn up by Hippolytus he appears as Cresces, Bishop of Charcedon in Gaul; while according to Sophronius he was the founder of the Church of Vienne in Gaul (*Encyclopaedia Biblica*).

CHAPTER VIII

ST. JOSEPH AND GLASTONBURY

'The Holy Grail.........What is it?
The phantom of a cup that comes and goes?'

'Nay, monk! what phantom?' answer'd Percivale.

'The cup, the cup, itself, from which our Lord
Drank at the last sad supper with His own.
This, from the blessed land of Aromat –
After the day of darkness, when the dead
Went wandering o'er Moriah – the good saint,
Arimathean Joseph, journeying brought
To Glastonbury, where the winter thorn
Blossoms at Christmas, mindful of our Lord.
And there awhile it bode; and if a man
Could touch or see it, he was heal'd at once,
By faith, of all his ills. But then the times
Grew to such evil that the holy cup
Was caught away to Heaven, and disappear'd.'

To whom the monk: 'From our old books I know
That Joseph came of old to Glastonbury,
And there the heathen Prince, Arviragus,
Gave him an isle of marsh whereon to build;
And there he built with wattles from the marsh

A little lonely church in days of yore,
For so they say, these books of ours, but seem
Mute of this miracle, far as I have read.
But who first saw the holy thing today?'

Tennyson, 'The Holy Grail'

THE BIBLE OF GLASTONBURY

The counterpart, or rather 'complement,' of the Provençal tradition is to be found in Aquitaine, in Brittany and in England.

In the Provençal legends, as we have seen, the name of St. Joseph of Arimathea occurs as that of one member of the group of Eastern missionaries who come to the Rhone Valley in the neighbourhood of Marseilles, but one who simply passed through Provence on his way to Britain.

Again we find his traces at Limoges (the ancient Lemovices and Augustoritum). The old Aquitaine legends concerning St. Martial the supposed first missionary Apostle of Limoges, which have a definite history reaching, at least, as far back as the tenth century (*Fastes Episcop.*, vol. ii, p. 104), mention the name of St. Joseph of Arimathea incidentally. St. Martial, accompanied by his father and mother (Marcellus and Elizabeth), St. Zaccheus (the publican of the Gospels) and St. Joseph of Arimathea – all Hebrews – are represented as arriving at Limoges in the first century. St. Martial is said to have remained at Limoges; the name of St. Zaccheus is permanently associated with the romantic village and pilgrimage of Rocamadour, while that of St. Joseph has no local resting-place.[1]

Again we find traces of the disciples or companions of St. Joseph at Morlaix in Brittany. The local tradition here is that Drennalus, a disciple

185

of St. Joseph of Arimathea and first bishop of Treguier, preached the Gospel in this district, about AD 72 (*North-Western France*, Augustus Hare).

Again, we find faint legendary traces of the presence of St. Joseph of Arimathea in Cornwall. He is represented as coming in a boat, as bringing the infant Jesus with him and as teaching the Cornish miners how to purify their tin. But here, too, St. Joseph had no settled resting-place.

Yet, again, we find his name at Glastonbury. Not only so, but the little town and adjacent country appear to be filled with ancient memories and traditions of his mission, in very much the same way as the Rhone Valley seems to be filled with traces of the family of Bethany.

'Weary all Hill,' the winter thorn, the story of the Holy Grail (or cup) he is said to have brought with him, the chalice spring, and last, but not least, St. Joseph's chapel, all remain traditionally associated with his reputed coming to the Britons. In short, the tradition here is not only a report of his coming but of his life, his labours, and his end.

But this is not all. The old romances or history – romances of the Middle Ages, compiled to a large extent from old records in the Abbey of Glastonbury – appear to carry us further still.

St. Joseph of Arimathea is never represented as coming to Britain alone but as accompanied by other Hebrews, and notably his son 'Josephes.' These companions and relations are said to have intermarried with the families of the British kings or chieftains, and from them, by direct descent, in something like four hundred years, are said to have arisen the greater heroes of King Arthur's Court – the Knights of the Round Table.

About the middle of the first century AD the western country on both sides of the Severn was held by the British in comparative security, being outside the main lines of Roman conquest, and it was purposely to these (as we are told) that St. Joseph and his companions came. Now in ancient British records – the very oldest we possess – a Christian mission of about this date is definitely mentioned. Gildas, who lived early in the sixth century, wrote as follows (referring to Great Britain):

'These islands received the beams of light – that is, the holy precepts of Christ – the true Sun, as we know, at the latter part of the reign of Tiberius Caesar, in whose time this religion was propagated without impediment and death threatened to those who interfered with its professors.

'These rays of light were received with lukewarm minds by the inhabitants, but they nevertheless took root among some of them in a greater or less degree, until the nine years' persecution by the tyrant Diocletian, when the Churches throughout the whole world were overthrown. All the copies of the Holy Scriptures which could be found were burned in the streets, and the chosen pastors of God's flock butchered, together with their innocent sheep, in order that (if possible) not a vestige might remain in some provinces of Christ's religion' (*History of Gildas*, sections 8, 9).

The account of Eusebius is quite in accordance with this. He writes: 'Tiberius . . . threatened death to the accusers of the Christians: a Divine providence infusing this into his mind, so that the Gospel, having freer scope at its beginning, might spread everywhere over the world.' Speaking of the events from AD 37-41, he goes on to say: 'Thus . . . the doctrine of the Saviour, like the beams of the sun, soon irradiated the whole world. Throughout every city and village Churches were found rapidly abounding and filled with members from every people' (*Eccles. Hist.*, bk. ii, chaps, ii, iii).[2]

As Tiberius Caesar died in AD 37 this very much antedates the earliest received record of any Christian mission to this country but the date need not be insisted on too rigidly; the more especially as the news of the death of one emperor and his succession by another would often take years before it filtered to the farthest corners of the Roman Empire and its dependencies. What we do know is that through the reigns of Tiberius, Claudius and the earlier years of Nero there was but little or no hindrance to the spread of the Gospel, and that troops were continually passing between Britain and Rome during all this time. No persecution of any importance reached Great Britain until the reign of Diocletian (AD 285) when, according to the Venerable Bede, 'The persecution was more lasting and bloody than all the others before it, for it was carried on incessantly for the space of ten years with burning of Churches, outlawing of innocent persons and slaughter of martyrs. At length it reached Britain also, and many persons, with the constancy of martyrs, died in the confession of their faith' (bk. i, cap. vi).[3]

Such persecutions would – and did, no doubt – destroy nearly all the earliest written records. In many places they not only did this but practically wiped out (as they were intended to do) the existing Christianity of the day, so that fresh missions had to be undertaken in later years, but none the less the earlier message most certainly had been delivered, and the second coming brought a revival of the older teaching rather than a new and original message.

This is the more easily understood when we remember that the earliest missionaries appear to have gone directly to the peoples of the various nations, and did not, so far as we can judge, seek to influence them through their conquerors.

In Britain, for example, the original message must have been delivered to the native Britons directly and not by means of Roman intercourse (or only accidentally in this way), for we have the historical evidence of Tertullian who, writing at the latter end of the second century, speaks of the 'places of the British inaccessible to the Romans' as having been already won for Christ (See Appendix E). But by what route leading to a district 'inaccessible to the Romans' could the early Christians of the first or second century have brought the news of the Gospel?

A complete answer to this question is found in the writings of Diodorus Siculus, who lived in the time of Augustus: it was the route of the tin traders.

The passage describing this ancient British industry of tin mining and tin smelting is as follows (bk. v, cap. ii):

'They that inhabit the British promontory of Belerium, by reason of their converse with merchants, are more civilized and courteous to strangers than the rest. These are the people that make the tin, which with a great deal of care and labour they dig out of the ground; and that being rocky, the metal is mixed with some veins of earth, out of which they melt the metal and then refine it. Then they beat it into four square pieces like a die and carry it to a British isle, near at hand, called Ictis. For at low tide, all being dry between them and the island, they convey over in carts abundance of tin. But there is one thing that is peculiar to these islands which lie between Britain and Europe: for at full sea they appear to be islands, but at low water for a long way they look like so many peninsulas. Hence the merchants transport the tin they buy of the inhabitants of Gaul, and for thirty days' journey they carry it in packs upon horses' backs through Gaul to the mouth of the river Rhone.'

And again:

'This tin metal is transported out of Britain into Gaul, the merchants carrying it on horseback through the heart of Celtica to Marseilles and the city called Narbo' (Narbonne, vol. v, cap. 2) (*Diodorus Siculus*, Booth's trans., vol. i, p. 311).

So that, before Christ was born, we find the very route exactly described by Diodorus that was afterwards traditionally chosen by St. Joseph of Arimathea.

We can retrace it step by step. From Marseilles up the Rhone as far as Arles or farther; then the thirty days' journey across Gaul, through the country of the Lemovices to the sea-coast; the stopping at Limoges; the arrival in Brittany at Vannes or Morlaix; the four days' sailing in the traders' vessels (Diodorus) across the English Channel to Cornwall and, finally, the journey inland to the British stronghold.

This well-known journey of the tin merchants presents no difficulty from the mouth of the Rhone to Cornwall, and it is only the journey beyond it – the inland journey from Cornwall to Glastonbury – that would call for the courage and determination of the explorer in an unknown land.[4]

The recognition of this route as almost certainly the route of the early missionaries, gives a special force to the Cornish tradition. Cornwall was not really Christianized until the end of the fifth or beginning of the sixth century, and then mainly by Christian missionaries from Ireland, so that we should not (prima facie) expect to find any tradition of St. Joseph here. Yet here is the tradition of the actual coming of St. Joseph preserved through all the centuries, and not only so, but the coming is especially associated with the old industry of the tin workers.

The legend is that 'Joseph of Arimathea came in a boat to Cornwall and brought the child Jesus with him, who taught him how to extract tin and purge it of its wolfram. When tin is flashed the tinner shouts,

"Joseph was in the tin trade" ' (*Cornwall*, S. Baring-Gould, p. 57).

Again, 'There is a traditional story that Joseph of Arimathea was connected with Marazion when he and other Jews traded with the ancient tin-miners of Cornwall' (*Guide to Penzance, Land's End and Scilly*, 5th edition, London, Ward, Lock & Co.).

Anyone who knows the eastern coast of Cornwall, the 'promontory' of the Lizard and Land's End, including Mount's Bay, cannot fail to identify Ictis with St. Michael's Mount. It is close to all the old tin-mining region and still answers exactly to the description of Diodorus. Every day, at low tide, the carts go across from the mainland to the Mount over the sand or by the old immemorial causeway, and every detail corresponds to the ancient history.

The only alternative offered is that of the Isle of Wight, and this is so far from the tin-producing region, and so very unlikely to have been accessible by land within two thousand years, that it is surprising to find anyone bold enough to suggest its claims as worthy of consideration.

All the best authorities, including the late Professor Max Muller, accept the identification of St. Michael's Mount with Ictis, and there can hardly be any reasonable doubt that they have the best grounds for doing so.

Whatever may have happened to the far Cornish coast toward Scilly – the supposed old Lyonesse – it is very evident that little or no change has taken place in Mount's Bay from immemorial times. We find quaint old pictures of the Mount in medieval times and histories of it under the Norman kings. 'Edward the Confessor found monks here serving God, and gave them by charter the property of the Mount.' Long before this it is said that St. Kayne, or Kenya,[5] who lived in the latter end of the fifth century, went a pilgrimage to St. Michael's Mount in Cornwall' (Borlase, *Antiquities*, p. 351 and notes; Carew, p. 130; and Capgrave, p. 204). So that the Mount through the whole of the Christian era has remained very much as we see it today, and from the very earliest times it was regarded as sacred and as a place of pilgrimage.

All the adjacent country is rich in remains of old mining works and debris. Some of these, like those of the Ding-Dong Mine, may be traced to a high antiquity; others, though long neglected, belong rather to medieval or almost modern times. The oldest rude pits containing smelted tin are called 'Jews' houses,' there being a tradition that the tin mines were in very remote periods 'wrought by the Jews with pickaxes of holm, box and hartshorn – tools sometimes found among the rubble of such works' (Edwards).

'There is scarcely a spot in Cornwall where tin is at present found that has not been worked over by the "old men," as the ancient miners are always called; . . . upon whatever spot the old miner has worked there we are told the Phoenician has been or the Jew has mined. The existence of the terms "Jews' houses," "Jews' tin," "Jews' leavings," "attall" and "attall Saracen," prove the connection of these strangers with the Cornish mines' (Hunt, *Romances of the West*).

From the supplement to Polwhele's *History of Cornwall* (Falmouth, 1803) we find that the oldest smelting-places are called 'Jews' houses,' the old blocks of tin occasionally found are called 'Jews' pieces,' and the stream works of tin that have been formerly deserted by the labourers are called 'Jews' works' or 'attall Saracen.' 'The Jews appear to have called themselves or were called by the Britons of Cornwall "Saracens".'

Now, although the ancient presence and influence of the Jew in Cornwall is marked and undeniable – names and places like 'Bojewyan' (abode of the Jews), 'Trejewas' (Jews' village) and 'Market Jew' being well-known examples of such influence, and these, as well as the historical 'Jewish windows' in St. Neot's church and other Jewish monuments and memories abundantly supplementing the older traditions of the 'Jews' houses' and 'Jews' leavings' – it is by no means easy to fix the date of the earliest Jewish appearance and influence on the country.

In the reign of King John we know that the Jews were working or farming the tin mines, not as slaves but as masters and exporters,[6] and whether the bulk of the Jewish traditions date from this time or from a much older period it is difficult to determine.

The tin used by the Greeks came from the 'Cassiterides,' and these islands were 'situated in the extremes of Europe toward the West' (Herodotus, 400 BC). Mr. Copeland Borlase, the best authority on the subject, unhesitatingly states that Cornwall is the country indicated by Herodotus. The earliest workers of the tin mines here, however, are really unknown.

They do not appear to have been the British themselves, nor do they appear to have been the Phoenicians, who were the commercial traders or middle-men rather than the actual workers of the tin. For, although occasional Phoenician antiquities have been discovered in Cornwall, there are no traces here of any genuine Phoenician graves. The oldest graves that have been found – those of the Harlyn Bay discoveries, near Padstow – are remarkable as showing that the earliest settlers in Cornwall and, as some think, the first tin workers, were buried exactly like the prehistoric Egyptians, in a crouching position on the left side with the knees almost touching the chin.[7]

All the graves have slanting lids, a method of covering still in common use among the Turks; and the race here buried, though prehistoric in Cornwall, need not be regarded as belonging to any very remote antiquity, but may have lived at any time from 400 BC to near the Christian era. Gold, bronze and iron ornaments, and Roman pottery have been found either within or in close proximity to these early graves.[8]

Such evidence and tradition as we have seem to point to the settlement in Cornwall of some pre-British Eastern race, who worked the tin mines, were buried, like some of the old Egyptians, in a crouching position on the side, and left an obscure but ineffaceable impress on the language, customs and work of the land and (by inter-marriage?) on the very race or races that succeeded them.[9] By the time of Diodorus or Christ these as well as the true Phoenician traders may have lost some of their chief national characteristics, and the natives of the Cassiterides, mentioned by Strabo (44 BC) as 'bartering their tin, lead and skins for pottery, salt and brazen manufactures,' were probably a mixed race or some combination of the British and the tin workers who had lived for so many ages in 'Belerium' that they possessed equal rights to the British tribes around them though still retaining marked traces of an Eastern if not Semitic origin. In the old records of the Saints we read of Solomon, 'Duke of Cornwall,' as living about AD 300. This not only suggests the presence of a Jewish population of tin workers, but that one of this race held a position of some local headship or Sovereignty.

Certainly the oldest traditions of the 'houses' and 'leavings' of the 'Jews or Sarasins' suggest a race of workers who kept themselves more or less distinct from the tribes around them, and whose tools of 'holm and box and hartshorn' point to a time long anterior to the dates of the Norman kings.

That they were an Eastern race seems to be borne out by the antiquarian studies of Mr. Bellows, of Gloucester, who in his travels in the Trans-Caucasus discovered specific 'Cornish' implements and customs in common use in this distant country, no similar pattern or use being known of elsewhere.

The shovel or spade and pick which he found used in the East at Tiflis and used by the miners of the Kedabek mines in the Caucasus are (he says) of exactly the same patterns as the ancient Cornish shovel and pick used in tin mining. He also says that at Akstapha, near Tiflis, 'what we call Cornish cream' was set before him, and adds, 'This helps to show, I think, that the Cornish people had their ways of making cream from Asia' (John Bellows, Kegan Paul, 1904, p. 210).

Mr. Bellows does not commit himself to anything beyond this, but it is remarkable that a distinguishing feature of the population of the Caucasus, especially in the neighbourhood of Tiflis, is the ancient Hebrew origin of many of their customs and habits, and the strong Hebrew traditions found there regarding the ancient coming of the Jews to the Caucasus. The well-known Hebrew writers and compilers of the *Jewish Encyclopaedia* state: 'It is certain that among the peoples of the Caucasus the Jewish type is everywhere represented, and that even among Christian and Mohammedan tribes many Jewish habits and customs have been preserved to the present day. . . Many of the villages bear Hebrew names, and the marriage and funeral ceremonies correspond in many respects with those of the ancient Hebrews . . . Some of the Caucasian Jews claim to be descendants of the tribes which were taken captive by Nebuchadnezzar, while others are equally certain of their descent from the Israelites who were taken from Palestine by Shalmaneser.'

Those who have studied the ancient Cornish language, and particularly Dr. Pryce, of Redruth, who in 1790 published his *Essay to Preserve the Ancient Cornish Language*, profess to have found in it strong indications of an Eastern impress or origin, Dr. Pryce's opinion being that 'Cornish and Breton were almost the same dialect of a Syrian or Phoenician root' (Preface of *Archaeologia Cornu-Britannica*, W. Pryce, M.D., 1790).[10]

This Eastern element or origin has generally been put down to the Phoenician trade with Cornwall, but the Phoenicians themselves were, as we have seen, only commercial travellers or visitors, and it seems far more likely that the old Jewish or 'Sarasin' tin workers of 400 BC and downwards, were the men who really left their impress on the race.

For the thoughtful visitor and student may well question whether it has really gone today. The language is dead, but the Eastern look of the old villages – such as Mousehole, beyond Penzance and Newlyn – the Eastern use and breed of the Cornish donkey, the facial and other characters of the people – so akin and yet so different from the red-haired men of Wales – the black hair and eyes, the profoundly nervous constitution – nervous with an intellectual antiquity and strain that tends toward disease as well as progress – the genuine indifference to, or delight in, long sea voyages, and the spirit of adventure in the fibre and the blood[11] – all of this seems to separate the Cornish from the rest of their British family, and increases the interest of the inquirer into the nature and origin of the 'old men,' 'the Jews' and 'Sarasins,' who are now mysteriously lost but have apparently left such strong and virile traces behind them. If they were of Jewish extraction, it is not improbable that they came from the great Jewish colonies of Egypt, which were originally contemporaneous with the Babylon dispersion to the Caucasus, and this would account for the alternative name of Saracen as applied to them by the British.[12]

If they were Jews – and the old name is more likely to have lived unaltered than any history – it is only reasonable to suppose that those who were connected in any way with the Phoenician tin trade would be cognizant of this Jewish colony in the Cassiterides. Much as St. James the Greater would necessarily know of the Jews who had been banished to Sardinia, so St. Joseph might hear and know of the Jewish tin workers, and his mission would be undertaken, in the first place, to preach the glad tidings of the coming of the Saviour to the 'lost sheep' of his own race.

If we turn to the account of the journeyings of St. Joseph, as given in the *Morte d'Arthur*, we come to some interesting details which seem to harmonize rather curiously with local tradition and nomenclature.

The narrative (bk. xiii, cap. 10) brings St. Joseph and his son to

'Sarras,' where the 'Saracens' under 'Tolleme la Feintes,' are fighting against the Britons under King Evelake. King Evelake is apparently a local king belonging to one of the provinces of Great Britain, and the Saracen, 'which was . . . a rich king and a mighty,' is spoken of as marching to meet him, so that the encounter must necessarily have been reported – or imagined – as taking place on this side of the Channel. Moreover – and this is of further interest – King Tolleme the 'Saracen' is said to have been the 'cousin' of King Evelake, so that although they were at war with each other and apparently of different nationality, ties of marriage had taken place between the 'Saracens' and the ancestors of King Evelake. Surely there are some fragments of history underlying this tale of the journey of St. Joseph!

Are not the rich 'Saracens' the Jewish or Jewish-Egyptian tin workers of the Cassiterides, and do we not gather, as the tale progresses, that these turned a deaf ear to the message of St. Joseph, while King Evelake and, later on, the greater king of Glastonbury (Arviragus?) were kindly disposed towards his company and more or less won over by the teaching of St. Joseph and his son?[13]

Both 'Saracens' and British were probably by no means so un-cultivated and barbarous as many have imagined.

Diodorus Siculus, although writing before the time of our Lord, describes them as civilized and courteous to strangers. He writes: 'They are of much sincerity and integrity, far from the craft and knavery of men among us, contented with plain and homely fare, and strangers to the excess and luxury of rich men.' His description, too, of their work shows that they had then made very considerable progress in the useful arts and in commerce. From other descriptions (of the British) we read that their ordinary clothing was of 'tartan, spun, coloured and woven by themselves. The upper classes wore collars and bracelets of gold and necklaces of amber. The chiefs were armed with helmets, shields and cuirasses of leather, bronze or chain mail, while their many weapons of defence – darts, pikes and broadswords – were often richly worked and ornamented' (Conybeare, *Roman Britain*, pp. 48-50).

The Druids, who were the ministers of religion, education and jurisprudence among the Britons, appear to have possessed some knowledge of the Greek language as well as that of their native tongue. Some of them sang to the music of harps (Diodorus). They professed to understand the movements of the stars (Pomponius Mela). They studied natural science and ethics (Strabo), and especially taught the doctrine of the Immortality of the Soul.

Again, in contrast to what is sometimes taught regarding British weakness and isolation at this date, we know that the coast was plentifully supplied with ports and harbours, that there was very considerable shipping, that much of the land was cultivated with corn, that a definite British coinage had existed for some two centuries before the Christian era (Brit. Museum), and that in spite of the small chieftaincies into which the government was broken up, the British 'kings and princes lived for the most part in peace and amity with one another, and the Romans had the utmost difficulty in subduing them.'

Some of these leaders were men of considerable cultivation and ability – men who would have been conspicuous in any age or country for character, for intellect and wit. This is abundantly shown by the remarkable and eloquent speech of Galgacus, the leader of the British forces in the battle with Agricola in AD 84. Tacitus, the historian, in his Life of Agricola, has preserved the whole of this wonderful address, and it would probably be difficult even in modern times to find language better chosen, more impassioned in its pathos, or more refined in its irony and satire.[14]

It must necessarily not only have been spoken by a man of very considerable intellectual force, but have been addressed to men who could understand and appreciate his arguments. It has been assumed by many writers that this address has been 'put into the mouth' of Galgacus by Tacitus. It bears the impress of a strong individuality, and is much more likely to have been directly repeated and preserved. Compare, too, with this the strikingly similar terse and epigrammatic speech of Caradoc before Claudius in Rome. 'Kill me,' he said, 'as all expect, and this affair will soon be forgotten; spare me, and men shall talk of your clemency from age to age.'

In much of this we have had the finger of actual history or of existing monuments to guide us. Beyond this we have some old but mostly undated writings, chronicles of the twelfth century, romances of the fifteenth century, and some monuments both in Wales and Somerset (then equally the strongholds of the British), which are more or less in harmony with the traditions we have found in Provence and in England.

The most connected account of the British mission of St. Joseph is that given by William of Malmesbury, the historian of Glastonbury.

This was probably written about 1126, and from it I have taken the following:

In the year of our Lord, 63, twelve holy missionaries, with Joseph of Arimathea (who had buried the Lord) at their head, came over to Britain, preaching the Incarnation of Jesus Christ. The king of the country and his subjects refused to become proselytes to their teaching,[15] but in consideration that they had come a long journey, and being somewhat pleased with their soberness of life and unexceptional behaviour, the king, at their petition, gave them for their habitation a certain island bordering on his region, covered with trees and bramble bushes and surrounded by marshes, called Ynis-wytren (and later Glastonbury), Afterwards two other kings, successively, although pagans, having information of their remarkable sanctity of life, each gave of them a portion of ground, and this, at their request, according to the custom of the country, was confirmed to them – from whence the "twelve Hides of Glastonbury," it is believed, derive their origin.

'These holy men, thus dwelling in this desert place, were in a little time admonished in a vision by the Archangel Gabriel to build a church in honour of the Blessed Virgin, in a place to which they were directed. Obedient to the Divine precept, they immediately built a chapel of the form of that which had been shown them: the walls were of osiers wattled together all round.

'This was finished in the one-and-thirtieth year (AD 64) after our Lord's Passion, and though rude and misshapen in form, was in many ways adorned with heavenly virtues; and being the first church in this region, the Son of God was pleased to grace it with particular dignity, dedicating it Himself in honour of His Mother.

'These twelve saints serving God with peculiar devotion in this place, making addresses to the Blessed Virgin, and spending their time in watching, fasting and prayer, were supported in their difficulties by the assistance and appearance of the Blessed Virgin (as it is reasonable to believe); and for the truth of this matter we have St. Patrick's charter and the writings of the ancients to vouch for us.'

The foregoing is an abridged account from Malmesbury's history. It will be noticed that he takes his authority from 'the writings of the ancients,' which he is said to have found in the Abbey Library, and very probably from the history of one Melchin, who wrote about the year AD 560, and who is quoted by John of Glastonbury as follows: 'The disciples . . . died in succession and were buried in the cemetery. Among them, Joseph of Marmore, named of Arimathea, receives perpetual sleep,

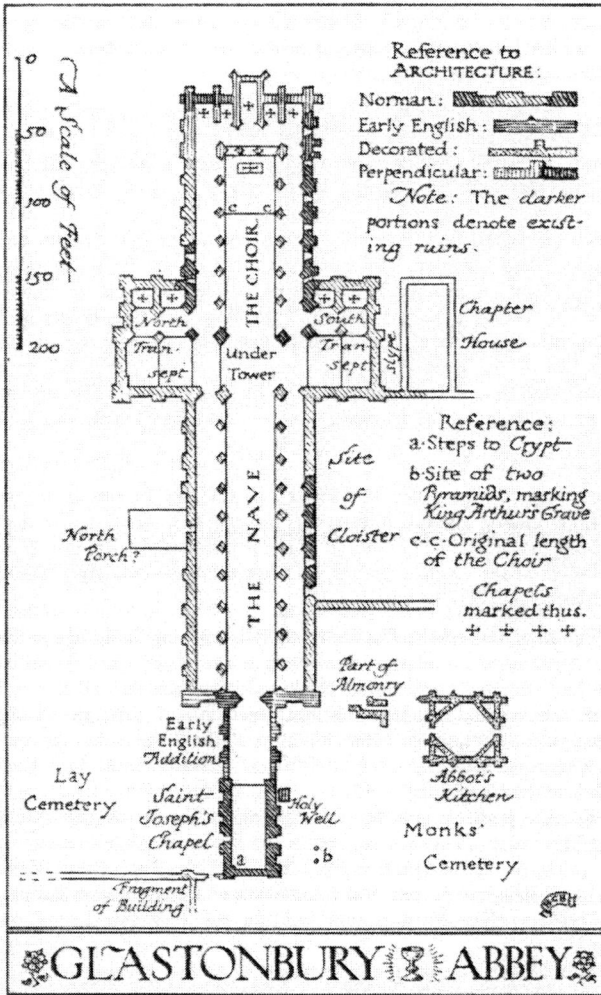

Reference to
ARCHITECTURE:

Norman:
Early English:
Decorated:
Perpendicular:

Note: The *darker*
portions denote *exist-
ing ruins.*

A scale of feet

0
50
100
150
200

THE CHOIR

North
Tran-
sept

Under
Tower

South
Tran-
sept

Chapter
House

THE NAVE

North
Porch?

*Site
of
Cloister*

Reference:
a. Steps to *Crypt*
b. Site of *two
Pyramids*, marking
King Arthur's Grave
c-c. Original *length*
of the *Choir*

Chapels
marked thus.
+ + + +

*Part of
Almonry*

Lay
Cemetery

Early
English
Addition

*Saint
Joseph's
Chapel*

*Holy
Well*

a

:b

Abbot's
Kitchen

Monks'
Cemetery

*Fragment
of Building*

GLASTONBURY ABBEY

201

and he lies in linea bifurcata near the south corner of the oratorio, which is built of hurdles.'[16]

The history of this 'oratorio of hurdles,' or wattled church, said to have been built by St. Joseph of Arimathea; the building of the great church of St. Peter and St. Paul to the east of it, so as not to interfere with the integrity of the older church; and the history of the Abbey buildings surrounding them is very remarkable. Professor Freeman writes:

'The ancient church of wood or wicker, which legend spoke of as the first temple reared on British soil to the honour of Christ, was preserved as a hallowed relic, even after a greater church of stone was built by Dunstan to the east of it. And though not a fragment of either of those buildings still remains, yet each alike is represented in the peculiar arrangements of that mighty and now fallen minister. The wooden church of the Briton is represented by the famous Lady Chapel, better known as the chapel of St. Joseph; the stone church of the West Saxons is represented by the vast Abbey church itself. Nowhere else can we see the works of the conquerors and the works of the conquered thus standing though but in a figure, side by side. Nowhere else, among all the churches of England, can we find one which can thus trace up its uninterrupted being to days before the Teuton had set foot upon English soil. The legendary burial-place of Arthur, the real burying-place of Eadgar and the two Edmunds, stands alone among English minsters as the one link which really does bind us to the ancient Church of the Briton and the Roman' (*The Origin of the English Nation*, by Professor Freeman, Macmillan's Magazine, 1860, p. 41).

The most remarkabe feature of the Glastonbury buildings is this continued representation of the wooden church of the Britons by the

Lady Chapel or chapel of St. Joseph. For, through all the ages since the wattled church was first erected, and through all the vicissitudes affecting the later buildings of the Abbey, the approximate size and shape of the first British church appear to have been religiously maintained.

There is, perhaps, nothing really corresponding to this to be found in Christendom. Every effort seems to have been made to preserve the original church, 'the first ground of God, the first ground of the saints in Britain, the rise and foundation of all religion in Britain, the burying-place of the saints, built by the very disciples of our Lord.'[17]

First we are told it was encased with boards and covered with lead then it appears to have been built over in stone, the interior being beautified with all manner of costly gifts, among which we read of an altar of sapphire presented by the Patriarch of Jerusalem.

All that was best in Great Britain came to it and, for a time, all who were noblest and kingliest sought to be buried here. Speaking of this oldest church, dedicated, as we have seen, to St. Mary, but later known as the Chapel of St. Joseph, William of Malmesbury says: 'Here are preserved the human remains of many saints, nor is there any space in the building that is free from their ashes, so much so, that the stone pavement and, indeed, the sides of the altar and the altar itself above and below, is crammed with the multitude of the relics. Rightly, therefore, is it called the heavenly sanctuary on earth, of so large a number of saints is it the repository.'

In 1184, it and the greater churches to the east of it – all the Abbey buildings – were destroyed by fire, and only a few of the treasures and relics were preserved.

Still, within two years the old church of St. Mary (or Chapel of St. Joseph) was rebuilt, 'where, from the beginning the "Vetusta"[18] has stood, with squared stones of the most perfect workmanship, profusely ornamented'; and lest there should be any later interruption or misconception of the old tradition, a brass plate was subsequently fixed to a pillar in the monk's churchyard, and on the south side of the chapel containing a representation of the original church of wattles, its dimensions (60 ft. in length and 26 ft. in breadth), and an inscription in Latin. The plate (or a copy of the original) is still preserved. It is of an octagon form, 10 in. by 7 in.; the holes by which it was riveted to the stone still remain. The old Latin inscription which covers it in black letters is of uncertain date, but said to be not later than the fourteenth century. It records the arrival of the first missionaries with Joseph of Arimathea in the year 31 after our Lord's Passion, and the Divine dedication of this first church to the Blessed Virgin. It records also the addition of a chancel at the east end of this church, and 'lest the place and magnitude of the (original) church should be forgotten by this augmentation, a column was erected on a line passing through the two eastern angles of that church protracted to the south, which line divided the aforesaid chancel from it.'

What was the reason of this continued careful preservation of the exact dimensions of the 'Vetusta Ecclesia,' for which I think there is scarcely any parallel to be found elsewhere?

If you go to Glastonbury today, still you see it. Shameful as has been the wreckage of the churches, the 'Chapel of St. Joseph' dedicated to the Blessed Virgin, that was finished in 1186, has suffered least; and there today is the site and shape of the little church of St. Joseph, 'the first ground of God . . . built by the very disciples of our Lord.' Its dimensions correspond roughly – roughly, for computations vary, and the size of the original church would necessarily be increased by its over-building – but, allowing for this, its dimensions correspond roughly with those of the Jewish tabernacle, and one cannot help wondering (if there is any truth in the legend) whether St. Joseph did not so design it, and impress upon all who helped him the value and significance of its shape and size.[19]

Standing on the half-pace or chancel steps of the ruins of the Abbey church, and looking from the choir-lawn down the long nave-lawn with the Chapel of St. Joseph at its farthest limit – whether intended so or not – one sees what I have ventured to call the Bible of Glastonbury.

There – reputedly built by Jewish builders – stood the original wattled church or Lady Chapel, built as the Tabernacle was set up, and as the Temple was built, with the House of God to the west of the sacred enclosure; and, opening out from it, directly continuous with it, toward the east where we are standing grew the great church – or what has been the great church – of St. Peter and St. Paul, one of the greatest, or perhaps the very greatest, of all English churches.

The sins of greed and cruelty have wrecked it – sins of both king and people – for until seventy years ago it is said that the stones were carted away at a shilling the cart-load and the coffins were melted down for cisterns; but it is the great church which has suffered most. St. Joseph's Chapel, though shattered and broken, is still standing and remains – if one may carry the illustration further – a type of that Jewish recognition and obedience of the Moral Law which often stands, thank God! when Christian faith is lost, and within the portals of which the honest heart may still find shelter until Faith returns and the Christian altar is again set up, as one hopes to see it yet, in the ruined Abbey church at Glastonbury.

For now, as of old, 'The fear of the Lord is the beginning of wisdom.'

The chain of traditions marking the journey of St. Joseph, the story of his mission at Glastonbury, and the historical writings referring to British Christianity in the first two centuries, are not without very considerable confirmations from the old Welsh records and traditions regarding British saints.

Three Jewish missionaries are definitely mentioned in these, though by their British names only, as bringing the Gospel into Britain at the close of the first century. The names of the missionaries are given as Ilid,[20] Cyndaf and Mawan, and the account is the more remarkable since all the names involved and the setting or story of the mission (from the British standpoint) are entirely different from those of William of Malmesbury, and yet in main essentials the two stories are in agreement.

Mawan, according to one of the copies of the Silurian Catalogue, is said to have been a son of Cyndaf, and Cyndaf (by his British name signifying chief, or head, or patriarch) is evidently recognized as the leader of the mission, and one who must have been honoured by the British in order to have been given this title. Both Cyndaf and Ilid are definitely stated to have been 'men of Israel,' and the account of their coming, together with Mawan, the son of the noble Cyndaf, is obviously directly paralleled in the later monkish record of the coming of St. Joseph and his son Josephes.

The actual references in Welsh literature are not easy to consult. Some are found in the third series of Triads published in the Myvyrian Archaeology, and others (according to Rees) are to be met with in the Silurian copies of 'Achau y Saint' (*Essay on the Welsh Saints*, by Professor Rees, London, 1836).

In the Welsh account the coming of the Hebrew missionaries is associated with the return from captivity in Rome of 'Bran the Blessed' (Bran Vendigaeth), for which there is but little or no good foundation, and also with the coming of Arwystli Hen, or Aristobulus, an Italian or Roman Christian (Rees), for whose presence in Britain and work as 'bishop of the Britons' we have the additional authority of the Greek martyrologies and the list of Hippolytus.[21]

Accordingly, although the 'setting' of the story in the British account is one in which a king of the Britons is supposed to share with Hebrew and Roman missionaries, the glory of bringing the Faith to Britain, the coming of the mission, its character as composed of several members, and the detail that the Jewish head of the mission was accompanied by his son, are absolutely identical in the two versions.

After examining both in the light of such contemporaneous or later history as is available, one is bound, I think, to admit that where there are discrepancies the balance of probability lies with the historian of Glastonbury.

There does not appear to have been any national or general acceptance of Christianity in Britain for over a hundred years after the corning of St. Joseph, although British missionaries (Mansuetus, Beatus and Marcellus) preached the Gospel in foreign countries during the century intervening. Mansuetus (St. Mansuy), an Irish or Caledonian Briton, became bishop of Toul in Lorraine, and is said to have died in AD 89.[22] His Commemoration is on September 3rd. Suetonius Beatus is said to have been converted in Britain, baptized by 'Barnabas,' a companion of Aristobulus, and to have afterwards become the Apostle of the Helvetians. He died at 'Under seven' in Helvetia, AD 110.[23] His Commemoration or Saint's Day is on May 9th. Marcellus, the first British martyr (though not martyred on British soil), became 'bishop' of Tongres and Triers, and is said to have been martyred in AD 166.[24]

These are remembered as British missionaries, and it is impossible to believe that they could have wandered about preaching the Gospel if their own country had meanwhile remained ignorant of the Faith. There can be but little doubt that Gildas is right in picturing the Britons as very slow in receiving Christianity, though it was brought to them in the very earliest years; and those in whom the Faith 'took root' at Glastonbury naturally turned (as Christ had commanded them) to those who were ready to receive their message, even at the cost of long journeys to distant cities and to far countries.

The 'Vetusta Ecclesia' of Glastonbury remained as a witness for the Faith; but it was not until the year of the great Gallican persecution at Lyons and Vienne in AD 177 (when several of the Gallican Christians would probably find refuge in Britain) that we find any indication of a national Christianity.

Then, according to several accounts, which probably have some basis in fact, a local king of the Britons, called Llewrwg, or Lucius, accepted the Faith, established an archbishopric in London, and wrote to Pope Eleutherius asking for counsel and direction in the government of his people.

Considerable doubt has been thrown on the existence and history of King Lucius, but without any adequate reason. Pope Eleutherius, a Greek, is said to have occupied the See of Rome from AD 177 to 192.

Two letters of his have been preserved in the records of the Church of Rome (Mansi). One is to the Christians of Lyons and Vienne at the time of the great persecution, and the other is directed to Lucius, King of Britain. This is in answer to a request from King Lucius for instruction in the right way of governing his people. This letter, and the occasion which called for it, appears to be in strict harmony with what we know of Roman occupation at this date, and of the opportunity it afforded a native chieftain or king (living in amity with his overload) of admiring and envying Roman discipline and order.

It is also in essential harmony with the Welsh account in the 35th Triad (Third Series), which records how the native king bestowed 'the freedom of country and nation with privilege of judgment and surety on all those who might be of the Faith of Christ, and how he built the first Church at "Llandaff" '(?). The only question that arises is whether the last word is not a mistake for Llundain, or London.

For, whether founded by Lucius or not, it must have been at this time or shortly after that the bishopric of London was instituted. About a hundred years afterwards it was the chief episcopal see; and the chief church in the kingdom is said (by an old tradition) to have stood on the present site of St. Peter's, Cornhill.[25]

However this may be, there can hardly be any doubt that it was toward the end of the second century that British Christianity received its main impetus, and that up to this time its progress had been slow. From the writings that have come down to us it may reasonably be gathered that few converts were made by the original missionaries, but that their holy lives (and possible descendants) had kept the memory of their religion green and fragrant, and that the Church of Glastonbury still remained a monument of their devotion. After they were dead further Christian teachers and guides were sent for, and these were astonished to find a Church already provided by God (as it was said), for the conversion of souls.

This keeps to very ancient authority and is a very probable résumé of the facts so far as these can in any way be gathered together.

From this date the British Church must have grown rapidly in numbers and importance, for at the end of the following century or the beginning of the next (300-305), when the great Diocletian persecution had begun, a great number of British Christians, according to Gildas, suffered for their faith, and among these Alban, Amphibalus, Julius, Aaron, Stephanus and Socrates are remembered by name as martyrs. Julius and Aaron are said to have been inhabitants of Caerleon-upon-Usk (the city of Legions), and churches in the neighbourhood were dedicated to their memory. These have been now destroyed, but there is still a chapel of Llanharan, in Glamorganshire, which probably owes its name to the British – or Hebrew-British – saint who suffered in the Diocletian persecution.

In spite of, or perhaps by reason of, this very persecution 'the blood of the martyrs being the seed of the Church,' the years immediately succeeding appear to show the British Church at the acme of her prosperity. The archbishopric of London became powerful and comparatively wealthy, Restitutus, who held the see in AD 314, heading the British contingent to the great Council of Arles. One of his colleagues, 'Adelphius' of Caerleon-upon-Usk, identified by Professor Rees with St. Cadfrawd,[26] a British saint of this period, appears to have belonged to the chief royal family of the Britons, being descended, like Lucius, from Bran and Caractacus, while (about the same time) in the far west of Cornwall where, if our theory be right, 'Saracen or Jewish' influence was paramount, we read that Kelvius, son of Solomon, Duke of Cornwall, not only accepted Christianity but became a Christian priest,[27] and 'Moses,' said to be a Briton, but presumably of some Hebrew relationship, became an 'Apostle to the Saracens.'

With the resignation of the Imperium by Diocletian in 305, and the consequent elevation of Constantius, a new era dawned for the Catholic Faith. Constantius had married Helena, a British princess (?), already favourable to Christianity, and when he died the following year (AD 306), at York, and was succeeded by his son Constantine, both mother and son became known adherents of the Cross.

It was under this banner, and as the first Christian emperor, that Constantine won his last great battle at the Milvian Bridge in AD 312.

So that the highest British influence – and this in more than one direction – the highest Roman influence – that of the Emperor himself – and even the highest unknown Jewish or Saracenic influence of the West Country, appear to have been alike enlisted at this date in the cause and spread of Christianity.

It is small wonder, therefore, that the national British Church during the first half (at least) of the fourth century somewhat suddenly increased in power and influence, until it seemed to enfold the whole of the land within its communion.

The Church of Britain became great, both at home and abroad, holding independent but sisterly relationship to the Church at Rome and bound by closer ties – by ancient intercommunication, custom and liturgy – with the Churches of Gaul, and again (through these) with the Churches of Asia.[28]

According to Geoffrey of Monmouth, at the beginning of the fourth century, there were three archbishops – those of London, of York and of the City of Legions (Caerleon-upon-Usk) – and under these there were twenty-eight bishops with their dioceses (*Hist.*, bk iv, cap. xix).[29]

However extraordinary this statement may appear, it must not be contemptuously or lightly dismissed as incredible, for it seems to be directly confirmed by the records of the Council of Arles in AD 314, when Restitutus of London, Eborius of York, and Adelphius of Caerleon attended as chief representatives of the British Church. These bishops evidently represented the three great provinces of Britain and were not casually chosen. Again, we have the authority of Athanasius that bishops from Britain were present at the Council of Sardica in Illyria, in AD 347, and that of Sulpicius Severus, that several bishops from Britain were present at the Council of Ariminum (in Italy) in AD 359.

Of the four hundred bishops of the Western Church there assembled he writes: 'Unto all . . . the Emperor had ordered provisions and appointments to be given. But that was deemed unbecoming by the Aquitans, Gauls and Britons; and refusing the Imperial offer they preferred to live at their own expense. Three only from Britain, on account of poverty, made use of the public gift after they had rejected the contribution offered by the others; considering it more proper to burden the exchequer than individuals' (*Sulpitii Severi Historiae*, 1. ii, c. 55).

These three, though forming, probably, only a small minority of the

British bishops present, show by the fact of their poverty that in some parts, at least, the life of the priesthood had become difficult, and by the end of the century we find that the period of success had been followed by one of failure and danger. For the sudden success and influence of the British Church was undoubtedly largely political and connected with the accession of Constantine to the Imperial purple. Among the great mass of the people the Christianity of the day was probably largely nominal and withered with the slow decadence of Roman authority and influence. Among the few it was a passion and a life worthy of the best ages of Christendom, and showing distinctive features characteristic of its special origin.

About AD 400, or slightly later, we come to the very earliest period touched by the literature of contemporaneous British Christianity. This literature, as found in the scattered writings of St. Patrick, is so remarkable and has been so little regarded in its bearing on the history and religious life of the period, that some extended notice of it seems necessary in order to bring out its value and full significance.

St. Patrick was born about AD 387, from an extended ancestry of Christians, his father, Calpornius, having been a deacon, and his grandfather, Potitus, a priest, so that he must have had a good practical acquaintance with the Christianity not only of his own age, but with that of previous ages.

His 'Confession' in the Book of Armagh, his 'Epistle to Coroticus' and his wonderful 'Hymn of the Deer's Cry,' are the chief writings which have been preserved to us, and we may find in these many valuable sidelights regarding British life and Christianity reaching back to the very beginning of the fifth century.

In his 'Confession' we find a brief word-picture of the British Church when he was sixteen years of age (about AD 400). It is that of a Church which had been powerful but had lost its first glory and love, and was now becoming decadent. He writes: 'We had gone back from God and had not kept His commandments and were not obedient to our priests, who used to warn us for our salvation.'[30]

In the hymn of the 'Deer's Cry' we find the Church fighting against the influence of the Druids, and in the conditions under which this was written, and in those which called forth the 'Epistle to Coroticus,' when this (local) king had suddenly made a raid on St. Patrick's converts, destroying many and carrying others into slavery, we get a historical picture of the life and times exceedingly similar to that portrayed in the (later) books of the Arthurian legends. But it is the hymn of the 'Deer's Cry' which demands the most attention, standing out, as it does, beyond and apart from all other contemporaneous Christian literature.

According to the account in the 'Liber Hymnorum' (eleventh century):

'Patrick made this hymn in the time of Laoghaire, son of Nial. The cause of making it . . . was to protect himself with his monks against the deadly enemies who were in ambush against the clerics. And this is a corselet of faith for the protection of body and soul against demons and human beings and vices. Everyone who shall say it every day with pious meditation on God, demons shall not stay before him.

'It will be a safeguard to him against every poison and envy; it will be a comna to him against sudden death; it will be a corselet to his soul after dying.

'Patrick sung this when the ambuscades were sent against him by Laoghaire that he might not go to Tara to sow the Faith, so that there seemed before the ambuscaders to be wild deer . . . and Faed Fiada is its name.'

ST. PATRICK'S HYMN OF THE 'DEER'S CRY'
(*c.* AD 450)

I bind myself today to a strong virtue,
An invocation of the Trinity. I believe in
A Three-ness with confession of an One-ness
In the Creator of the Universe.

I bind myself today to the virtue of
Christ's birth with His baptism.
To the virtue of His crucifixion with His burial,
To the virtue of His resurrection with His ascension,
To the virtue of His coming to the Judgment of Doom.

I bind myself today to the virtue of ranks of Cherubim,
In obedience of angels,
In service of archangels,
In hope of resurrection for reward,
In prayers of patriarchs,
In predictions of prophets,
In preachings of Apostles,
In faiths of confessors,
In innocence of holy virgins,
In deeds of righteous men.

I bind myself today to the virtue of Heaven,
In light of sun,
In brightness of snow,
In splendour of fire,
In speed of lightning,

In swiftness of wind,
In depth of sea,
In stability of earth,
In compactness of rock.

I bind myself today to God's virtue to pilot me,
God's might to uphold me,
God's wisdom to guide me,
God's eye to look before me,
God's ear to hear me,
God's word to speak for me,
God's hand to guard me,
God's way to lie before me,
God's shield to protect me,
God's Host to secure me.

Against snares of demons,
Against seductions of vices,
Against lusts of nature,
Against everyone who wishes ill to me
Afar and anear,
Alone and in a multitude.

So have I invoked all these virtues between me and these.

Against every cruel merciless power which may come against my
        body and my soul,
Against incantations of false prophets,
Against black laws of heathenry,
Against false laws of heretics,

Against craft of idolatry,
Against spells of women, and smiths, and Druids,
Against every knowledge that denies men's souls.

Christ to protect me today
Against poison, against burning,
Against drowning, against death-wound,
Until a multitude of rewards come to me!

Christ with me, Christ before me,
Christ behind me, Christ in me,
Christ below me, Christ above me,
Christ at my right, Christ at my left,
Christ in breadth, Christ in length, Christ in height!

Christ in the heart of everyone who thinks of me,
Christ in the mouth of everyone who speaks to me,
Christ in every eye who sees me,
Christ in every ear who hears me.

I bind myself today to a strong virtue, an invocation of the Trinity.
I believe in a Three-ness with confession of an One-ness in the
    Creator of the Universe.
Domini est salus, Domini est salus, Christi est salus.
Salus tua Domine, sit semper nobiscus.[31]

What is it that gives this hymn its peculiar power and charm?

Is it not the cultivated Hebrew model on which the construction of
the hymn is based, and the late Hebrew note which rings mysteriously
and repeatedly through all the gradations of this strange prayer-poem?

The old angel invocations brought from Persia are translated into Christian phraseology or, rather, turned into the material for a purely Christian hymn; and the whole is in strange accord with such influence and impress as might well be handed down from the teaching of the high-born 'men of the race of Israel' mentioned in the old Welsh writings, and left (perhaps by St. Joseph) in the oldest liturgies of Glastonbury.

East and West seem both to be united in this hymn, and through the long line of St. Patrick's Christian ancestry and through the traditions of Glastonbury, where St. Patrick is said to have spent a good portion of his life, we may perhaps trace living notes of that music which made the harp of Erin to sound in unison with that of the descendants of King David.

From the distinctly Hebrew invocation of 'Creator of the Universe' at the beginning of the hymn – through the 'ranks of Cherubim,' 'angels' and 'archangels,' 'patriarchs' and 'prophets' of the second part, down to the final measure of

> 'Christ before me,
> Christ behind me, Christ in me,
> Christ below me, Christ above me,
> Christ at my right, Christ at my left,'

the Hebrew form or modelling, and sometimes the very words of the 'Cry,' recall the voices of the later Hebrew poets and prayer writers as they invoked the protection of the great Creator and His holy angels.[32]

A much less romantic but more direct connection between St. Patrick and St. Joseph is that afforded by the old tradition that it was St. Patrick who drove the venomous reptiles out of Ireland, for it is worthy of note that there is another legend regarding this which gives the first place to St. Joseph of Arimathea.

According to Ussher (vols. v, vi and xvii),[33] it is stated to have been through the wisdom and advice of St. Joseph of Arimathea (learnt from the teaching of King Solomon) that Ireland was freed from venomous reptiles (vol. vi, p. 300). If St. Patrick was the Saint who accomplished the work, the source of his knowledge is directly attributed to St. Joseph.

So through all the whole course of the British Church, the history of which, I venture to think, was very much as I have described: first, difficult; secondly (under kingly protection and encouragement), exceedingly prosperous; thirdly, decadent or largely nominal; and, finally, oppressed or militant, we seem to find repeated traces of a quite special Hebrew influence, almost regal in its claims and associations; lofty, refined and poetic in its bearing on thought and on literature, and bravely aristocratic in its consciousness of high lineage and of moral strength.[34]

And if we seem to find traces of this in the Christian names and scanty records of the earlier centuries, there can be no mistake about its insistence in the work of the later writers – the history romancers or legend reciters of the thirteenth, fourteenth and fifteenth centuries.

All the extensive literature of the 'Grail-Quest,' which dates from about 1200 onwards, is grouped around the tradition of St. Joseph and his son Josephes who came to Glastonbury, bringing the Holy Cup of the Last Supper with them, and full of the idea that these were the ancestors of those great knights who formed the flower of Arthur's court.

In the 'Grand St. Grail,' one of the earliest of these histories, we are told that after the death of St. Joseph and Josephes the keeping of the Holy Grail was confided to Alain, the son of Brons and cousin to Josephes. At Alain's death his brother Josue becomes Grail keeper, and after him six kings, the last of whom is Pelles.

The daughter of King Pelles has a son named Galahad, who

becomes the special hero of the Holy Grail. His father is said to have been Lancelot, and this makes him ninth or tenth in descent from the time of St. Joseph.

Galahad is one of the knights of King Arthur's Round Table, and it is worthy of note that the ten generations described as intervening between the times of St. Joseph (AD 60-90) and King Arthur (500) are seriously consistent with such measure of history as may well underlie the romance.

In the most readily accessible books of the 'Sangreal' (apart from the *Morte D'Arthur*), *The High History of the Holy Grail*, which was probably compiled about 1220 from the book of Josephes in the Abbey Library at Glastonbury (see Appendix M), and has been translated by Dr. Sebastian Evans (extracts from which are given in the Appendix M), it is impossible not to recognize the important and essential part played by this Hebrew lineage or descent. Every book bears witness to this, and the very names of many of the knights or their associates seem to imply their Jewish origin. Elinant of Escavalon, Joseph, Josephes, Lot, Joseus, Josuias (p. 249), Galahad (?), Alain (?), Petrus, Brons or Hebron, Bruns Brundalis, Urien, Jonas (ii, 39), Pelles and Pelleas and Ban may be taken either as examples of Hebrew names or as indicating some special Hebrew association.[35] (The sons of *Bani* or *Ban* returning with Ezra to Jerusalem were 648. *Pelias* (or *Pelleas*) put away his wife at the command of Ezra.)

However apocryphal many of the legends may be regarding them, their names are, I believe, the names of historical persons, and the stories of their lives are in rough harmony with that imperfect militant Christianity which was not only the ideal of the medieval compilers, but may well have been the actual achievement of these distant descendants of the Judean Maccabees.

In the *Morte D'Arthur*, which contains almost entire the *Quest of the*

Sangreal ('Quête del St. Graal'), and in the *High History of the Holy Grail*, we find curious and startling digressions regarding King David, King Solomon and Judas Maccabees. These are mixed with the legends of the Arthurian Knights, and no direct explanation is offered or has been offered for their presence.

But if, as many of the old writers affirm, King Pelles, Sir Perceval, Sir Lancelot and Sir Galahad might be considered as descendants of these Hebrew kings, their chief ancestors being St. Joseph of Arimathea himself and the Brons or Hebron who married the sister of St. Joseph (Sir Percyville, Robert de Borron, Grand St. Graal, *High History, etc.,* and others), not only do these interpolations become less unintelligible, but the fusion of cultivated Hebrew with Celtic stock may to some extent account for that wonderful achievement in moral ideal and Christian chivalry which characterizes the story of King Arthur's court and the quest of the Holy Grail.

Mr. Alfred Nutt, who has made a special study of the Grail legends, considers them to be essentially British in origin, and suggests that they were carried from Britain to France at the time of the Celtic immigration into Brittany (between the fourth and sixth centuries). He professes to trace their beginnings from pre-Christian or Pagan times in Britain, but recognizes that the Joseph of Arimathea history is undoubtedly one of the conversion of Britain. Regarding this he writes:[36]

'If what may be called the Joseph of Arimathea Early History be considered closely, it will be seen that in both its two main forms it is essentially a legend of the conversion of Britain. Both forms start with Joseph, but at a later stage go widely asunder. In Borron, it is kinsmen of Joseph, Brons, or Alain, or Petrus who are the leaders of the evangelizing emigration: it is to them that the Holy Vessel is confided. In the Grand St. Graal Quête version of Joseph's son,

Josephes, is the leading spirit, and the fortunes of the Grail are bound up with those of Joseph's direct descendants or with the converted heathens Mordrains, Nasciens and their kin. This second is the popular version, the one which affected the later stages of the Conte del Graal. The fact that what may be called the Vulgate Early History (whether in its Brons or Josephes form) is in reality a conversion of Britain legend is important when we recollect that the personages of the Conte del Graal and allied versions are British and that the scene of the story is Britain.'

Later on, in a somewhat lengthy argument, which is very difficult to follow, Mr. Nutt appears to advance several theories in explanation of the Grail legends. None of these, however, are very illuminating or satisfactory, and although Mr. Nutt appears (in Celtic and medieval romance) to acknowledge an historic King Arthur who 'died in the first third of the sixth century,' he attempts nowhere to explain that insistence on Hebrew lineage and wonderful atmosphere which may be regarded as among the distinguishing features of the legends of the Holy Grail. In the *High History* this Hebrew relationship is repeatedly mentioned. Sir Perceval; his mother Yglais; his sister, Dindrane; Sir Lancelot, the hermit knight; Joseus; King Pelles, the Fisher King; and the King of the Castle Mortal, are all represented as being directly of the lineage of Joseph, and in one or two passages[37] this appears to include Gawain and King Arthur also. In the Grand St. Graal we read that Gawain was the son of Lot of Orcaine, and that King Lot was descended from Petrus. If so (as Gawain was the nephew of King Arthur), the King himself and nearly all his Table Round are represented as having Hebrew relationship and being for the most part of Hebrew lineage.

For my own part, after reading Mr. Nutt's book and heartily acknowledging his work and scholarship, I turn with greater confidence to the simple accounts given us in the old Histories.

If the medieval writers had not found the historical groundwork of their writings already recorded for them, they would never have dreamed of Jewish characters as types of British knighthood. There was not so much love for the Jew in medieval times that his people or the descendants of Briton and Jew should be exalted as the greatest heroes of contemporary fiction. The medieval romancers only invented new and prolonged adventures for recognized heroes whose reputed lineage and even names they did not dare to alter.

There is, after all, but little reason to disbelieve the tale we are told by the compiler of the *High History*, viz., that the Latin original, written by a scribe named Josephus, was in the Abbey Library of the Isle of Avalon (or Glastonbury), *where the bodies of King Arthur and Guinevere were buried*, and that the names and relationship of the chief actors and the main outlines of their adventures were regarded as historical and worthy of belief (see Appendix M).[38]

1. In addition to the legend we find quasi-historical references to the mission of St. Martial in ecclesiastical literature: "Martialis, Lemovicum in Gallia episcopus et apostolus, una cum St. Petro (ut volent) ex Oriente Romani venit, indeque ab eo in Gallias amandatur; ubi Lemovicensibus, Turonnensibus, aliisque ad-fidem conversis, abiit (ut exactis ejus liquet) Ann. 74 (G. Cave, *Script. Eccles. Hist. Liter. Basileae*, 1741, vol. i, p. 36).

2. Messrs. Haddan and Stubbs (and some other critics) speak of Gildas as copying Eusebius and applying his remarks to Britain without reason or authority. A close examination of the writings of both does not support this view, for Gildas and other old English writers, who follow him in their statements that 'the British were very slow to receive the gospel, and that it made but little progress among them for many years,' strike a special note which cannot be found in other writers on the spread of early Christianity. This certainly supports some definite historical source for the account (see also William of Malmesbury).

3. In this persecution they not only destroyed the churches, but they prejudiced Church history beyond recovery, for as Velserus observes, 'They burnt all the monuments which concerned the Christian Church' (Wm. Borlase, *Antiquities of Cornwall*, Oxford, Jackson, 1754).

4. On closer study of the probable route it even appears that the last part of the journey was by no means dangerous or through an unknown country. There is an old tradition that a trading route existed from pre-Roman times between the tin mines of Cornwall and the lead mines of the Mendips. Traces of this 'way' may perhaps still be found in the 'Here path' over the Quantocks.

5. Kenia, 'daughter of Braganus Prince of Brecknock.' She died on the eighth day before the Ides of October, AD 490 (Cressy's *Saints*).

6. 'In the time of King John, the tin mines (were) farmed by the Jews for 100 marks,' and later, 'the Jews being banished they' (the tin mines) 'were *neglected*' (Camden's *Britannia*, vol. i, p. 9).

7. Mr. J. B. Cornish, of Penzance, writes: 'The idea that these (Harlyn skeletons) are the remains of the pre-Cornish tin workers is my own explanation of the mystery that whereas we know that tin was worked in and exported from Cornwall in the time of Julius Caesar, on the other hand the earliest of modern historical records and all subsequent evidence go to show that the Cornish people themselves did not work the metal.'

8. *Harlyn Bay and the Discoveries of its Pre-historic Remains*, by R. A. Bullen, B.A., London Swan, Sonnenschein & Co., 1902. See also British Museum, Egyptian Room No. 1. No. 3, 275.

9. It is noteworthy that John of Fordun, the Scottish historian (1384-1387), describes the original Irish or 'Scots' as coming from Egypt. Bede, on the other hand, speaks of Great Britain as containing five nations – the English, Britons, Scots, Picts, and Latins – and says that it was the Picts who came from Scythia by sea and settled in Ireland and the adjacent coasts of Britain.

10. In Jago's *Glossary* 'Punic' (Phoenician) and Cornish sentences are compared. So late as 1730 the Cornish dialect near Penzance and the Breton dialect at Morlaix were so similar that a Cornish boy, using the Cornish language, was able to make his wants known at Morlaix better than when using the same language at home (see Jago's *Glossary*, p. 21, and Pryce's *Essay*).

11. 'Many Cornishmen seem to think less of a voyage to America or the Cape than of a railway journey to London' (local conversation).

12. Some of the older writers mention the Jews as coming out of Egypt, and appear sometimes to regard them as Egyptians (Strabo). Compare the speech of the 'chief captain' to St. Paul – 'Art thou not that Egyptian?' (*Acts* 21:38).

13. The name of the Saracen leader, 'Tolleme la Feinte,' meaning 'Tolleme the False,' seems to suggest that he had usurped the name and title of Ptolemy, a name which might well have special attraction for an Egyptian Jew at this date (see *Morte d'Arthur*, bk. xiii, cap. x).

14. See Appendix A.

15. Compare Gildas 'received with lukewarm minds by the inhabitants.'

16. Melchin, or Melkyn, is said to have lived before Merlin, and to have recorded the coming of St. Joseph in a book (see the *Flores Historiarum*, London, 1890, p. 127).

17. In the charter granted by Henry II (1185) for rebuilding Glastonbury, he styles it 'the mother and burying-place of the saints, founded by the very disciples of our Lord' (Hitchins, *History of Cornwall*, vol. i, p. 349); and in the charter of Edgar it is said to be 'the first church in the kingdom built by the disciples of Christ' (Conybeare's *Roman Britain*, p. 254).

18. 'Vetusta,' or 'Vetusta Ecclesia,' the ancient church.

19. The latest and perhaps the best computation of Tabernacle measurements (by the Revd. W. S. Caldecott) makes the length of the Tabernacle from the beginning of the inner court to the extreme limit of the 'Holy of Holies' 55 1/2 ft., or to the centre of the Great Altar of Sacrifice nearly 60 ft. The width of the covered portion or tent of the Tabernacle would be exactly 24 ft. (see Caldecott's *Tabernacle*, pp. 171, 183).

20.   'Hast thou heard the saying of St. Ilid?
          One come of the race of Israel,
          There is no madness like extreme anger.'
          (Chwedlau y Doethion, Iolo-morganwg MS.)

21. Cressy states that 'St. Aristobulus,' a disciple of St. Peter or St. Paul in Rome, was sent as an Apostle to the Britons, and was the first Bishop in Britain; that he died in Glastonbury, AD 99, and that his Commemoration or Saint's Day was kept in the church on March 15th (Rees, *Welsh Saints*, p. 81).

22. This is confirmed by a second century Christian sarcophagus which has been discovered at Malaincourt, in Lorraine, and which bears an inscription indicating (according to M. l'Abbé Narbey) that it was the tomb of one of St. Mansuy's friends who accompanied him from Ireland (see *Acta Sanctorum*, Supplement, vol. i, pp. 313, 343, 349).

23. This is confirmed by local traditions and the cave of St. Beatus on the borders of Lake Thun. St. Beatus is remembered as a British missionary; the site of his first church is still shown, and the district around Interlaken, 'Unterseen' and Beatenberg is fairly full of old traditions regarding him.

24. This is confirmed by one of the traditional records of the bishops occupying

the see as given by F. Godfrey Henschen, in his *De Episcopatu Tungrensi* (*Acta Sanctorum*, v. 20). The list is as follows: 1. Maternus, 2. Navitus, 3. Marcellus, 4. Metropolus, 5. Severinus, 6. Florentius, 7. Martinus, 8. Maximus, 9. Valentinus and 10. Servatius. Maternus is said to have lived in the Apostolic age, being sent by St. Peter as first missionary priest, so that Marcellus may well have finished his work as third in succession among the Tungri. Tongres is the ancient Aduatica, the capital of the 'Tungri,' mentioned by Caesar in his Commentaries. It was certainly the seat of a bishop about AD 300. Trier (Trèves) sent Agroesius, a bishop, and Felix, an exorcist, to the Council of Arles in AD 314.

25.   The episcopal succession of the old London see, according to Jocelyn of Furness (twelfth century), quoted by the late Bishop Stubbs in *Episcopal Succession in England*, Oxford, 1859 (p. 152), is as follows:

N.B.—Compare the names in Cressy.

1. Theanus.	1. Theanus, about 185.
2. Elvanus.	2. Elvanus.
3. Cadar.	3.
4. Obinus.	4.
5. Conan.	5.
6. Palladius.	6.
7. Stephanus.	7. Stephanus, d. 300.
8. Iltutus.	8. Augulus, d. 305.
9. Theodorus.	9. Restitutus, about 314.

26.   The Welsh or British 'Cadfrawd' means 'brother in battle,' for which the Greek Ἀδελφός or Latin-Greek Adelphius would be a natural synonym, the more warlike prefix 'Cad' being dropped on adopting a religious life.

27.   He is said afterwards to have been appointed as bishop to the see of Anglesea, where he died in AD 370 (Cressy's *Church History*).

28.   The ruined chapel at Tintagel and some other old western churches were dedicated to the memory of *St. Julitta of Tarsus*, but the immediate link of association appears to have been lost.

29.   For further information on Caerleon see *The Legacy of Arthur's Chester*, by R. B. Stoker.

30.   See Appendix H.

31.   Version by Whitley Stokes in his *Goidelica*, and quoted by Dr. Magnus Maclean in the *Literature of the Celts*.

32.   Compare with the old Hebrew invocations:

'O Lord our God, King of the Universe!
Let me not be affrighted by thoughts,
Bad dreams, or evil imaginations.

Protect us and remove from us foes, pestilence, sword,
    hunger, and troubles.
Remove Satan from before and behind us.
In the shadow of Thy wings shalt thou hide us.
God our Keeper and our Preserver!
        St. Michael on my right hand;
        St. Gabriel on my left hand;
        St. Raphael in front of me;
        St. Uriel behind me;
        The majesty of God above me.'

33. On the authority of Valdes.

34. What is the source of the curious minor chanting of the 'hwyl' in the impassioned religious sermons of the Welsh? The only thing it really resembles (and resembles very closely) is the minor chanting of the Hebrew Rabbis in the public reading of the *Psalms*. Anyone who has heard both cannot fail to be struck by the striking likeness between these methods of quaint prose-poem singing.

35. See Apocrypha, I *Esdras* 5:12, 37; 9:34.

36. *The Legends of the Holy Grail*, pp. 39, 40.

37. See p. 251 (possibly wrongly translated?).

38. 'About 1280 the trouveur, Sarrazin, cites the Grail (li Graaus) in verification of the then accepted truism that King Arthur was at one time Lord of Great Britain. This appeal to the Grail as the authority for general belief shows that it was at that time recognized as a well-spring of authentic knowledge' (Sebastian Evans in his epilogue to the *High History of the Holy Grail*).

CHAPTER IX

THE CONNECTED STORY OF THE LEGENDS

Once in a dream I saw the flowers
    That bud and bloom in Paradise;
    More fair they are than waking eyes
Have seen in all this world of ours.
And faint the perfume-bearing rose,
    And faint the lily on its stem,
And faint the perfect violet
    Compared with them.

I saw the gate called Beautiful;
    And looked, but scarce could look within;
    I saw the golden streets begin,
And outskirts of the glassy pool.
Oh, harps, oh crowns of plenteous stars,
    Oh green palm branches many-leaved –
Eye hath not seen, nor ear hath heard,
    Nor heart conceived.

I hope to see these things again,
    But not as once in dreams by night;
    To see them with my very sight,
And touch and handle and attain:
To have all heaven beneath my feet
    For narrow way that once they trod;
To have my part with all the saints,
    And with my God.

Christina Rossetti

In attempting to gather together the various threads of love, of sympathy, of work and of adventure which run through the foregoing pages, I recognize that it is quite impossible to form with them any perfect picture or story. There are serious breaks in the tapestry, and no one can tell with any certainty whether the threads should be continuous or whether some of the material may be patchwork of a later date. But one thing is clear to me: no one is likely to read the picture aright who has not some real knowledge of Christian life and character, some definite appreciation of the great work done by unnoticed lives in the spread of the Gospel of Jesus, some recognition of the profound truth contained in the passage, 'the foolishness of God is wiser than men, and the weakness of God is stronger than men.'

The loom may be of this world, but the tapestry, the colours and the inscription upon it are only partly of this world. They belong essentially to the spiritual and the heavenly.

We read the story of the Gospels and watch the slow unfolding of the spiritual character in the various disciples, and especially (apart from 'Peter, James and John') in Salomé, in Mary Cleopas, in Mary Magdalene and Martha, in Lazarus and the man born blind, and cannot readily believe that all this had but little earthly sequel.

Somewhere, whether in East or West, God, Who had called them, lived with them and taught them in the Person of His Son, must have used them as His messengers and missioners. It was not in the Holy Land or in the immediate East, or we should read of them in the *Acts of the Apostles* or Epistles. The silences of history (as in the case of St. James the Greater) correspond with the voices of tradition.

We watch the 'Seventy' proceeding two by two upon their journeys for some time previous to the crucifixion. We see them in the towns and villages of Galilee and Samaria, and in the Syro-Phoenician towns on the border.

228

We remember the many ties of friendship and common work between Syro-Phoenicia and Judea; we see these renewed and sanctioned by the loving presence and healing power of Jesus.

Across the 'great sea' of the Mediterranean we trace the various Hebrew or Phoenician and Hebrew colonies, though their greatness and activity at this time were slowly waning – in Asia Minor (as at Tarsus), in Cyprus, in Africa, in Crete, Sicily, Sardinia and Spain – and as we read authoritatively in the *Acts of the Apostles* of the establishment of Christian missions in the great Syrian capital of Antioch and in all the eastern colonies of the Phoenicians (Cyprus, Crete, Sicily and Africa) we cannot fail to recognize that such missions (essentially Semitic, between Jews and Jews or Canaanites) must have inevitably spread before long to the more distant colonies also.

At this stage we pick up the thread of the 'Recognitions,' inter-lacing, as it does, with that belonging to the historian St. Luke. We see the best-known friends of Jesus hunted out of Jerusalem, and some of these finding a temporary shelter at the Roman capital and seaport Caesarea. Peter, Philip, Zaccheus, Joseph of Arimathea and the 'Holy Women' are of this company, and early Christian visitors from distant parts (such as Barnabas and Clement) are coming or going, calling to comfort, or be comforted by, the brethren dwelling or sheltering there.

The next important thread is one of great adventure – the mission of St. James the Greater to Sardinia and to Spain. The source of it is traditional, but the supposed date of it exactly corresponds with the almost necessary absence of St. James from Jerusalem; the tradition of it is immemorially ancient, and even adverse critics are constrained to admit its strength and importance. But if we accept this, and trace the return and martyrdom of St. James as briefly recorded in history and pictured for us here, we seem bound also to recognize another thread closely connected with this – a delicate thread of human love – which

229

accompanies, or rather continues, the thread of adventure. We find this in the beautiful tradition of St. Mary Salome or 'the three Maries.'

Perhaps, if we consider this portion of the tapestry or picture by itself, there may appear to be something far-fetched or unlikely in the presentation. As we watch the aged women, St. Mary Salome and St. Mary Cleopas, depicted as going with St. Mary Magdalene, and her reputed company on their long journey from East to West, the unlikeliness of such a far expatriation in the latter years of life is marked and almost startling.

But when we trace the intimate association almost certainly existing between this tradition and the tradition of the previous mission of St. James the Greater, all the difficulties vanish.

We remember how St. Salome's life was wrapped up in her sons, how she came to Jesus worshipping Him, and praying that one should sit on His right hand and the other on His left hand in His Kingdom (*Matthew* 20:21). We recall also that St. John had taken the blessed Mary under his special protection after the crucifixion of our Lord. Remembering these things, anyone who understands something of a mother's self-sacrificing but still not self-less love – who knows the power of the distant missionary field in calling on the love of those who have loved the labourers – will see at once the reasonableness, the naturalness, the almost inevitable consequence of the following of Salome.

Whether she undertook the journey while her son was still preaching in Spain, or whether – as some of the legends affirm – she and St. Mary Cleopas took the martyred body of her son back towards the scene of his former labours, it matters little. The spiritual love of the mother for her boy is quite enough to account for what is otherwise unreasonable in the distant journey.[1]

And the writings of St. Paul are, at all events, in harmony with such interpretations. If, as I have already suggested, the later labours of St. Peter and St. Paul were much more for the gathering together of the scattered Christians, for the building up and confirming of the Churches, a new light is thrown on St. Paul's anxiety to go to Spain. He knew that St. James had suffered martyrdom, and that whatever may have been intended by those who followed him to the West, but little or no further progress had been made in Spanish missionary effort, and he would necessarily be anxious lest the interrupted work of the Apostle James, for want of the organizing and directing power of the Church, should suffer loss or be swept away as though it had never been. The coupling, too, of this work with the work he promised himself in Rome suggests a similarity in both that has certainly not received the attention it deserves.

Another thread or clue of some importance is that afforded us by the name of 'Austroclinianus' in the *Acts of Barnabas*. For some centuries the thread seems lost, and then it reappears in the traditions of South-Western France. In both places Austroclinian is spoken of as a convert of Antioch, and in the *Acts of Barnabas* we read of him as a native of Cyprus, and as having been ordained to missionary work in Cyprus. No direct mention is made of this in the French chronicles, but it is a significant fact that two other names are traditionally remembered in the same neighbourhood as missionaries from Cyprus. These are Lazarus, whose first century (?) crypt is preserved at Marseilles, and Sergius Paulus (mentioned by St. Luke in *Acts* 13:7-12), whose relics are said to rest in the old church dedicated to his memory at Narbonne.

Much in the same way, if we turn back to the early records of the Church at Caesarea and find again the first thread of the 'Recognitions' – Philip, Zaccheus, Joseph and the Holy Women – if we take up also part of the second thread connected with this town given us by the historian St. Luke in the history of St. Paul and Trophimus, and slowly follow these onwards, we can trace the same threads, or something very like them, in the history of Rabanus and in the corresponding traditions of the Rhone Valley, of Rocamadour, of Brittany and England. For we find these not only related to the reputed previous mission of St. James and the following of St. Mary Salome, but in the further pictures presented to our view by the extended series of traditions, the threads we are holding appear again and again, and one of them can be traced through the whole of the series. The one thread is the track of the journey of St. Joseph of Arimathea, and the other is formed by the apostolate or bishopric of St. Trophimus. This latter is, I believe, historical, and has already been sufficiently considered in the chapters on Caesarea and St. Trophimus. The track of St. Joseph's journey brings all the remaining traditions together and demands some further notice, for in it we find the strongest ground for believing that there must be some historical basis underlying them.

The traditional sites of the earliest missions across the Mediterranean from East to West – from Palestine to Gaul, and again from Gaul across the Continent and Channel to Great Britain – form when connected a map or missionary route (extending from Caesarea in Palestine as far as Glastonbury in England) rational, almost direct, and following the probable lines of the commercial traffic of the period.

Each chief place of stopping has its own reputed 'Apostle' or set of missionary teachers. These are said to have remained, and round them gather the local traditions and legends of the neighbourhood. Through most of these main traditional sites or missionary stations (Jerusalem, Caesarea, Marseilles, Limoges, Morlaix and Cornwall) there passes, as we have seen, the figure of St. Joseph of Arimathea to his final resting-place at Glastonbury.

Some traces – of varying value – but some traces of the reputed early Hebrew missionaries are apparently found immemorially attached to each place or district on the line of journey, and accepting these as landmarks we are in a position to construct or reconstruct the following itinerary:

1. At Caesarea we find the residence of St. Philip, the first Hebrew missionary to the Gentiles (New Test.), the sender of St. Joseph (Chronicles of Glastonbury) and the missionary to the Gauls (St. Isidorus). Here, too (according to the 'Recognitions' and 'Homilies' of St. Clement), we find the temporary residence of Zaccheus, Joseph, Lazarus and the 'Holy Women.'
2. At Cyrene we find the residence of several Jewish missionaries of the same date as St. Philip (New Test.).
3. At Crete (Phenice) we find one of the earliest missionary stations (New Test.).
4. At Syracuse we find the tradition of a mission sent from Antioch from AD 40.
5. At Rome we find the history of a mission quite as early as that of Antioch (or earlier) ('Recognitions' and 'Homilies'), and evidence of a Church formed there before either St. Peter or St. Paul had visited it (New Test.).
6. At Marseilles and Ste. Baume we find cave churches or hermitages of the early Christians, immemorially held as such and identified with the names of St. Lazarus and St. Mary. St. Joseph of Arimathea is said to have come with them and passed on (Local tradition and *Life of Rabanus*).
7. At Limoges and Rocamadour we find a similar cave-shelter and the traditional coming of Jewish missionaries in the first century, one of whom is St. Joseph of Arimathea. Two remain (St. Zaccheus and St. Martial), St. Joseph passes on (Tradition).
8. At Morlaix a companion or disciple of St. Joseph of Arimathea (St. Drennalus) is said to have preached in AD 72.[2] Again, at Fécamp, at

some distance along this coast, we find the legend of the washing ashore of the trunk of a fig-tree belonging to Joseph of Arimathea. The name (Ficus Campus) Fécamp is said to have arisen from a belief in the legend.

9. In Cornwall we find a tradition that St. Joseph of Arimathea came in a boat and brought the infant Christ with him. He passes on (Tradition).

10. At Glastonbury we find the tradition that St. Joseph came here, lived here, built a church of wattles here, and died here (Chronicles of Glastonbury, supported by Welsh Triads, etc.).

Such a summary is certainly remarkable. The fact that the various histories and traditions do not conflict with or contradict one another but, on the contrary, combine to substantiate the traditional journey of St. Joseph, is one which demands some explanation. Are we not almost forced to the conclusion either that as early as the eighth or ninth century (or before this) a worldwide conspiracy of fiction was undertaken (and undertaken successfully) by the deliberate planting of local traditions which should combine to form a harmonious whole, or that behind these local traditions there has always existed a substream of historical fact which itself is the reason of their mutual harmony and support? For my own part the first hypothesis appears to me to be wild and 'singular' and unbelievable; the second hypothesis, on the contrary, is consistent with the known relations of tradition and history in all ages and countries, and is in the strictest harmony with all the earliest Christian literature.

A few subsidiary or finer threads remain to be considered.

I have already referred to the importance of Christian names as bearing on contemporary or previous Christian association. One definite consequence of the Christian conversion of Britain seems to have been the taking of old Hebrew names by British converts.

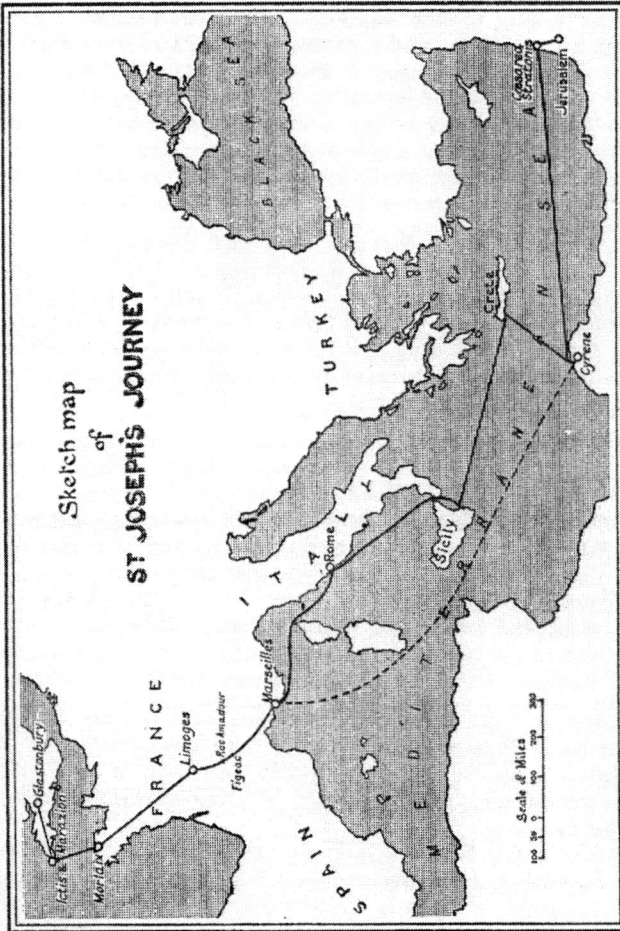

Sketch map of ST JOSEPH'S JOURNEY

Nearly all the great heroes of Hebrew history appear to have been chosen as namesakes. We find:

'Moses,' a British Apostle of the Saracens, Com. February 7th.
'Aaron,' native of Caerleon, martyred with Julius, July 1st, *c.* 287.
'Samson,' son of Caw, lived about 500.
'David,' first bishop of Menevia. Died March 1st, 544, aet. 82.
'Daniel,' first bishop of Bangor, died 534, Com. December 10th.
'Baruch,' a hermit, 600-700.
'Judoc,' *c.* 650.
'Stephanus,' martyred in the persecution of Diocletian.
'Petrock,' or Peter, died 564.
'Paulinus,' or Paul, disciple of St. Germanus.[3]

Most of these names must have been taken because of special interest in Hebrew history. Whence came the knowledge of this history, if not from Hebrew teachers? And why is the Hebrew interest apparently more marked in Christian Britain than in Christian Gaul?

Side by side with these names we notice some examples of the more usual class of Christian names, those chosen from the names of honoured forebears or Christian saints, and especially those chosen from the names of the early missionaries.

We do not find the name of St. Joseph among the early British Christians, for he is supposed to have been given (as we have already seen) the British appellation of 'Cyndaf,' implying 'head or chief,' and no one could voluntarily assume the same name after him, but we find the recurring names of Mawan, of Arwystli, of Cadfarch and of Rhystyd, the Welsh equivalent for Restitutus. The name of the British 'Restitutus' who was bishop of London in 314 is somewhat remarkable. He was perhaps of Roman birth (Restitutus being a fairly common Latin name, as we know from the letters of Pliny), but it is quite as likely that he was the descendant of some Gallican convert who came over to Britain at the time of the great persecution, and that his name was given in honour of that older Restitutus who, according to tradition, was known and beloved in Provence and had been a fellow-pilgrim with St. Joseph when they both left Palestine.

Most of the children, then as now, would be given the names of their relatives or more immediate friends, but occasionally the Christian convert or the child of Christian parents would take the name of some missionary or saint, and especially of one who was connected with the local religious life of the preceding age.

Of these 'namesakes,' again, only a small number might grow up to fulfil the promise of their childhood, and it may well have been the children or grandchildren of these (named after their fathers), rather than the namesakes themselves, who attained both a holy life and high distinction.

It is very much in the proportion suggested by this that we find the names of the saints recurring among the prominent early Christians. For 'Restitutus' does not stand alone in relation to the traditions of the Provençal saints. At Aix, after the (doubtful) names of St. Maximin and St. Sidonius, the first, or one of the first, historical bishops whose identity cannot be questioned, is one who lived about AD 400, and who bears the name of Lazarus. At Arles, the fifth known bishop after Trophimus has the name of Crescens; Crescens himself, at Vienne, was followed by Zacharias; at Trèves in 344 the name of the bishop is Maximinius, or 'Maximin.' Euodius is one of the signatories of the Council of Valence in 374, and the earliest known bishop of Besançon is Chelidonius, who was contemporary with Hilary of Arles.

Frail as they are – frail as gossamer, if you like – these are still fine threads which bind together the Christianity of tradition with the

Christianity of the Bible, and both of these with the histories of Gaul and of Britain. When you realize that within some two or three hundred years, over a limited tract of country, you find in convert bishops the names of the reputed teachers of their fathers – of Lazarus, of Maximin, of Restitutus, of Chelidonius, of Crescens and Euodius – and out of the list of names of contemporary bishops you can form no artificial combination so striking – not even one of the names of the Apostles – the work of Rabanus and the legends of the saints cannot but gain in value and demand a greater consideration.

In nearly all the earliest missions out of Palestine Hebrews and Gentiles appear to have worked together – at Ephesus, at Athens, at Rome, at Marseilles and at Glastonbury; and it is interesting to find in this and in immediately succeeding ages a transient time when Jew and Gentile forgot their differences, and Gentile children gladly took the names of Jewish missionaries.[4]

The one weak point in the credibility of the traditions we have been considering is (as I have said before) the silence of the first five centuries regarding them.

But before we consider this as fatal we have to determine, as far as possible, what is the natural history of the beginnings of any foreign unrecognized and largely unsuccessful mission.

Do we not find over and over again that every detail of its earliest history is absolutely unrecorded and practically lost: that for three or four centuries the thoughts of all the chief adherents have been fixed on growth and on success: that tentative efforts and failures have been deliberately forgotten, and that even historians toward the end of such a period either hear nothing of, or regard as unimportant, any local accounts of those who first began to teach the Faith, but had few converts, built no churches, and established no permanent centres of government? In Africa, where the Church developed most rapidly, where great writers such as Tertullian, Cyprian and Origen are to be found engaged in compiling books and treatises from the very earliest times; in Spain, where in AD 306 there was a great Council of Spanish clergy at Elvira, attended by 'nineteen bishops, thirty-six priests and many deacons'; in Gaul, the country of the great persecution in AD 177; in Germany and Britain, the history is still the same. We have to depend almost entirely on legend and tradition for any account of the earliest beginnings of the Faith, and these records being mainly oral, can rarely, if ever, be traced to anything like the higher limits of antiquity.

Long before the date of any published records regarding these, we find historical notices (whether dependable or not) of the great successes of the Faith; of churches and of seas, of great writers and controversies, of martyrs and of saints.

It is not until a long time after such historical records that the traveller and antiquarian, finding some almost unknown names and legends connected with the local history of Christianity in certain districts, begin to find in these and in local monuments and local memories some traces of a history older than that recorded by the better-known books and parchments.

And then we get some record of the tales 'told by our forefathers' – full, it may be, of unintentional inaccuracies and of unintentional additions but, because not designedly untruthful, still enshrining definite truths and often the only truths we can ever obtain about the very beginnings of missionary effort.

What is the great picture that all this unfolding 'tapestry' of the legends presents to us but a most rational portrayal of what is otherwise a mystery of blankness? We *have* to account in some way for the great Gallican Churches of the early martyrs in the second century, and for the early knowledge of the Faith in Spain and England as well as in Italy. We have, too, to account in some way for the fact that nowhere outside of Asia is Christianity so pure and so advanced as in the Valley of the Rhone, at only the distance of one or two generations from the times of the Apostles.

No other histories are known to us. On the one hand we find a blank wall of impenetrable darkness; on the other a pictured and written surface, on which many hands have laboured, the whole, however, forming a connected story with harmony of colouring and perspective in which it seems difficult to find the least conflicting element.

We see 'the Holy Women' who have attended their Lord and Master throughout the whole of His ministry – Mary Salome, Mary Cleopas, Mary Magdalene, Martha and Joanna – not neglectful or disobedient after His ascension, but gladly accepting danger, toil and suffering for the hope and the joy set before them, knowing, as no one else could know, the blessedness of the daily walk with Jesus, and longing to tell others of that constant Light and leading which His presence brings to those who follow Him. We see them ministering to strangers in a distant country and, associated with them in their labours, we see the very men who, in the Gospels, had received most from Jesus or given most to Him: the dead whom Christ had raised to life, the blind whose sight the Saviour had restored, and the rich from whom the Lord of all things had deigned to receive the shelter of the sepulchre and spices of His burying. We see those among whom they lived and laboured growing day by day to understand more and more of that sweet self-sacrificing love which draws all men to the feet and heart of Jesus – we see them becoming disciples of the disciples of their Master – we see their grandchildren strong in choosing death rather than the denial of their Lord – we see St. Trophimus from Ephesus and Caesarea organizing the Church and bringing with him that rich and subtle tincture of the cultivated East which has never entirely faded from Gallican and British Christianity – we see his spiritual successors, Pothinus and Irenaeus, carrying on the work which the gates of hell are powerless to withstand.

And 'above all, and through all, and in all' we mark the presence of the unseen but ever-living Christ redeeming His chosen 'from among men – the first-fruits unto God and to the Lamb' (*Revelation* 14:4).

> As one who came with ointments sweet;
>> Abettors to her fleshly guilt,
>> And brake and poured them at Thy feet
>> And worshipped Thee with spikenard spilt:
> So from a body full of blame,
> And tongue too deeply versed in shame
> Do I pour speech upon Thy Name.
>
> O Thou, if tongue may yet beseech,
> Near to Thine awful Feet let reach
> This broken spikenard of my speech!

Laurence Housman

1. The earliest Christians, who were firm believers in the resurrection of the Lord, and who had (many of them) seen Him after He had risen from the dead, must have been at first uncertain as to what might be expected regarding the bodies of those they loved, and especially the bodies of those who had died for the Faith. Might they not hope that these would finally undergo the triumph and glory of a resurrection? Until they could be certain about this, such a dream or hope would of itself account for the jealous way in which they guarded the bodies of their dead, hoping not for themselves (conscious as each might be of failure), but hoping against hope for those whom they had loved and honoured and revered, that some morning the lifeless clay might have vanished from its resting-place and the risen master or father or son be waiting to greet the watching disciple.

2. The Latin name of the town, Mons Relaxus, came from its fortress which existed at the time of the Roman occupation. Drennalus, disciple of Joseph of Arimathaea and first Bishop of Treguier, is said to have preached the gospel here, AD 72 (*North-Western France*, Augustus Hare. George Allen, 1895).

3. On looking over the early Welsh pedigrees and the genealogical tables constructed by Professor Rees, many of the relatives of St. Cadfrawd, or 'Adelphius,' appear to have had names suggestive of some strong Hebrew strain or relationship, derived, perhaps, from the first Christian missionaries. Among such names are the following: Aron, Teon, Urien, Pasgen, Owain (John), Iago (James), Androenus (Andrew), Asaf, Sawyl, Dewi (David), Jestin and Arwystli.

4. Other names that may have some bearing in this argument are the following:

Marcellus	4th	Bishop of	Die (463).
	5th	"	Bourges.
Marcellinus	1st	"	Embrun.
Maternus		"	Milan (*c.* 300-400).
Maternianus		"	Rheims (*c.* 300).
Marcellinus	5th	"	Rouen (*c.* 360).
Marcellinus	2nd	"	Sens.
Maximus	2nd	"	Valence (419).
	2nd	"	Riez (433).
Maximus	6th	"	Cahors (549).
	10th	"	Lyons.
	4th	"	Geneva (520).
Austriclianus	3rd	"	Limoges (Austroclinian or Aristoclinan).
Adelphius	9th	"	" (after Adelphius of Caerleon?),
Anianus	2nd	"	Perigeuex ⎫ After Annianus the first Hebrew
	5th	"	Chartres ⎬ Bishop of Alexandria (after St.
	5th	"	Orleans ⎭ Mark).
Illidus	4th	"	Auvergne (after St. Illid of the Welsh?).
Petrus	6th	"	Rouen (380?).
	4th	"	Saintes (511).
Paulus	1st	"	Narbonne (Sergius Paulus?).
	1st	"	Chalons.
		"	St. Paul Trois-Chateaux.
Sergius	7th	"	Narbonne.
		"	Carcassonne (589).
Marcus	4th	"	Paris.
Rufus	4th	"	Sion (541).

Sanctus	1st	"	Tarantaise (after the deacon of Vienne, 177?)
Euodius	9th	"	Rouen.
Crescens	13th	"	Rouen.
Isaac	1st	"	Geneva (c. 400).

There are other examples of similar nomenclature. The names of the bishops of Antioch in the second century appear to bear out the relation of this see to Jerusalem and Caesarea, and, perhaps, the historical intimacy between the Churches of East and West, as shown in AD 177. The fourth bishop is Cornelius, the sixth Theophilus, the seventh Maximin.

CHAPTER X

ON PILGRIMAGE

In the fair Church of Amiens
There lies the relic of St. John
Some say it is the skull of him
Beheaded, as the Gospels tell,
By Herod for a woman's whim
What time her daughter danced so well.
    (St. John the Baptist, ever blest,
    Bring me to his eternal rest.)

But some adore it as the head
Of John Divine, the same who said,
'My little children, love each other,'
And lay upon the Lord Jesu's heart
And took in trust the blessed Mother
Till see in glory and did depart.
    (St. John Divine, the son of love,
    Preserve me to his peace above.)

For John the Baptist's head, they say,
Was broken up in Julian's day.
One bit is in Samaria's town
And two beneath Byzantium's dome,
And Genoa has half the crown,
The nose and forehead rest in Rome.

(St. John the Baptist's scattered dust,
Bring me to kingdoms of the just.)

But there are others say again
St. John Divine escaped the pain
Of death's last conflict; for he lies
Still sleeping in his bishopric
Of Ephesus, until his eyes
Shall ope to judgment with the quick.
 (St. John the Divine, who sleeps so fast,
 Wake me to Paradise at last.)

For me, a poor unwitting man,
 I pray and worship all I can,
Sure that the blessed souls in heaven
Will not be jealous of each other,
And the mistake will be forgiven
If for one saint, I love his brother.
 (St. John Divine and Baptist too,
 Stand at each side whate'er I do.)

And so that dubious mystery
Which of the twain those relics be
I leave to God. He knows, I wis;
How should a thing like me decide?
And whosesoever skull it is,
St. John, I trow, is satisfied.
 (May God, who reads all hearts aright,
 Admit my blindness to His sight.)
 Henry W. Nevinson, from 'Between the Acts'

I am pale with sick desire,
  For my heart is far away
From this world's fitful fire
  And this world's waning day;
In a dream it overleaps
  A world of tedious ills
To where the sunshine sleeps
  On the everlasting hills –
    Say the Saints: There Angels ease us
      Glorified and white.
    They say: We rest in Jesus,
      Where is not day nor night.

Christina Rossetti

Some measure of faith is necessary for the pilgrim. It may not be a very active or polemic faith; it may trouble itself but little about the noisy arguments of the 'heretic' and the 'orthodox,' but the 'bloom of the rose-petal belongs to the heart of the perfume-seller,' and it is only fitting that the breather of the incense from the rose-casket should be gentle and gracious and sympathetic. The pilgrim will not lightly regard – or disregard – traditional sites, traditional reverence and traditional names (which alter least when all beside them change and pass). He will not refuse to listen to the voices of almost countless generations of his predecessors, or to inhale the subtle fragrance left by their worship and devotion, their vows and sufferings.

They did not undertake pain and difficulty and danger for the sake of foisting a lie upon posterity, and the luminous cloud of witness which their memory forms about each sacred shrine has not only light within itself, but undoubtedly throws some light on the object of their veneration and devotion.

So when we know that many Popes and kings have gone in pilgrimage to Ste Baume – John XXII, Benedict XII, Clement VI, Innocent VI, Urban V, Gregory XI, Clement VII and Benedict XIII – Louis IX, Louis XI, Charles VIII, Louis XII, Francis I, Charles IX, Louis XIII and Louis XIV – when, in one day, Philip of Valois, King of France, Adolphus IV, King of Arragon, Hugo IV, King of Cyprus, John of Luxembourg, King of Bohemia and Robert, King of Sicily, stood or knelt within the cave of Mary Magdalene as humble pilgrims, we may take it for granted that all of these firmly believed in the truth of the Provençal tradition, and that those, therefore, who lived nearer to the times of Rabanus than we do had the strongest belief in the credibility of his history.

So, too, when we find that King Henry II of England went twice on pilgrimage to Rocamadour in old Aquitaine, and the great Roland laid down his sword, 'Durandal,' on the altar of the Blessed Virgin of Zaccheus, we know that some strong belief must have brought them to the shrine.

So, too, in our own land, if we look back through Norman and Danish and Saxon and Roman or British times, and watch the long procession of pilgrims pass to our earliest shrine of Glastonbury – Gildas, who ended his days here, St. Patrick, St. Benignus, St. David, St. Dunstan, King Ine of the West Saxons, King Edgar, King Edmund, King Edmund Ironsides and King Canute, we may take it for granted that all of these firmly believed in the ancient British church of wattles, 'Vetusta Ecclesia,' or 'ealder chirche,' raised here (according to tradition) by Joseph of Arimathea, and therefore that those who lived nearer to his time than we do had the strongest belief in the credibility of St. Joseph's mission.[1]

In England today, fortunately, we are content to leave the legends and traditions of the countryside unsullied by futile controversy, and Tennyson's matchless poem of the Holy Grail is none the less read and valued by thousands because they know that it is forever impossible to decide either the truth or the falsity of the Arthurian idylls and the story of St. Joseph.

In France of today it is quite as impossible to determine the truth or the falsity of the 'Legends of the Saints' but, unfortunately, critics and apologists, not content to leave the priceless legacy of their forefathers wrapped in its silk and rose-leaves, appear to be continually quarrelling over its value, and between them have done much to tarnish if not to destroy the freshness and beauty of the ancient story.

So, if we go on pilgrimage at all, I think it safer to follow in the wake of the older pilgrims – to stand with them in the holy places, and do nothing to forfeit that spirit and atmosphere of which the subject is really worthy.

For if the Provençal legends be nothing more than legends, their antiquity, their vitality, their power of penetration and the wideness of their influence are so remarkable that no study of them can be too sympathetic or too appreciative.

The whole circle of legendary history, of tradition and of monuments, would still form one of the most poetical and, at the same time, the most wonderful of romances which the world has ever known – a romance which has affected whole populations and generations for centuries; which has coloured the face of history, as at Vezelai in the Second Crusade; which has raised shrines and great churches and pilgrimages and, in spite of hostile criticism, is living now as an active faith in the hearts and minds of both clergy and people all through the South of France.

But if it is more than this – as it may well be – if the writings of Strabo, of St. Paul, of Clement, of Tertullian, of Isidorus and of Eusebius are in harmony with the old tradition and rather support the theory of Jewish missions reaching all parts of the Roman Empire in the very earliest years of Christianity – if the Saints themselves, companions of our Lord, toiled and suffered and died within the borders of the country to which we are going – if, recognizing this probability, we follow them, not in imagination only, but in deed and truth – if their spirit and life may arouse and animate our spiritless and lifeless Christianity of today – then, indeed, though 'the light be neither clear nor dark,' yet 'living waters shall still go forth from Jerusalem, and it shall come to pass that at evening-time there shall be light' (*Zechariah* 14:6, 7, 8).

It is not only or chiefly at Arles where history and monuments are found to support the story, but all over the Provençal district one finds the names of nearly all our little band of early Christians still living in the names of towns or of churches or of caves, and all these names are either immemorial or can be definitely traced to the earlier centuries of Christendom.

We find the Holy Maries (Les Saintes Maries) in the Camargue, St. Lazarus at Marseilles, St. Martha on the outskirts of Marseilles and at Tarascon, St. Maximin at the town and church of St. Maximin, and St. Mary Magdalene at Ste Baume.

All this country is the country of the olive and the vine, but many do not know of the hidden olive gardens and the secret vineyards. Come, if you are not weary of the quest, and let us see what fruit we can gather in the Provence of today.

If you land at Marseilles and go by the Quai de la Joliette to the bottom of the Rue de la Cannabière, and then take any of the lower turnings on the right, you will find that you are skirting the older quay of Marseilles, and that as you bear again to the right and follow the Rue Sainte at some little height above the sea, directly in front of you, on an eminence, is the old church of St. Victor.

It has rather the appearance of some old dungeon or fortress than that of a church, but the church you enter is only of secondary importance. It conceals something far more interesting underneath it. A door on the south side of the nave leads down to a subterranean church, large and lofty, which dates from the fourth century. This was built by the Cassianite monks, and from its position has been untouched and could not well be destroyed through all the centuries since.

And all this vast fourth century church has been visibly built around a still older natural cave or grotto known as the original first century church or refuge of St. Lazarus.

Near the entrance to this is a carving of vine-leaves dating from the fourth century, and grouped near are old chapels dedicated to St. Cassian, St. Victor and other saints. The bodies of the saints, however, have been removed. Two sarcophagi stones, said to date from the second century, were too solid to be rifled of their contents, and still remain.

The great height of this underground abbey church, its darkness, its stillness, the few scattered but perfect round pillars supporting the roof, and the 'first century chapel' which is enshrined by it, all combine to produce a picture of early Christian life and architecture, striking and irresistible.

No explanation that I know of has been, or can be, offered other than that offered by tradition – that here was the place where Lazarus of Bethany lived and preached and ministered and died, and that therefore within some two hundred or three hundred years afterwards this church was built in honour of his memory and to enshrine his body which was then present here.

And all through the ages ever since this faith has been firmly held, and lives as strong today as ever. If we come back from the crypt or subterranean church into the (upper) church of St. Victor, at the west end of the nave, under the organ-loft, we find a life-sized statue of St.

Lazarus, his left hand holding the crosier, his face upturned to heaven, and underneath the statue two pieces of stone removed from the old sepulchre at Bethany out of which our Saviour raised him. On the pediment of the statue is this inscription:

'Divo Lazaro
a Christo suscitato
qui Massiliensium primus Apostolus
hujus ecclesiae cryptam
ministerio et passione
illustravit.
In memoriam missionis
A.D. MDCCCXCVII
grato animo parochus fidelesque
S. Victoris dedicant.'

(Kneeling underneath this statue above his own church on St. Lazarus' Day, September 1, 1901 (Solemnité de St. Lazare), I attended the Eucharistic service and heard the priest speak of him as 'le premier évêque de cette ville' – 'the first bishop of this city.')

St. Maximin is probably some thirty of forty miles distant from Marseilles. We take the train from Marseilles on a beautiful moonlighted evening in the later summer or early autumn, the season of the vintage, and as we alight at the station, which is on an eminence at some little distance from the town, the one striking feature of the landscape – made still whiter by the moonlight – is the large white church of St. Maximin. Indeed, one sees this and nothing else, and it is not until we get quite into St. Maximin itself that the church disappears from view.

The village of St. Maximin is a quiet, semi-Eastern-looking town, with high white houses, every window of which is closed with *'persiennes.'* There is a small central 'Place,' with a fountain in the middle and four sets of trees to form a promenade, one larger road leading into this 'Square,' and two or three narrow streets straggling out of it. At the corner of one of these is the chief hotel or inn, and two doors from this, down the side street, is the second little inn quiet, homely and comfortable.

On the opposite side of the 'Square' or 'Place' is a lane or little street leading to the church. If we follow this we come suddenly upon the church in a mean square, with dirty and rather squalid surroundings. It is difficult to say exactly the impression it produces from this close aspect. It is almost entirely one of size. The western part is unfinished, and all the details are severely and peculiarly plain. There are nine buttresses on each side, a reddish tiled roof and a small turret tower at one side of the apse – or rather three apses – which finish the eastern end, but no carving or special beauty that one could desire in it.

Viewed at a distance, all this is changed – the great effect is wonderful, as I have already hinted. The country is surrounded on almost every side by distant high mountain or hill ranges. All the centre is an extensive cultivated plain, full of vineyards and olive gardens, and in the centre of this plain is one vast towering structure – the big white church of St. Maximin. In comparison with it there is no visible town surrounding it. The roofs of the adjoining houses seem to barely touch the final pediments of the buttresses, and the church, by reason of its height and size, commands the whole prospect as no other church or cathedral that I remember can in any way be said to do. Distance glorifies it, the barrenness and meanness of its finish, or want of finish, is lost sight of, and the white, clear-cut wonderful church rears its magnificent façade in the centre of the plain, and becomes a very type and realization in outline of all that can be meant architecturally by power and beauty.

This, then, is the continuous voice of all the centuries since it was a building – from 1295 to 1480 – a book to be opened and read of all men today as on the day when it was founded – a silent, solemn witness of faith and devotion which cannot be gainsaid. No one can pretend, I think, that the church of St. Maximin was built as it was for any other reason than as a fitting monument or shrine for the relics of St. Mary Magdalene, some of which have been preserved in it from that day to this.

The interior of the church is fine, but severely plain. The loftiness of the groined roof, with the apse at the eastern end (for we cannot get any collective view or idea of the treble apse from the nave of the church) is striking and impressive, but there are no transepts, and none of the side altars are visible on looking towards the chancel; one sees nothing but the high altar surmounted by a kind of urn, which is said to have formerly contained the body or bust of St. Mary. According to the sacristan, this was rifled at the time of the Revolution, and the ashes were scattered to the winds. Reaching for some distance down the church are heavy wooden stalls with handsome medallion floral and figure carvings, the number of these appearing to lengthen somewhat unduly the choir or chancel. This is finished towards the nave by a heavy carved wooden screen of similar design to the stalls.

To the left of the nave, shortly behind the chancel screen, is a railed enclosure, the entrance to the little crypt containing the relics of St. Mary. We enter this by a gateway at the eastern end and, passing down a short flight of steps, turn inwards (at right-angles) towards the centre of the church, entering a small crypt-chapel with sarcophagi on each side. One of these (of alabaster ?) is said to have originally contained the body of St. Mary. At the farther end (south end) of the little arched crypt is a kind of altar, and on it, behind a grille, are the sacred relics. The grille is opened, and we see the skull, small and especially well formed, clothed with a casing of gold representing the hair and natural outer configuration of the human head. This is held or supported by a pedestal representing angels with wings outstretched. On the left side is a golden arm and hand containing a relic of one arm-bone of the saint, and on the opposite side is another relic, enclosed in glass. In yet another casket is a small portion of her hair. Of all these the most important is, of course, the skull. The face of this is imperfect, the upper ramus or ascending portion of the lower jaw (inferior maxilla) being wanting on both sides. This gives a rather curious appearance to the side of the face. In all other respects the skull appears to be perfect, and as the sacristan holds his lighted candle to illuminate the forehead, he asks you to notice the spot on the right frontal eminence where the bone is perhaps lighter in colour, and where it is asserted that for several hundred years a piece of flesh still adhered. This was believed to be the spot which touched, or was touched by, our Lord after His resurrection.

At the present date it is difficult or impossible to make out any real difference in the two frontal eminences.

To us, who are inclined to attach but little value to relics, it is perhaps difficult to realize the care with which they have been guarded, and especially to credit the peculiar reverence and esteem in which the very earliest Christians held the bodies of their saints.

A strict history has been kept of these, and I do not know that there is the slightest reason for doubting either the bona fides or the accuracy with which this history has been recorded. Certainly, from the date of the re-discovery by Charles II there has been unbroken custody, and the relics seen today are undoubtedly those (or part of those) which were preserved by him, and in honour of which the church of St. Maximin was built.

St. Louis came, as we are told by the Sire de Joinville, to St. Maximin (at a little distance from Aix), where St. Mary Magdalene was interred, and then went to 'Le Basme,' where there is a deep cave in a rock in which it is said the holy Magdalene lived for a long time. Countless pilgrims have done the same before and since, and what William, the son of Otho, is said to have done in 935, and what Louis de Joinville did in 1254, one naturally does today if staying at St. Maximin. 'La Sainte Baume,' as it is now called, is about eighteen kilometres from St. Maximin.

We go back through the 'Place' towards the station, then turn sharply to the right, and almost immediately the rugged mountain range which is our goal presents itself directly in front of us. About two kilometres out we pass, on the left, an old stone pillar or cross called St. Pilon, which is said to mark the place to which St. Mary Magdalene was brought when dying, in order to receive a last communion of the Body and Blood of our Lord from the hands of St. Maximin. Beyond this the road passes through some miles of vineyards and olive-trees – the vines with large bunches of beautiful purple grapes showing under the lower branches or resting on the ground. The olive-trees are, of course, recognized at once by the peculiar greyish or dusky colour of their foliage. These, too, are in fruit and covered with olives. Farther on we pass through a kind of avenue of mulberry-trees. They line each side of the road and, though short and pruned, are topped by luxuriant fresh and vivid green leaves which form a marked contrast to the dusky foliage of the olives. Almond-trees, firs, oaks, and blackberry bushes are also occasionally seen, but the oak-trees are small. One or two large almond-trees in fruit are particularly beautiful.

About ten kilometres out we come to the village of Nans – a large village (considering its isolation) with a 'Place,' trees, fountain (surmounted by an image of St. Mary), and a narrow street.

Shortly after leaving this the road begins to ascend, and for six or seven kilometres there is a continuous up-hill winding way. As we gradually come nearer to the foot of the mountain we see clearly outlined against the darker colour of the rock-wall, the two white erections of the small monastery and guest-house, one on each side of the entrance to the 'grotto.'

The walk through the forest is rather trying from its steepness, but very pleasant; the shade is grateful, and though 'the road winds up-hill all the way,' one can take it easily. After some twenty minutes of fair walking we find a stone stairway with occasional breaks of level ground. Some ninety-nine of these steps are passed, and then we come to the platform of the grotto – an open space or terrace apparently cut out of the mountain, and on which are built the houses already mentioned. In the rock-wall itself is the entrance to the grotto and church. This is simply a large natural cave, lofty and damp, with water dripping in many places from the roof, and it is in this cave that St. Mary Magdalene is supposed to have lived for many years before her death. It has been converted into a church with several chapels and six altars, to the more or less spoiling, I think, of the original cave. On one side, now railed off, there is a portion of the cave quite under water, and here one sees the remains of a very ancient altar of uncertain date. Behind the high altar is a piece of sculpture representing St. Mary reclining on a rock, and on one side of this is a shrine with a relic of St. Mary (femur).

Outside the church, on the terrace in front of the grotto, there is a wonderful view over the surrounding country. Apparently close below the mountain range, on a ledge of which we are standing, is the Hotellerie, and spreading out from this a fairly large plain open to the east – the plain of St. Maximin. Beyond this is a broken range of hills, running in nearly a parallel direction to that on which we are standing, and beyond this still another stretching to the west as far as we can see.

The mountains are rugged and sometimes bare, but the lower slopes are covered with trees, and the plain itself is fertile with vines and olives. In spite of the season of the year (late August) there is a beautiful cool breeze. The air is fresh and dry, and there is the sense of peace and rest which is rarely absent from high altitudes. Such is La Sainte Baume of today – 'le Basme' of de Joinville.

'Les Saintes Maries,' in the Camargue (the traditional landing-place of the first Hebrew missionaries), is no longer the inaccessible place it used to be. There is a railway from the 'Trinquetaille' station at Arles, and the little town, which was formerly only known as a place of pilgrimage, appears to be developing as a seaside resort.

The Camargue, through which one passes during the journey, is low and flat and sparsely inhabited. In some places vines grow luxuriantly, and poplars, elms, and small oaks break the monotony of the landscape; in others, nothing seems to grow except tall reeds and coarse grass. Low-lying pools of water, rushes, half-submerged but waving in the wind, and startled wildfowl – these are the chief things which engage the eyes as the train goes slowly onward. Here and there the expanse is broken by some rough homestead or dwelling-house. This is often a thatched cottage with a curious apse-like 'annex' at one end, suggesting the thatched chancel of some primitive church. Occasionally three or four houses grouped together appear to form the nucleus of a village, but through all the thirty kilometres from Arles to Les Saintes Maries there is nothing more than this visible in the way of human habitation, and the railway stations are little more than resting-places at the cross-roads leading to some farm. On reaching Les Saintes Maries (the terminus of the little line) the first noticeable feature is the strange old fortress-church of the ninth century – indeed, for some miles before you reach it this is the chief feature of the landscape. It is hardly like any other building in the world of which I am aware. The upper chapel of the Holy

Maries above the choir gives the church a towering height at this end that is both curious and imposing. In the church itself, beyond a few slits or 'squints' in the solid masonry of the wall, there is no avenue for light except at the west end, and the darkness of the choir and apse, lit only from a shaft of sunlight behind the kneeling worshippers, is a special and striking feature of the interior of the church. There are no side aisles or transepts. In the centre of the nave, surrounded by an iron railing, is a well, which, whether used originally for baptism, or as a water-supply for the defenders of the church, was evidently purposely included in the sacred building. The choir is raised above the nave, and several steps on both sides lead up into the chancel. In the centre of this division between nave and chancel is an open archway with steps descending from the nave into a lower chapel or crypt underneath the choir. In this are kept the relics of St. Sara, the traditional handmaid of the holy Maries. All round the church is a plain wooden gallery, and it is very evident that on special occasions (as at times of pilgrimages) every available nook and corner is needed for the accommodation of the worshippers. The nave is enriched by several fine paintings fastened to the walls; one in particular by M. Henri de Gaudemaris, representing the holy Maries in a boat conducted by angels to the coasts of Provence, is very beautiful, both in conception and in execution. This was exhibited in the Salon at Paris in 1886. No relics of the Saints appear to be kept in the (visible) apse or chancel of the church. The supposed bodies of St. Mary Salome and St. Mary Cleopas are found in a chapel above this, wholly concealed from the interior of the church. There is, however, an opening from this chapel in the church above the apse of the choir. This is closed by doors, and every year (on May 24th) the double coffer, or case, containing the relics is lowered by a kind of windlass into the church below for the adoration of the pilgrims.

An outside stairway leads to the high chapel or shrine. Here in a closed chamber, which the curé kindly opened for us, is the double case of wood containing the chief relics, together with the apparatus by means of which it can be lowered into the church below. On the altar facing this, at the east end of the chapel, is a further reliquary of silver called the 'Saint bras,' containing the radius and ulna of one of the Saints. This is carried in procession on the greater festivals.

Near the 'high chapel' is to be seen the chief monumental record afforded by the church of the existence of the tradition at its building. This is the remains of a sculptured representation of two female figures in a boat at sea, and the almost necessary deduction from this appears to be that the church was built early in the ninth century in honour of two female Saints who drifted to the Camargue coast in an open boat. Some three hundred years later, but a long time before the re-discovery of the bodies of the Saints, we find the full tradition recorded by Gervais of Tilbury (as already mentioned); and in the will of St. Cassaire, written in 542, we find the church then existing on this site called the church of St. Mary of the Boat (Sanctae Mariae de Ratis).

A short walk from the church through the one street of the little town leads us directly to the seashore or beach, a wide expanse of fine sand where a boat might anywhere drift ashore with little or no danger.

A little higher up the Rhone Valley from Arles are Avignon and Tarascon – both towns traditionally associated with St. Martha. Avignon – the City of the Popes – is over weighted by the traditions and past glories of its lost Papacy, and the cathedral of Notre Dame des Doms, though said to have been originally founded by St. Martha on the ruins of a Pagan temple, is chiefly remarkable for its monuments and memories of the Avignon Popes.

At Tarascon, on the other hand, the legend of St. Martha dominates both town and church, and in spite of M. Duchesne and other sceptics is apparently as fresh and living as at any period of the Faith.

The whole of the church of St. Martha in Tarascon – the church itself with its crypt and various monuments – forms a remarkable record of belief of many past generations and centuries in the tradition of St. Martha.

In the crypt of St. Martha (to the left of the nave as you enter the church) there is an altar, and behind this the sixteenth century tomb of St. Martha surmounted by a life-size statue of the Saint. She is figured as lying on her back (from east to west) with her head against the wall of the crypt and her feet resting behind the altar. The body of St. Martha is said to lie beneath this, or rather beyond it to the east, the crypt having formerly extended farther to the east.

To the right of the crypt is a very fine twelfth century tomb, which formerly took the place of that which I have just described. Four standing figures in stone guard the sarcophagus; one of these is distinguished as that of St. Lazarus, the brother of St. Martha and bishop of Marseilles. On the same side of the crypt one sees what is known as the well of St. Martha; for it is said to be in this crypt that St. Martha lived during the greater part of her residence in Provence.

On the opposite or north side of the crypt is a small chapel, called the 'Chapelle Royale' because a daughter of Louis II is buried here. This chapel is chiefly remarkable for the very fine carving representing the raising of Lazarus. Each figure is full of expression, the treatment of the subject being exceedingly graphic and original.

As you ascend from the crypt, on the same side as this chapel, there is a very old altar, nearly square, remarkably small in size with a central depression for the deposition of relics. This is said to have belonged to the primitive church. On the opposite wall is a tablet commemorating the cure and gift of King Clovis (in AD 500), and in the church above the crypt is a replica of the third century sarcophagus which held the body of

St. Martha before this was translated to its later resting-place. From the first to the third century the body is said to have rested in a simple rock grave – a hole corresponding to the shape of the body being cut in the solid stone of the cave. Similar early Christian graves can be seen, and have been described as a feature of the entrance to the cells of St. Trophimus at Montmajour.

The later church above the crypt is full of interest. As pointed out to us by the Vicaire Administrateur, the whole of this great church is built to commemorate the coming of the Saints by sea to Provence.

The church is built in the form of an inverted boat. The pillars of the nave are not vertical but spread outward as they rise to the vaulted roof, so as to convey the idea of the masts of a ship; while the rolling and pitching of the vessel on the sea is ingeniously suggested by the graduated irregularity of the bases of the columns. For example, on one side of the church the shaft of the column enters the ground directly with no pediment, the opposing pillar of the aisle on this side has a slight pediment of one or two inches; the corresponding pillar on the opposite side of the nave has a bold pediment of a foot or more, while the opposing pillar of the farther aisle has an exaggerated pediment of nearly double the size. The conception is interesting and curious, and the effect – when the mind grasps the central idea – is far more striking than any that can probably be conveyed by mere description.

I know of no similar architectural features, and unless there be any other explanation of these special characters of the building, the whole must be recognized as a wonderful architectural monument of belief that is probably without a parallel.

The more important historical monuments of the church are undoubtedly the various sarcophagi which are said to have contained the body of St. Martha – that of the sixteenth century, that of the twelfth century, and that of the third century – the oldest (or its facsimile) being of chief importance.

Now, although the carvings of this oldest sarcophagus are much disfigured (all the heads of the figures being wanting) there can be no doubt, I think, that one can trace on the front of the tomb a representation (1) of the raising of Lazarus; (2) the prostration of either St. Mary or St. Martha at the feet of the Saviour; and (3) a central female figure in the act of prayer or of blessing.

There is nothing perhaps peculiarly distinctive in these groups as especially referring to St. Martha, but the sarcophagus is necessarily a Christian one of the third or fourth century, and was probably intended to hold the remains of some female saint who was very especially honoured by those who raised this monument to her memory. It is quite consistent with its reputed history – that it formerly enshrined the body of St. Martha.

Still journeying northward up the Rhone Valley (as the Saints went journeying before him) the pilgrim now changes at the station of Pierrelatte for St. Paul Trois-Chateaux (the Roman 'Augusta Tricastinorum') and the district especially associated with the memory of Restitutus.

St. Paul Trois-Chateaux is a picturesque old town. Plane-trees shade the borders of the larger roads or streets, vines festoon many of the houses. Narrow gateways leading to the narrower streets of the ancient town beyond them afford glimpses of quaint buildings flecked with patches of sunlight and shadow. In one or two tiny squares fountains are plashing and gurgling ceaselessly and delightfully, and in the centre of this crowded little city one finds the cathedral, a massive church, with but little claim to beauty, but large, lofty and cool, testifying to a larger life in the past.

Roman remains are found at odd corners. Here a gateway and there a wall with portions of a tower, but these seem to be disappearing or becoming incorporated with the buildings of a later date.

About one kilometre beyond St. Paul one turns to the right across the railway in order to reach the village of St. Restitut. The road winds upward over sand and rock, and the last part of the ascent is made by means of rough steps, worn for ages in the rock. The village clusters round the church, which dates from the ninth century, the architect Hugo being the builder of it.

At the western end of the church stood an old temple of Diana, and the form of this has been preserved through all the centuries since. It was here, in the lower part of this building, that Restitutus, the man born blind of the Gospel, is said to have lived and died, and underneath the ground of its lower bay (near the present baptistery of the church) he was buried.

In the earlier centuries an altar was formed above his tomb, and until the fifteenth, pilgrimages were made to this shrine and to a fountain then existing (the fountain of St. Restitut), which possibly may have been used for baptism.

During the religious wars of the Middle Ages, however, the church was pillaged, the body of the Saint was burnt, his ashes thrown to the winds, and now there is no relic connecting the church with its most ancient past save the place where the body of the Master lay.

By a winding stone stairway M. Algoud led us to the upper bay or gallery of this western chapel of St. Restitutus, and then to the roof of the church and belfry. The roof is of stone and in perfect condition, though untouched (as I understood) for nearly a thousand years. The church stands high, and from its roof a very fine view is obtained of the surrounding country.

To the east are the distant Alps, showing clearly beyond the borders of the mountains encircling the Valley of the Rhone, while almost illimitable stretches of country are spread out as in a picture at one's feet, the land on the hills poor and sparsely cultivated, that in the valley rich with grapes and fig-trees and olives. If it was anything like this in the days of the Hebrew pilgrims it must surely have reminded them of their own country at its best, for figs and grapes and olives (as at Eschol) are characteristic of all the country.

Returning to the interior of the church, we notice that its east end takes the form of an apse, as do most of the churches in the district. It is plain, but has a beauty of proportion and of carving that is dearer, perhaps, to the eyes of an Englishman than the colouring and ornamentation of richer buildings. The carving of the pillars supporting the apse is particularly worthy of notice, each capital being different in design.

There is a churchyard cross outside the south entrance to the church, and around this is the only space in the village. Most of the houses are poor, old and dilapidated, and some of them appear to be built in the rock itself, and to be almost rock-dwellings. Near the church is a somewhat romantic-looking old 'chateau,' but with this exception, all the surroundings of the church are mean and decaying, and the village seems to be waiting in vain for the return of that faith and devotion that has passed it by since the days of the fifteenth century.

Again, still following the great river northwards, we come to Vienne, one of the earliest known strongholds of primitive Christianity.

Traditionally associated with the names of Archelaus, Pontius Pilate and Crescens, and its Christianity historically linked with that of the greater city of Lyons beyond it (by the well-known Epistle of the two Churches of Lyons and Vienne to the Churches of Asia and Phrygia in the second century), one might expect to find here Christian monuments or sites professedly dating from apostolic times. So far as I know, however, none have been preserved.

The Temple of Augustus and Livia – somewhat similar to, but much less beautiful than the Maison Carrée at Nîmes – is still standing as an entire edifice, and having been built under the Emperor Claudius Caesar especially marks for us the epoch of earliest Christian missions. The so-called 'Arc de Triomphe,' which is probably the ancient entrance to the Roman Forum (still standing in a small passage near the theatre), and the monument of the 'Aiguille,' also dating from the Roman period, still further link the present city (with its modern shops and busy life) to its more ancient past; but although these give considerable foundation for the imaginative reconstruction of the Roman Vienne, all beyond appears to be vague and problematical. Even the beautiful but ruined or greatly injured cathedral of St. Maurice, begun in the eleventh and finished in the sixteenth century has, I believe, no certain connection with the church of the earlier centuries, and the pilgrim, in this city of the Saints, finds no relics of them here as he wanders through the narrow streets or by the ever swiftly-flowing river.

The city of Vienne is some twenty miles distant from Lyons, and this of itself seems sufficient to prove the practical independence of the two Churches in the second century. The river was perhaps more used for traffic than it is today, but the return journey to Lyons would be a difficult one, and for all practical purposes, except on special occasions of rejoicing or of persecution, the two Churches, like the two cities, must each have had a separate existence.

The traces of early Christian sites and monuments that the pilgrim fails to discover in Vienne, he finds in abundance at Lyons.

Strange as it may seem, this great and populous city, remaining as it has done a centre of industry and commerce throughout all the ages that have passed since the coming of our Lord, has yet lost but little of its ancient features, and the rivers of the Rhone and the Saône and the dominating hill of Fourvière not only make the city perennially beautiful, but give it such a marked and distinct individuality that we can immediately and confidently recognize the city of Pothinus and Blandina and Irenaeus in its modern dress, and know that here, and here, and here, stood the martyrs of Christ, teaching the people, confessing Him in the forum, and suffering for His sake in the prison.

The old city was built mainly about the River Saône, and on the western bank of this, quickly rising to a considerable height and still, in places, beautifully wooded, the great hill of Fourvière guards the city at its foot. Built on the very heights of this, on a magnificent plateau overlooking the surrounding country, was the Roman Forum. Here it is almost certain that Pothinus and Blandina, and all the Christian martyrs of AD 177, were tried and sentenced, and on the site of this now stands the fine and stately basilica of Notre Dame de Fourvière.

You reach this today by a funicular railway (for the hill is very steep), and as you stand and gaze at the great panorama below, the larger features of the landscape are so evidently permanent that it is quite possible for one who knows the history of the city to forget for a moment the centuries intervening, and to dream himself back into the days when Rome was lord and master.

Here, spread out beneath you, is the old Lugdunum of the Gauls with its rivers Rhodanum and Arar. Above, near where you stand, are the heights held by the Romans, the buildings of the Roman colony and the Imperial Palace or residence of the Prefects, while (to complete the illusion) the outward form of the basilica, with its stately procession of steps before the chief entrance, reproduces immediately before you some of the more essential features of the Roman Forum.

From this general survey of the city and of the Hall of Judgment on the hill of Fourvière, as it existed in the first and second centuries, it is only natural to pass to a more detailed description of the historical monuments still existing that are connected with the history of the early Christians.

Perhaps the finest of these is the prison of Pothinus and Blandina, still preserved in a crypt underneath the Hospice de l'Antiquailles. This is situated on the farther side of Notre Dame de Fourvière, and is of the greatest interest, first, because its claim to historical accuracy appears to be well founded: the Hospice itself being built on the site of and partly from the remains of the old Imperial palace, and the prisons of the palace being naturally found underneath this; and, secondly, because a considerable portion of this prison is said to have been untouched, and can be observed today as it was in the second century.[2]

In the centre of this chamber or rough cavern made in the solid rock, one sees a stone column to which it is said St. Blandina was chained, the old ring to which the chain was attached being still seen in the top of the pillar. To the left of this a small opening with a grille in front of it leads to a shallow chamber in the rock in which, according to tradition, St. Pothinus was confined. A man could only be forced into it in a crouching position as it is too small either for sitting or for lying, and it is not surprising that Pothinus, who was ninety-one years of age, succumbed in three days to the torture of his incarceration.

On the right side is a large opening which is the entrance of a subterranean passage, supposed to have led either to the Judgment Hall of the palace or to the old amphitheatre.

Still farther away, but on the same side of the River Saône, is the church of St. Irenaeus. This, or rather an older crypt or church below it, connects us with a slightly later page of ecclesiastical history.

Here the successor of Pothinus, the great Irenaeus, gathered together the disciples remaining after the first great persecution (of 177), dedicating the new church to the memory of St. John the Evangelist, whom he held in special veneration as his own great leader through St.

Polycarp.

Here, in spite of continued persecution (for thirty-six more of the Christians suffered martyrdom in AD 178), Irenaeus ministered to the disciples for some thirty years.

Finally, in the reign of Septimius Severus, on the 28th of June, 208 (according to M. l'Abbé J. Huguet), an extensive massacre of Christians was carried out under the personal direction of the Emperor, when St. Irenaeus and 'nineteen thousand Christians, not counting women and children,' were put to death. 'The blood ran in torrents down the length of the "Gourgillon" (*gurges sanguinus*), and so reddened the waters of the Arar that henceforth it took the name of the Saône' (in Low Latin 'Sagono,' *sanglante*).

The old church or crypt is entered by a door in the outside of the chancel of the present church of St. Irenée. As you pass down a flight of stone steps you see on the right a chamber closed by a grille, before which a lamp is burning. This is filled with the remains of the bones of these martyrs. For a long time (until 1562) they were preserved intact, but then the Calvinists destroyed the crypt and profaned the relics, mixing other bones with those of the martyrs. Some of them were saved from destruction and carefully separated out, and these can be seen today between the bars of the grille. Beyond this we enter the old church of Irenaeus, altered and restored, but still retaining the wall of the old baptistery, while beyond this are the scanty remains of an ancient burial-ground with some of the Latin inscriptions still legible.

A sketch of the Christian antiquities of Lyons would not be in any way complete without a description of the church of St. Nizier and its crypt, for this crypt, or the original church represented by it, was the scene of St. Pothinus's early labours before the persecution of 177. This is the oldest historical Christian ground in Lyons, and the church above it is worthy of its association. It is not so grand or so inspiring as Notre Dame de Fourvière, but its west front is fine, and the church, with its high vaulted ceiling and rich triforium, is both impressive and beautiful.

To the left of the high altar is a chapel with a fine statue of St. Pothinus, and close to this, directly in the floor of the church and closed only by a hinged iron covering, is the entrance to the crypt. This lower church of St. Pothinus has also been considerably enlarged and restored, but the east end of it is undoubtedly the place where the original altar stood, and the space immediately around this represents the chapel or cell where Pothinus ministered in the early or middle part of the second century. The original altar was preserved until the thirteenth century, and there is still shown in this crypt a tablet of stone which is supposed by some to have formed part of the altar of Pothinus.

Away to the west, more than half-way between the Rhone Valley and the coast, we come to the old country of the Lemovices with its capital 'Limoges,' where St. Martial, the cousin of St. Stephen, is said to have laboured and died. Not very far from this, but difficult to get at, is the curious and romantic sanctuary of Roc-Amadour, the traditional dwelling-place of Zaccheus, who is said to have journeyed with Joseph of Arimathea and St. Martial as far as this country, and to have stayed here because of its resemblance to his old home in Palestine.

As pilgrims to Rocamadour we spent the night at Perigueux. It was the 'quatorze Juillet' and France was everywhere *en fête*. At Perigueux the central Boulevard was prettily decorated with masts and variously coloured paper lanterns. Simple festoons were made of these from mast to mast, and at every crossing or open space, these were arranged diagonally, and a complex globe of many-coloured lights was suspended overhead in the centre of the pavé. Fountains were playing and various booths with flags and fairings had been set up on either side of the

'Place.' At the upper part of the 'Grand Place,' within the gardens, a military band was playing popular airs, and a whole crowd of peoples – old people, young people and babies in arms – surrounded the band and stand. Somewhat later a procession of soldiers carrying lanterns and torches, and occasionally showing flares of variously coloured lights, marched round the town followed by an enthusiastic crowd of young women and boys, but through it all the gaiety seemed to be simple and innocent. There was no visible drunkenness or immorality, and no disturbances or quarrels among those who were assisting in the *fête*.

We turned in about 9 p.m., as we were leaving at five in the morning for Rocamadour, but through the night until after 1 a.m. some echoes of the merrymaking came floating upwards through the open casements, and a young troubadour, with tambourine for sole accompaniment, made the night musical, but in no wise hideous with light-hearted song.

Called about 4.30 and away to the 'Gare' at 5 a.m., we started for Rocamadour. The journey lies through a rich agricultural district. We cross the Dordogne, and perceptibly rise to a higher elevation among the hills, which are more or less enveloped in the morning mist. We change at Brive and reach the station for Rocamadour at 9.25 a.m.

A short distance from the station, over high stony ground where the rock continually breaks through the scanty field grass, and we suddenly come to the edge of the plateau overlooking a narrow but deep little gorge or valley; and on the opposite side of it, nearly on a level with our road, but towering high above the valley and the villages at its foot, we see the picturesque buildings and chateau of Rocamadour. These, fashioned out of or clinging to the rock, with steep stone stairways ever mounting higher – the old gateways and village at the foot of the rocky heights, the great churches and other sanctuaries toward the middle of the ascent, and the chateau at the summit – form a picture that is striking and not easily forgotten.

The whole is rather curiously like in its grouping to the buildings of the Mont St. Michel in Normandy, but on a smaller scale, and whereas the latter is an island erection and striking from every point of view, Rocamadour, crowning the highest point of a deep gulf or hollow in the stony plateau (for the valley seems to have no true ingress or egress), is not really isolated and, though always effective, is only seen to best advantage from the valley at its base.

Here it is said that Zaccheus of the Gospels built a little church and, either because he loved the rocks where he lived or the people among whom he dwelt, was called 'St. Amadour' by his disciples.

Here he is said to have been visited by St. Martial of Limoges, and here he is said to have died and been buried.

On passing through the gateway of the village and along the whole course of its one winding street, we come to the great stone stairway of the pilgrims. This leads us to the first open courtyard of the sanctuaries or religious buildings that cover the mountain. Again, a shorter flight of steps and we see before us a chamber in the rock with a recumbent statue of Zaccheus at its base. Over it is a white stone tablet with the following inscription:

'Ici fut découvert
en 1166
le corps parfaitement conservé
de Zachée
l'ami de Notre Seigneur.'

Close by is the entrance to the chapel of the Blessed Virgin. This contains an ancient statue of the Blessed Virgin and her Child, carved in wood. This is venerated by pilgrims as having been made by Zaccheus (?). It also contains a 'miraculous bell' of very ancient date, supposed to have been used by Zaccheus in calling his people to worship. This is said to sound of itself in times of special danger, and these times have been recorded.

Beyond this chapel one passes into a spacious church which, however, contains nothing especially associated with the old tradition. The remaining monuments are found in the 'crypt of St. Zachée,' on a lower level. This is reached by a special stairway descending to it. In the crypt there is a vertical chamber which for some four or five hundred years is said to have contained the body of Zaccheus after it was removed from the grave. This chamber was rifled by the Huguenots, and the body was burnt. Some of the ashes were collected, and these are now preserved above (or beneath) the altar of the crypt. The whole of the interior of this chapel is rich with various paintings and carvings representing the life of Zaccheus. In one he is waiting in the fig-tree for the passage of the Saviour, in another he is opening the door of his house for the Saviour's entrance. The local tradition of his life is set forth in a series of tableaux accompanied by the following inscriptions:

1. Zachée, parce qu'il était petit, ne pouvant voir Jésus au milieu de la foule, monta sur un sycamore. Jésus l'aparcevant lui dit: 'Zachée, descends vite, Je viens loger chez toi.'
2. Zachée était disciple de Jésus. Véronique sa femme, se mit a la suite de Marie. Ils furent persécutés pour la foi; mais un ange vint les delivrer de la prison où ils avaient été enfermés.
3. Un ange ordonne à Zachée et à Véronique de se mettre en mer, et de s'arrêter où le navire prendrait port, afin d'y servir Jésus Christ et Marie, sa sainte Mère.
4. Leur navire vint aborder sur la côte du Médoc, au lieu appelé Soulac; ils y vécurent dans le jeûne et la prière, Saint Martial les y visita, et bénit un oratoire qu'ils avaient élevé à Saint Etienne.

5. Saint Amadour (Zachée) sur l'ordre de Saint Martial, alla à Rome auprès de Saint Pierre. Sainte Véronique resta au pays bordelais, où elle trépassa. Saint Amadour, revenu a Soulac, y érigea deux monastères et se retira du monde.

6. Ce fut l'an 70 de la nativité de Notre Seigneur que Saint Amadour choisit pour ermitage et retraite le rocher que l'on a appelé depuis Roc-Amadour. Ce rocher était alors inhabité et peuplé de bêtes féroces.

7. Les habitants du pays étaient presque sauvages: Saint Amadour les catéchisa et leur fit connaître la religion de Notre Seigneur Jésus Christ.

8. Saint Amadour érigea, dans le rocher un autel en l'honneur de Marie. Cet autel, si humble mais depuis si glorieux fut consacré par le B. Martial, apôtre, qui visita plusieurs fois notre saint dans sa retraite.

The chief monuments which are supposed to connect the present sanctuaries with the first century and with Zaccheus are this altar, the statue of the Blessed Virgin and Child and the bell.

All are undoubtedly of extreme antiquity, and the type of the statue seems to mark it as belonging to one of the earliest centuries. The bell, though not generally used until very much later, is not necessarily an anachronism in the first century. The Hebrews had been accustomed to the use of bells on the vestment of the High Priest during the course of many centuries, and it would be both natural and appropriate that Hebrew Christians should use the bell to denote the coming of Christ in the Holy Eucharist.

The 'body' is much more difficult to believe in, but its 'invention' (in 1166) may reasonably be taken as confirmatory of the older tradition.

Pilgrimages to Rocamadour were undertaken long before this, and at the end of the eighth century the great Roland is said to have visited Rocadamour, and to have laid his sword 'Durandal' on the altar of our Lady of Zaccheus. The local account of this states that he redeemed his sword afterwards by the gift of its weight in gold, but after his death, at Roncevalles, the sword was returned to Rocamadour. There it remained until 1183, when 'Henri au Courtmantel' took it away.

A representation of the sword is chained to the wall on the plateau of St. Michel, which overlooks the valley, and is in front of the chapel of the Virgin.

The Pilgrimage to Rocamadour is one of the very oldest (if not the oldest) of French pilgrimages, and traces of the pilgrims' way and of their resting-place in medieval and earlier times may still be recognized near Figéac, and for many miles in the surrounding country.[3]

The scene of the labours of St. Maternus (the traditional son of the widow of Nain) lies far away to the north or north-east, on the borders of Belgium and Germany; the two chief towns associated with his name being Tongres and Trier (or Trèves). Tongres is a rather sleepy agricultural town – probably of far less importance now than it was in the days of Caesar – and so far as I could find there is no local monument now standing to confirm or illustrate the old tradition. We cannot even recognize with any certainty the site of the oldest church, 'the first beyond the Alps dedicated to the Virgin Mary,' and the present fine church, though standing presumably on the holy ground of former ages, is comparatively modern, much of it dating from the sixteenth and seventeenth century only.

The city of Trèves or Trier is a much more interesting centre for the religious pilgrim, and especially so, I think, for one of English nationality and Catholic sympathy. One Sunday I spent at Trèves will always remain a happy memory to me. The type of Catholic worship found in nearly all the churches was sober, manly and devout, approximating much more to the Anglican than to the Latin ideal. In every church we entered, including the cathedral or Dom, there were no side-chapels and only the one 'high altar,' at the eastern end. In some (as in the Dom) the church and service had some of the defects as well as the virtues of soberness – part of the nave was 'pewed' and, save for the necessary ritual of the Mass, the services were almost puritanical in their simplicity. 'Vespers' was sung without the usually accompanying rite of 'Benediction,' and one of the distinguishing features of this service was the quiet and spiritual German sermon, listened to with intense interest, not only by the regular worshippers who filled the seats, but by many who came in rather later and crowded as near to the preacher as they could, standing until the whole of the service was finished.

Within the Dom are kept the relics of St. Maternus, and in a closed chapel to the south-west of the high altar is kept the 'Holy Coat,' said to have been worn by our Lord and presented to Agritius, bishop of Trèves, by St. Helena in AD 326.

In the church of St. Gangolf, close to the market-place, the morning congregation, on the Sunday of our visit, was mainly composed of men (due probably to some guild festival), and the service of the Mass was enriched and followed by the singing of a number of German hymns, the whole congregation joining in with marked devotion and enthusiasm. Directly facing the entrance to this church, on the opposite side of the market-place, is St. Simeon Strasse, which leads to the Porta Nigra and the St. Paulinuskirche.

The Porta Nigra, the old city gate in the time of the Romans, is one of the finest examples of Roman remains to be found so far north. It is of great size, having three, and in one part four storeys, and is built of big blocks of stone, now black with age and girded together with iron braces. It dwarfs the modern houses near it, and speaks of a past civilization greater, or on a larger scale, than any that has succeeded it. Between here and the Paulinuskirche, farther on, is the scene of the first great Christian persecution in Trier; for Trier, like Lyons, had its early days of trial and martyrdom, although this did not take place until a hundred years later (in AD 286), and the persecution of Trèves began in the ranks of the Roman army. Here it was that one of the chief divisions of the well-known Theban legion, under Thursus and Bonifacius, refused to sacrifice to the heathen gods, and all so refusing were martyred by order of the prefect, Nitius Varus, on one of the early days in October, computed to be October 4, AD 286. The next day Palmatius, the burgomaster of Trier, seven councillors of the city, and four well-known burghers of good birth and position – all Christians – were haled before the judgment-seat and, like the Christian soldiers before them, refusing to do heathen sacrifice, were bound to a stake, beaten with rods, and beheaded.

On the third day, 'October 6, AD 286,' the prefect, finding that the greater part of the inhabitants of the city were Christians, summoned all of them before him and commanded them to sacrifice to the Emperor and the gods.

A vast crowd of men and women, old people and little children, testifying boldly to their faith in Christ, and refusing to deny Him, were butchered by the heathen soldiers. Torrents of blood are said to have flowed over the field of Mars and to have coloured the waters of the Mosel for the space of many miles down the river as far as Neumagen. The St. Paulinuskirche or, as some call it, the Church of the Martyrs, was first erected to commemorate the martyrdom of these noble confessors by Paulinus, bishop of Trier, about AD 354.

The present church is quite modern. At the time of our visit the morning Masses were over, but a quaint little service was still going on in the nave. There was, I think, Exposition of the Blessed Sacrament, and a knot of worshippers, led by an old peasant (with a lad beside him to start the singing), were reciting litanies and prayers and singing hymns. No clergy were present.

Quite on the opposite or south side of the city, about a mile or more from the market-place, and practically in a suburb of the present city, is the district which is known as the earliest Christian ground of Trier. Here is the St. Matthiaskirche erected on or near the ground where St. Eucharius, St. Valerius and St. Maternus are said to have preached and laboured in apostolic times. The local tradition is that one of the most important converts of their mission was the widow of a councillor named Albana, and that she presented her villa to St. Eucharius as a meeting-place and church for the early Christians. The villa remained standing till the year AD 303, when it was destroyed, but a church was built upon its site, and some of the Roman masonry or marbles of the villa were used in the building of the church. These may still be identified as forming part of the pillars of the crypt where St. Eucharius and St. Valerius are buried.

You enter the precincts of the church from the high-road by an open arch of masonry. This leads to a wide courtyard or 'close,' terminated by the west front of the church. On the left side of this is a gate opening into the churchyard, surmounted by statues of the three evangelists – St. Maternus, St. Eucharius and St. Valerius.

The church inside is of plain stone, well proportioned and lofty. On each side of the chancel a flight of steps leads down into the crypt, and on the sides of these stairways several Christian monuments of the Roman period have been built into the walls. The crypt contains the stone tombs of St. Eucharius and St. Valerius, which lie almost directly under the high altar, and near them are the pillars visibly containing relics of the Roman period, and said to date from the first century church of the Villa Albana. At the eastern end of the crypt is a kind of altar with carvings representing the coming of the early missionaries.

The churchyard, badly kept and neglected, possesses two small crypts containing old graves of the Roman period, and in the west wall near the entrance is a curious old tablet with an inscription in Latin and German. This refers to the statue of a heathen deity which formerly was kept in the churchyard and which has been removed to the Trier Museum. The inscription, which is of interest not only as referring to the mission of St. Maternus, but also as fixing the reputed or traditional date of the mission (AD 50), runs as follows

'Wolt ihr wissen was ich bin
Ich bin gewessen ein Abgottin
Da S. Eucharius zu Trier kam
Er mich zerbrach, mein Ehr
    abnam
Ich was geehret als ein Gott
Jetz stehen ich hier der Welt zu
    Spot
In Jahre 50 nach Christi geburt
Seint diese 3 h. Bischoffe von
Rom. zu Trier komen. Euch.
    Val. Mat.'

'Me pridem Treviris coluit
Profanis aris, iam truncus
Sacrilegi numinis prostrata
Spernor inanis. Et dum (Petrus)
Piscator legat Eucharium,
Valerium, Maternum, tunc
(Huius superstitonis) tollitur
    error.
A° post Christum natû Roma
    missi a St. Petro 50
Treveros venerunt Euch. Val.
    Mat.'

Dear Saints of Christ the Lord, who passed through grievous trial,
    Here, where today I stand, your holy feet have trod;
Here you chose pain and death, rather than base denial,
    And passed rejoicing through the awful flames to God.

Dear Saints, to whom the very name of Jesus Christ
    Was breath of healing and the kindling of a fire,
Whose service was a passion that alone sufficed
    For every need and craving, every heart's desire,

Look down on us in pity for our groundless fears,
    Whose Christian faith and courage have grown old and dim,

The feeble, spell-bound creatures of decadent years,
 Who in the name of Christ have heaped reproach on Him.

You wholly trusted Him and in His service wrought
 Wonders and signs at which the worldly-wise were dumb;
We live for pleasure as if this were all we sought,
 Heedless of death, and judgment, and the life to come.

Clear-brained and always ready, patient, strong and sane,
 You drank as from a stream the life-draughts of God's grace,
And gladness changed to glory through the gate of pain
 For you, who saw the open Vision, face to face.

Such vision and such gladness might be ours today
 But for the rising mist of selfish sins between,
A noxious blinding mist which hides from us the Way
 By which the earth-bound seeker enters the Unseen.

Dear Saints, arouse in us the spirit of your vow,
 Pray for us, us who love you, that our starless night
May flush the traces of the Dawn, and even now
 Our dead may wake from sleep and Christ may give us light.

J.W.T.

1. This was so generally accepted in the Middle Ages that at the Council of Constance, in 1419, precedence was actually accorded to our bishops as representing the Senior Church of Christendom (Conybeare).
2. How far this is reliable I cannot say.
3. Is not this 'pilgrim's way' also the way of the old tin-traders? Figéac and Roc-Amadour are in the direct line of march from Marseilles or Narbonne to Limoges and Morlaix.

APPENDIX A

AD 84. 'SPEECH OF GALGACUS, THE NORTH-BRITISH OR CALEDONIAN LEADER, BEFORE THE BATTLE WITH AGRICOLA, AS REPORTED BY TACITUS IN HIS *LIFE OF AGRICOLA*

When I reflect on the causes of the war, and the circumstances of our situation, I feel a strong persuasion that our united efforts on the present day will prove the beginning of universal liberty to Britain. For none of us hitherto debased by slavery; and there is no land behind us, nor is even the sea secure, while the Roman fleet hovers around.

'Thus the use of arms, which is at all times honourable to the brave, now offers the only safety even to cowards. All the battles which have yet been fought with varying success against the Romans, had their resources of hope and aid in our hands; for we, the noblest inhabitants of Britain, and therefore stationed in its deepest recesses – far from the view of servile shores – have preserved even our eyes unpolluted by the contact of subjection. We – at the farthest limits both of land and liberty – have been defended to this day by the remoteness of our situation and our fame. The extremity of Britain is now disclosed; and whatever is unknown becomes an object of importance. There is no nation beyond us; nothing but waves and rocks, and the still more hostile Romans, whose arrogance we cannot escape by obsequiousness and submission.

'These plunderers of the world, after exhausting the land by their devastations, are rifling the ocean: stimulated by avarice, if their enemy be rich; by ambition, if poor; unsatiated by the East and by the West; the only people who behold wealth and indigence with equal avidity. *To ravage, to slaughter, to usurp under false titles, they call Empire; and whence they make a desert, they call it "peace."*

'Our children and relations are, by the appointment of Nature, rendered the dearest of all things to us. These are torn away by levies to serve in foreign lands. Our wives and sisters, though they should escape the violation of hostile force, are polluted under names of friendship and hospitality. Our estates and possessions are consumed in tributes; our grain in contributions. Even our bodies are worn down amid stripes and insults in clearing woods and draining marshes. Wretches born to slavery are once bought and afterwards maintained by their masters: *Britain every day buys, every day feeds her own servitude.* And as among domestic slaves every new-comer serves for the scorn and derision of his fellows, so, in this ancient corner of the world, we, as the newest and vilest, are sought out to destruction. For we have neither cultivated lands, nor mines, nor harbours which can induce them to preserve us for our labours. The valour, too, and unsubmitting spirit of subjects only renders them more obnoxious to their masters; while remoteness and secrecy of situation itself, in proportion as it conduces to security, tends to inspire suspicion.

'Since then all hopes of forgiveness are vain, let those at length assume courage to whom safety as well as to whom glory is dear.

'The Trinobantes, even under a female leader, had force enough to burn a colony, to storm camps and, if success had not induced negligence and inactivity, would have been able entirely to throw off the yoke: and shall not we, untouched, unsubdued, and struggling not for the acquisition but the continuance of liberty, show at the very first onset what men Caledonia has reserved for her defence? Can you imagine that the Romans are as brave in war as they are licentious in peace? Acquiring renown from our discords and dissensions, they convert the errors of their enemies to the glory of their own army – an army compounded of the most different nations which, as success alone has kept together, misfortune will certainly dissipate.

'Unless, indeed, you can suppose the Gauls and Germans and (I blush to say it) even Britons, who, though they lavish their blood to establish a foreign dominion, have been longer its foes than its subjects, will be retained by loyalty and affection!

"Terror and dread alone are their weak bonds of attachment: these once broken, they who cease to fear will begin to hate. Every incitement to victory is on our side. The Romans have no wives to animate them, no parents to upbraid their flight. Most of them have either no home or a distant one. Few in number, ignorant of the country, looking round in silent horror of woods, seas, and a heaven itself unknown to them, they are delivered by the gods, as it were imprisoned and bound, into our hands. Be not terrified with an idle show and the glitter of silver and gold which can neither protect nor wound. In the very ranks of the enemy we will find our own bands. The Britons will acknowledge their own cause. The Gauls will recollect their former liberty. The rest of the Germans will desert them as the Usipii have lately done. Nor is there anything formidable behind them – ungarrisoned forts, colonies of old men, municipal towns distempered and distracted between unjust masters and ill-obeying subjects.

'Here is a general: here an army. There, tributes, mines, and all the train of punishments inflicted on slaves, which, whether to bear eternally or instantly to revenge, this field must determine. March then to battle and think of your ancestors and your posterity.' (From the *Life of Agricola*, written by his son-in-law, C. Cornelius Tacitus, in the year of Rome 850, in that of Christ 97; during the third Consulate of the Emperor Nerva, and the third of Virginius Rufus – Aitkin's translation.)

APPENDIX B

ST. CLEMENT, AD 97. FROM THE FIRST EPISTLE OF ST. CLEMENT TO
THE CORINTHIANS (CHAP. V)

L et us take the noble examples furnished in our own generation. Let us set before our eyes the illustrious Apostles. Peter . . . endured not one or two but numerous labours, and when he had at length suffered martyrdom departed, to the place of glory due to him . . . Paul also obtained the reward of patient endurance, after being seven times thrown into captivity, compelled to flee, and stoned. After preaching both in the East and West, he gained the illustrious reputation due to his faith, having taught righteousness to the whole world, and come to the extreme limit of the West, and suffered martyrdom under the prefects.'

FROM THE 'RECOGNITIONS OF CLEMENT'
(*Possibly dating from AD 90 in the original. The work has come to us in the form of a translation by Rufinus of Aquileia, written in AD 410*)

'A certain report which took its rise in the regions of the East in the reign of Tiberius Caesar gradually reached us' (in Rome).

'For it was spread over all places . . . that there was a certain person in Judea who . . . was preaching the Kingdom of God to the Jews, and saying that those should receive it who should observe . . . His commandments and His doctrine . . . . He made the deaf to hear and the blind to see and the lame to stand erect, and expelled every infirmity and all demons from men; yea, He even raised dead persons who were brought to Him.

'At length meetings began to be held in various places in the city and this subject to be discussed in conversation, . . . until about the same year a certain man, standing in a most crowded place in the city, made proclamation to the people, saying:

'"Hear me, O ye citizens of Rome. The Son of God is now in the regions of Judea, promising eternal life to every one who will hear Him, but upon condition that he shall regulate his actions according to the will of Him by whom He hath been sent, even of God the Father. Wherefore turn ye from evil things to good, from things temporal to things eternal." . . .

'Now, the man who spoke these things to the people was from the regions of the East, by nation a Hebrew, by name Barnabas, who said that he himself was one of His disciples, and that he was sent for this end, that he should declare these things to those who would hear them.

'He did not confirm his assertions by the force of arguments, but produced from the people who stood round about him many witnesses of the sayings and marvels which he related.

'As the day was declining to evening I laid hold of Barnabas by the right hand and led him away, although reluctantly, to my house, and there I made him remain less perchance any of the rude rabble should lay hands on him.

'While we were thus placed in contact for a few days, I gladly heard him discoursing the word of truth; yet he hastened his departure, saying that he must by all means celebrate at Judea a festal day of his religion which was approaching.

'At length I said to him . . . "If you wish it, I will even sail along with you, for I am extremely desirous to see Judea, and perhaps I shall remain with you always." To this he answered, "If, indeed, you wish to see our country and to learn those things which you desire, set sail with me even now; or, if there be anything that detains you now, I shall leave with you directions to my dwelling, so that when you please to come you may easily find me, for tomorrow I shall set out on my journey." When I saw him determined I went down with him to the harbour, and carefully took from him the directions which he gave me to find his dwelling. I told him that (but for the necessity of getting some money that was due to me) I should not at all delay, but that I should speedily follow him . . .

'Having then stopped for a few days, and having in some measure finished the business of collecting what was owing to me, . . . I set sail for Judea, and after fifteen days landed at Caesarea Stratonis, which is the largest city in Palestine. When I had landed and was seeking for an inn I learned from the conversation of the people that one Peter, an approved disciple of Him who appeared in Judea . . . was going to hold a discussion . . . the next day with one Simon, a Samaritan. Having heard this I asked to be shown his lodging; and having found it and standing before the door, I informed the doorkeeper who I was and whence I came; and, behold, Barnabas coming out, as soon as he saw me rushed into my arms, weeping for joy, and seizing me by the hand, led me to Peter. . . . "This," said he, "is Peter, of whom I spoke to you as the greatest in the wisdom of God, and to whom also I have spoken constantly of you. Enter, therefore, as one well known to him. . . . Therefore I present you to him today as a great gift." At the same time presenting me he said, "This, O Peter, is Clement."

'But Peter, most kindly, when he heard my name, immediately ran to me and kissed me. . . .' (Book I).

'When the day dawned . . . Peter, rising at the first cock-crowing, aroused us also, for we were sleeping in the same apartment, thirteen of us in all, of whom next to Peter Zaccheus was first, then Sophonius,

Joseph and Michaeus, Eliesdrus, Phineas, Lazarus and Elisaeus; after these I (Clement) and Nicodemus; then Niceta and Aquila, who . . . were converted to the faith of Christ under the teaching of Zaccheus. Of the women there was no one present. As the evening light was still lasting we all sat down, and Peter . . . having saluted us, immediately began to speak' (Book II).

'At this announcement all the people wept, hearing that he was going to leave them; and Peter, sympathizing with them, also shed tears and, looking up to heaven, he said:

' "To Thee, O God, who hast made heaven and earth and all things that are in them, we pour out the prayer of supplication that Thou wouldest comfort those who have recourse to Thee in their tribulation. For by reason of the affection that they have towards Thee, they do love me who have declared to them Thy truth. Wherefore guard them with the right hand of Thy compassion; for neither Zaccheus nor any other man can be a sufficient guardian to them."

'When he had said this and more to the same effect, he laid his hands upon Zaccheus and prayed that he might blamelessly discharge the duties of his bishopric. Then he ordained twelve presbyters and four deacons, and said:

'"I have ordained you this Zaccheus as a bishop, knowing that he has the fear of God and is expert in the Scripture. You ought, therefore, to honour him as holding the place of Christ, obeying him for your salvation, and knowing that whatever honour and whatever injury is done to him redounds to Christ and from Christ to God.

Hear him, therefore, with all attention, and receive from him the doctrine of faith, and from the presbyters the monitions of life, and from the deacons the order of discipline. Have a religious care of widows, vigorously assist orphans, take pity on the poor, teach the young modesty and, in a word, sustain one another as circumstances shall demand. Worship God, who created heaven and earth; believe in Christ; love one another; be compassionate to all; and fulfil charity not only in word but in act and deed."' (Book III, cp. 66.)

APPENDIX C

The servants of Christ dwelling at Lyons and Vienne, in Gaul, to those brethren in Asia and Phrygia, having the same faith and hope with us, peace and grace and glory from God the Father and Christ Jesus our Lord.

'The greatness, indeed, of the tribulation, and the extent of the madness, exhibited by the heathen against the saints, and the sufferings which the martyrs endured in this country, we are not able fully to declare, nor is it indeed possible to describe them. For the adversary assailed us with his whole strength, giving us already a prelude how unbridled his future movements among us would be. And, indeed, he resorted to every means to accustom and exercise his own servants against those of God, so that we should not only be excluded from houses, and baths, and markets, but everything belonging to us was prohibited from appearing in any place whatever. But the grace of God contended for us, and rescued the weak, and prepared those who like firm pillars, were able, through patience, to sustain the whole weight of the enemy's violence against them. These, coming in close conflict, endured every species of reproach and torture. Esteeming what was deemed great but little, they hastened to Christ, showing in reality "that the sufferings of this time are not worthy to be compared with the glory that shall be revealed in us." And first, they nobly sustained all the evils that were heaped upon them by the populace, clamours and blows, plundering and robberies, stonings and imprisonments, and whatsoever a

288

savage people delighted to inflict upon enemies. After this they were led to the forum, and when interrogated by the tribune and the authorities of the city, in the presence of the multitude, they were shut up in prison until the arrival of the governor. Afterwards they were led away to be judged by him, from whom we endured all manner of cruelty. Vettius Epagathus, one of the brethren who abounded in the fulness of the love of God and man, and whose walk and conversation had been so unexceptionable though he was only young, shared in the same testimony with the elder Zacharias. He had walked, therefore, in all the commandments and righteousness of the Lord blameless, and with alacrity in kind offices to man, abounding in zeal for God, and fervent in spirit. As he was of this high character, he could not bear to see a judgment so unjustly passed against us, but gave vent to his indignation, and requested also that he should be heard in defence of his brethren, whilst he ventured to assert that there was nothing either at variance with religion or piety among us. At this those round the tribunal cried out against him, for he was a man of eminent standing. Nor did the governor allow a request so just and so properly made, but only asked whether he also were a Christian? He confessed in as clear a voice as possible, and he, too, was transferred to the number of martyrs, being publicly called the advocate of the Christians. But he had the Paraclete (Advocate) with him, viz., the Spirit, more abundant than Zacharias, which, indeed, he displayed by the fulness of his love; glorying in the defence of his brethren, and to expose his own life for theirs. He was, indeed, a genuine disciple of Christ, following the Lamb whithersoever He would go. After this the others were also set apart, and the first martyrs endured their sufferings with promptness and alacrity, most cheerfully finishing the confession of martyrdom. They appeared, indeed, unprepared and inexperienced, and yet so weak as to be incapable of bearing the intensity of the mighty contest. Of these, indeed, about ten also fell away, causing great sorrow and excessive grief to our brethren, and damping the ardour of those who had not yet been taken. These, however, although they endured all manner of affliction, nevertheless were always present with the martyrs, and never left them. Then, indeed, we were all struck with great fear, on account of the uncertainty of their holding out in the profession, not, indeed, dreading the tortures inflicted, but looking at the end, and trembling lest they should apostatize. Those, indeed, that were worthy to fill up the number of the martyrs were seized from day to day, so that all the zealous members of the two Churches, and those by whose exertions the Church had been there established, were collected. Some domestics that were heathen belonging to our brethren were also seized, as the governor had publicly commanded search to be made for all of us. But these, at the instigation of Satan, fearing the tortures that they saw the saints suffering, and the soldiers besides this urging them, charged us with feasts of Thyestes, and the incests of Oedipus, and such crimes as are neither lawful for us to speak nor to think; and such, indeed, as we do not even believe were committed by men. These things being spread abroad among the people, all were so savage in their treatment of us, that if before some had restrained themselves on account of some affinity, they now carried their cruelty and rage against us to a great excess. Then was fulfilled the declaration of our Lord "that the day would come when everyone that slayeth you will think he is doing God a service." The holy martyrs, after this, finally endured tortures beyond all description; Satan striving with all his power that some blasphemy might be uttered by them. Most violently did the collective madness of the mob, the governor and the soldiers rage against the holy deacon of Vienne and against Maturus, a new convert, indeed, but a noble champion of the faith. Also against Attalus, a native of Pergamus, who was a pillar and foundation of the Church there. Against Blandina also, in whom Christ made manifest that the things that appear mean and deformed and contemptible among men are esteemed of great glory with God on account of love to Him, which is really and powerfully displayed, and glories not in mere appearance. For whilst we were all trembling and her earthly mistress, who was herself one of the contending martyrs, was apprehensive lest through the weakness of the flesh she should not be able to profess her faith with sufficient freedom, Blandina was filled with such power that her ingenious tormentors, who relieved and succeeded each other from morning till night, confessed that they were overcome and had nothing more that they could inflict upon her. Only amazed that she continued to breathe after the whole body was torn asunder and pierced, they gave their testimony that one single kind of the torture inflicted was of itself sufficient to destroy life without resorting to so many and such excruciating sufferings as these. But this blessed saint, as a noble wrestler, in the midst of her confession itself renewed her strength, and to repeat "I am a Christian, no wickedness is carried on by us" was to her rest, refreshment and relief from pain. But Sanctus himself, also nobly sustaining beyond all measures and human power the various torments devised by men, whilst the wicked tormentors hoped that by the continuance and the greatness of the tortures they would get to hear something from him that he ought not to say, withstood them with so much firmness that he did not even declare his name, nor that of his nation, nor the city whence he was, nor whether he was a slave or a freeman, but to all the questions that were proposed he answered in the Roman tongue, "I am a Christian." For this he confessed, instead of his name, his city, his race, and instead of everything. No other expression did the heathen hear from him. Whence, also, an ambitious struggle in torturing arose between the governor and the tormentors against him, so that when they had nothing further that they could inflict they at last fastened red-hot plates of brass to the most tender parts of his body. But he continued unsubdued and unshaken, firm in his confession, refreshed and strengthened by the celestial fountain of living water that flows from Christ. But the corpse itself was evidence of his sufferings, as it was one continued wound, mangled and shrivelled, that had entirely lost the form of man to the external eye. Christ suffering in him exhibited wonders, defeating the adversary, and presenting a kind of model to the rest, that there is nothing terrific where the love of the Father, nothing painful where the glory of Christ, prevails. For when the lawless tormentors tortured the martyr again during the day, and supposed that whilst the wounds were swollen and inflamed, if they applied the same torments they would subdue him, as if he would not then be able to bear even the touch of a hand, or else that dying under his tortures he would strike a terror into the rest, not only was there no appearance like this, but, beyond all human expectation, the body raised itself and stood erect amid the torments afterwards inflicted, and recovered the former shape and habit of the limbs, so that his second tortures became, through the grace of Christ, not his torment, but his cure. But the devil also led forth a certain Biblias to punishment, who was one of those that had renounced the faith, thinking that he had already swallowed her, was anxious to increase her condemnation by blasphemy, and constraining her as a frail and timid character, easily overpowered to utter impieties against us. But in the midst of the torture she repented and recovered herself and, as if waking out of a deep sleep, was reminded by the punishment before her of the eternal punishment in hell. And accordingly she contradicted the blasphemers in her declarations. "How," said she, "could such as these devour children who consider it unlawful even to taste the blood of irrational animals?" After that she professed herself a Christian, and was added to the number of martyrs. But as all the tortures of the tyrants were defeated by Christ, through the patience of the martyrs, the devil devised other machinations; among these were their confinement in prison, in a dark and most dismal place, their feet also stretched in the stocks and extended to the fifth hole, and other torments which the enraged minions of wickedness, especially when stimulated by the influence of Satan, are accustomed to inflict upon the prisoners. Numbers of them were therefore suffocated in prison, so many, viz., as the Lord would have to depart, thus showing forth His glory. Some of them, indeed, had been cruelly tormented, so that it appeared they could scarcely live, though every means were applied to recover them. Though confined in prison, devoid of all human aid, they were strengthened by the Lord, and filled with power from Him, both in body and mind, and even stimulated and encouraged the rest. But the new converts, and those who were recently taken, whose bodies were not exercised in trial, did not bear the oppression of incarceration, but died within the prison.

'But the blessed Pothinus, who had faithfully performed the ministrations of the episcopate at Lyons, and who was past his ninetieth year and very infirm in body, who, indeed, scarcely drew his breath so weak was he in body at the time, yet in the ardour of his soul and his eager desire for martyrdom he roused his remaining strength and was himself also dragged to the tribunal. Though his body, indeed, was already nearly dissolved, partly by age and partly by disease, yet he still retaining his life in him that Christ might triumph by it. When carried by the soldiers to the tribunal, whither the public magistrates accompanied him, as if he were Christ Himself, and when all the mob raised every outcry against him, he gave a noble testimony. When interrogated by the governor who was the God of the Christians? he said, "If thou art worthy, thou shalt know." After this he was unmercifully dragged away and endured many stripes, whilst those that were near abused him with their hands and feet in every possible way, not even regarding his age. But those at a distance whatsoever they had at hand every one hurled at him, all thinking it would be a great sin and impiety if they fell short of wanton abuse against him. For they supposed they would thus avenge their own gods. Thus scarcely drawing breath he was thrown into prison, and after two days he there expired. A wonderful interposition of God was then exhibited, and the boundless mercy of Christ clearly displayed a thing that had rarely happened among brethren, but by no means beyond the reach and skill of Christ. For those that had fallen from the faith on the first seizure were also themselves imprisoned, and shared in the sufferings of the rest. Their renunciation did them no good at this time, but those that confessed what they really were were imprisoned as Christians, no other charge being alleged against them. But these at last were confined as murderers and guilty culprits, and were punished with twice the severity of the rest. The former, indeed, were refreshed by the joy of martyrdom, the hope of the promises, the love of Christ, and the Spirit of the Father; but the latter were sadly tormented by their own conscience. So that the difference was obvious to all, in their very countenances, when they were led forth. For the one went on joyful, much glory and grace being mixed in their faces, so that their bonds seemed to form noble ornaments and like those of a bride, adorned with various golden bracelets, and impregnated with the sweet odour of Christ, they appeared to some anointed with earthly perfumes. But the others, with downcast look, dejected, sad, and covered with every kind of shame, in addition to this were reproached by the heathen as mean and cowardly, bearing the charge of murderers, and losing the honourable, glorious and life-giving appellations of Christians. The rest, however, seeing these effects, were so much the more confirmed, and those that were taken immediately confessed, not even admitting the thought suggested by diabolical objections.'

'After these things their martyrdom was finally distributed into various kinds; for, platting and constituting one crown of various colours and all kinds of flowers, they offered it to the Father. It was right, indeed, that these wrestlers, who had sustained a diversified contest, and had come off with a glorious victory, should bear away the great crown of immortality. Maturus, therefore, and Sanctus, and Blandina and Attalus were led into the amphitheatre to the wild beasts, and to the common spectacle of heathenish inhumanity, the day for exhibiting the fight with wild beasts being designedly published on our account. Maturus, however, and Sanctus again passed through all the tortures in the amphitheatre, just as if they had suffered nothing at all before, or rather as those who in many trials before had defeated the adversary, and now, contending for the crown itself, again as they passed bore the strokes of the scourge, usually inflicted there, the draggings and lacerations from the beasts, and all that the madness of the people, one here and another there, cried for and demanded, and last of all the iron chair, upon which their bodies were roasted, while the fumes of their own flesh ascended to annoy them. The tormentors did not cease even then, but continued to rage so much the more, intending, if possible, to conquer their perseverance. They could not, however, elicit or hear anything from Sanctus besides that confession which he had uttered from the beginning.

'These two, therefore, in whom life for the most part had remained through the mighty conflict, were at last despatched. On that day they were made an exhibition to the world, in place of the variety of gladiatorial combats. Blandina, however, was bound and suspended on a stake, and thus exposed as food to the assaults of wild beasts, and as she thus appeared to hang after the manner of the cross, by her earnest prayers she infused much alacrity into the contending martyrs. For as they saw her in the contest with the external eyes, through their sister they contemplated Him that was crucified for them, to persuade those that believe in Him that everyone who suffers for Christ will forever enjoy communion with the living God. But as none of the beasts then touched her, she was taken down from the stake and remanded back again to prison to be reserved for another contest, so that by gaining the victory in many conflicts she might render the condemnation of the wily serpent irrefragable, and though small, weak and contemptible, but yet clothed with the mighty and invincible wrestler Christ Jesus, might also encourage her brethren. Thus she overcame the enemy in many trials, and in the conflict received the crown of immortality. But Attalus himself, being vehemently demanded by the populace, as he was a distinguished character, came well prepared for the conflict, conscious as he was of no evil done by him, and as one who had been truly exercised in Christian discipline, and had always been a witness of the truth with us. When led about in the theatre with a tablet before him on which was written, in Latin, "This is Attalus the Christian," and the people were violently incensed against him, the governor, learning that he was a Roman, ordered him to be remanded back again to prison with the rest concerning whom he had written to Caesar, and was now awaiting his determination. But he (Attalus) in the meantime was neither idle nor unprofitable to them, but by their patient endurance the immeasurable mercy of Christ was manifested. For by means of those that were yet living were things dead made to live. And the martyrs conferred benefits upon those that were no martyrs (i.e., upon those that had fallen away). Much joy was also created in the Virgin Mother (the Church), for those whom she had brought forth as dead she recovered again as living. For by means of these the greater part of those that fell away again retraced their steps, were again conceived, were again endued with vital heat, and learned to make the confession of their faith. And now living again and strengthened in their faith, they approached the tribunal where that God that willeth not the death of a sinner, but inviteth all to repentance, sweetly regarding them, they were again interrogated by the governor.

For as Caesar had written that they should be beheaded, but if any renounced the faith these should be dismissed, at the commencement of the fair which is held here, which indeed is attended by an immense concourse of people from all nations, the governor led forth the martyrs, exhibiting them as a show and public spectacle to the crowd. Wherefore he also examined them again, and as many as appeared to have the Roman citizenship these he beheaded. The rest he sent away to the wild beasts. But Christ was wonderfully glorified in those that had before renounced Him, as they then, contrary to all suspicion on the part of the Gentiles, confessed. And these, indeed, were separately examined, as if they were soon to be dismissed; but as they confessed they were added to the number of the martyrs. Those, however, who had never any traces of the faith, nor any conception of the marriage garment, nor any thought of the fear of God, remained without, who, as the sons of perdition, blasphemed the way by their apostasy. All the rest, however, were attached to the Church, of whom, when examined, a certain Alexander was found to be one, a Phrygian by birth and physician by profession. Having passed many years in Gaul, and being well known for his love of God, and his freedom in declaring the truth, for he was not destitute of apostolical grace, he stood before the tribunal, and by signs encouraged them to a good confession, appearing to those around the tribunal as one in the pains of childbirth. The mob, however, chagrined that those who had before renounced the faith were again confessing, cried out against Alexander, as if he had been the cause of this. And when the governor urged and asked him who he was, and he replied that he was a Christian, in his rage he condemned him to the wild beasts and, accordingly, on the following day, he entered the arena with Attalus. For the governor, to gratify the people, also gave up Attalus a second time to the beasts. Thus, enduring all the torments that were invented as punishment in the amphitheatre, and after sustaining the arduous conflict, these were likewise finally despatched. As to Alexander, he neither uttered a groan nor any moaning sound at all, but in his heart communed with God; and Attalus, when placed upon the iron chair, and the fumes from his roasting body arose upon him, said to the multitude in Latin, "Lo, this is to devour men what you are doing, but as to us, we neither devour men nor commit any other evil." And when asked what was the name of God, he answered God has no name like a man. After all these, on the last of the show of gladiators, Blandina was again brought forth, together with Ponticus, a youth about fifteen years old. These were brought in every day to see the tortures of the rest. Force was also used to make them swear by their idols; and when they continued firm, and denied their pretended divinity, the multitude became outrageous at them, so that they neither compassionated the youth of the boy nor regarded the sex of the woman. Hence they subjected them to every horrible suffering, and led them through the whole round of torture, ever and anon striving to force them to swear, but were unable to effect it. Ponticus, indeed, encouraged by his sister, so that the heathen could see that she was encouraging and confirming him, nobly bore the whole of these sufferings, and gave up his life. But the blessed Blandina, last of all, as a noble mother that had animated her children and sent them as victors to the great King, herself retracing the ground of all the conflicts her children had endured, hastened at last, with joy and exultation at the issue, to them as if she were invited to a marriage feast, and not to be cast to wild beasts. And thus, after scourging, after exposure to the beasts, after roasting, she was finally thrown into a net and cast before a bull, and when she had been well tossed by the animal and had now no longer any sense of what was done to her by reason of her firm hope, confidence, faith and her communion with Christ, she, too, was despatched. Even the Gentiles confessed that no woman among them had ever endured sufferings as many and great as these. But not even then was their madness and cruelty to the saints satisfied, for these fierce and barbarous tribes, stimulated by the savage beast Satan, were in a fury not easily to be assuaged, so that their abuse of the bodies assumed another novel and singular aspect. Not abashed when overcome by the martyrs, but evidently destitute of all reason, the madness both of the governor and the people, as of some savage beast, blazed forth so much the more to exhibit the same unjust hostility against us; that the Scriptures might be fulfilled, "He that is unjust, let him be unjust still, and he that is righteous, let him be righteous still" (*Revelation* 22:11). For those that were suffocating in the prison they cast to the dogs, carefully watching them night and day lest any should be buried by us, and then also cast away the remains left by the beasts and the fire, howsoever they had either been mangled or burnt. They also guarded the heads of the others, together with the trunks of their bodies, with military watches, for many days in succession, in order to prevent them from being buried. Some, indeed, raged and gnashed their teeth against them, anxious to find out some better way of punishment. Others, again, laughed at and insulted them, extolling their idols, and imputing to them the punishment of the martyrs. But others, more moderate, and who in some measure appeared to sympathize, frequently upbraided them, saying, "Where is their God, and what benefit has their religion been to them, which they preferred to their own life?" Such was the variety of disposition among the Gentiles, but among our brethren matters were in great affliction for want of liberty to commit the bodies to the earth. For neither did the night avail us for this purpose, nor had money any effect to persuade, nor could any prayers or entreaties move them. But they guarded them in every possible way, as if it were a great gain to prevent them from burial.'

'The bodies of the martyrs, after being abused in every possible manner, and thus exposed to the open air for six days, were at length burned and reduced to ashes by the wretches, and finally cast into the Rhone, that flows near at hand, that there might not be a vestige of them returning on the land. These things they did as if they were able to overcome God and destroy their resurrection.

'As they themselves gave out, "that they might not have any hope of rising again, in the belief of which they have introduced a new and strange religion, and contemn the most dreadful punishments, and are prepared to meet death even with joy. Now we shall see whether they will rise again, and whether their God is able to help them and rescue them out of our hands".'

(Such were the occurrences that befell the Church of Christ, under the above-mentioned Emperor, from which it is easy to conjecture what was the probable course of things in the remaining provinces. It may be well here to add to these accounts other extracts from the same epistle, in which the moderation and benevolence of these martyrs whom we have mentioned is recorded in the following words): 'They were also so zealous in their imitation of Christ, who, though in the form of God, thought it not robbery to be equal with God, that though they were esteemed in the same light, and had neither once nor twice but frequently endured martyrdom, and had been again taken away from the beasts to prison, and had brands and scars and wounds spread over them, they did not proclaim themselves martyrs, for it did not become us to apply this name to them; but if any one of us either by letter or in conversation called them martyrs they seriously reproved us. For they cheerfully yielded the title of martyr to Christ, the true and faithful Martyr (witness), the First-begotten from the dead, the Prince of Divine life. They also made mention of those martyrs that had already departed and said, "They are now martyrs whom Christ has thought worthy to be received in their confession, setting the seal to their martyrdom (testimony) by the issue. But we are but indifferent and mean confessors," and with tears did they entreat the brethren that they should offer up incessant prayers, that they might be made perfect. They exhibited, indeed, the power of martyrdom in fact, exercising much freedom in declaring themselves to all people, and manifesting their noble patience and fearless intrepidity; but the name of martyrs (witnesses) they declined receiving from the brethren, filled as they were with the fear of God. . . . They humbled themselves under the mighty hand by which they were now highly exalted. Then, however, they pleaded for all, they accused none, they absolved all, they bound none, and prayed for those that were so bitter in their hostility, like Stephen that perfect martyr, "Lord, impute not this sin to them"; but if he prayed for those that stoned him, how much more for the brethren! . . . This was their greatest conflict against him (the devil) on account of the genuine character of their love, that the beast being choked and throttled might be forced to return alive again (to vomit up) those whom he had already thought to have swallowed. For they did not arrogate any superiority over the backsliders; but in those things wherein they themselves abounded, in this they supplied those that were deficient, exercising the compassion of mothers and pouring forth many prayers to the Father on their account. They implored life and He gave it to them, which they also shared with their neighbours; coming off victorious over all, to God; always lovers of peace, they always recommended peace, and with peace they departed to God. Not leaving grief to their mother (the Church), no discord or dissensions to the brethren, but joy and peace, unanimity and love. This account may be profitably added, respecting the love of those blessed brethren towards those that fell away, on account of those also who, after these events, unsparingly exercised an inhuman and merciless disposition towards the members of Christ.'

(The same epistle of the above-mentioned martyrs also contains another account worthy of record, which no one could regret to be presented to the knowledge of our readers. It is as follows): 'A certain Alcibiades, who was one of these (martyrs), and who had led a hard and rough kind of life, partook of no food usually eaten, but merely bread and water. When cast into prison, and he attempted to lead the same kind of life, it was revealed to Attalus after the first conflict which he finished in the amphitheatre that Alcibiades did not do well in not making use of the creatures of God, and affording an example of offence to others. Alcibiades, therefore, in obedience to this, partook of all kinds of food, and gave thanks to God; for neither were they destitute of Divine grace but the Divine Spirit was their counsellor.' But let this suffice concerning these. Now as Montauris and Alcibiades and Theodotus in Phrygia, then first began to be esteemed by many of their gifts (as there were many other wonderful powers of Divine grace yet exhibited even at that time in different Churches), they created the belief with many that they also were endued with prophecy. And as there was a discussion in consequence of these men, the brethren in Gaul again presented their own pious and correct judgment also concerning these, and published several letters of the martyrs that had been put to death among them. These they had written whilst yet in prison, and addressed to the brethren in Asia and Phrygia. And not only to these, but likewise to Eleutherus, who was then bishop of Rome, negotiating, as it were, for the peace of the Churches. But these same martyrs recommending also Irenaeus, who was then a presbyter of the Church at Lyons, to the bishop of Rome before mentioned, bear abundant testimony in his favour, as the following extracts show: 'We pray and desire, Father Eleutherius, that you may rejoice in God in all things and always. We have requested our brother and companion, Irenaeus, to carry this epistle to you, and we exhort you to consider him as commended to you as a zealous follower of the testament (covenant) of Christ. For if we knew that any place could confer righteousness upon any one, we would certainly commend him among the first as a presbyter of the Church, the Station that he holds.'

Why should we here transcribe the list of those martyrs given in the above-mentioned epistles, of whom some were made perfect by decapitation, some cast to be devoured by wild beasts, and others again fell asleep in prison? Why repeat the number of confessors still living? For whoever wishes to learn these can more easily obtain the fullest account by consulting the epistle itself, which, as I said, has been inserted by us in our collection of martyrs. But such were the events that happened under Antonine.

APPENDIX D

THE EARLY GALLICAN COUNCILS

AD 177-197

'Concilia Lugdunensis: Irenaei
'Synodus divina et sancta provincialis,
dudodecim episcoporum, collecta
Lugduni metropoli Galliae, ad
Rhodanum flumen, ab Irenaeo
sancto martyre, ejusdem urbis
episcopo, contra praescriptos haereticos.'

'Concilia Lugdunensis: Irenaei
'Synodus divina et sacra provincialis
collecta Lugduni Galliae ab Irenaeo
sanctissimo ibedem episcopo,
aliisque trederim episcopis: . . .
quae similiter de divino mystico
pascha constituit.'

('Mansi,' vol. i, pp. 723, 726)

c. AD 190

The following is a part of a letter (preserved by Eusebius in his *Ecclesiastical History*, bk. v, chap. 24) from Irenaeus, bishop of Lyons, to Victor, bishop of Rome:
'An epistle . . . of the Churches of Gaul over whom Irenaeus

presided' (*E.H.*, bk. v, c. 23) in which Irenaeus, 'in the name of those brethren over whom he ruled throughout Gaul, maintains the duty of celebrating the mystery of the resurrection of our Lord only on the day of the Lord,' and holds that the Churches of Gaul 'observed' in this 'the tradition of an ancient custom' (*E.H.*, bk. v, c. 24).

c. AD 190

'The controversy is not merely as regards the day, but also as regards the form itself of the fast. For some consider themselves bound to fast one day, others two days, others still more, while others do so during forty; the diurnal and nocturnal hours they measure out together as their (fasting) day. *And this variety among the observers (of the fasts) had not its origin in our time, but long before in that of our predecessors, some of whom probably, being not very accurate in their observance of it, handed down to posterity the custom as it had, through simplicity of private fancy, been introduced among them.* And yet nevertheless all these lived in peace one with another, and we also keep peace together. Thus, in fact, the difference in observing the fast establishes the harmony of our common faith. And the presbyters preceding Sotor in the government of the Church, which thou dost now rule – I mean Anicetus and Pius, Hyginus, with Telesphorus and Xystus – did neither themselves observe it (after that fashion) nor permit those with them to do so. Notwithstanding this, those who did not keep (the feast in this way) were peacefully disposed towards those who came to them from other dioceses in which it was so observed, although such observance was felt to be in decided contrariety as presented to those who did not fall in with it. And when the blessed Polycarp was sojourning in Rome in the time of Anicetus, although a slight controversy had arisen among them as to certain other points, they were at once well inclined towards each other with regard to the matter in hand, not willing that any quarrel should arise between them on this head. For neither could Anicetus persuade Polycarp to forgo the observance in his own way inasmuch as these things had been always so observed by John the disciple of our Lord, and by other Apostles with whom he had been conversant; nor on the other hand could Polycarp succeed in persuading Anicetus to keep the observance in his way, for he maintained that he was bound to adhere to the usage of the presbyters who preceded him. And in this state of affairs they held fellowship with each other, and Anicetus conceded to Polycarp in the Church the celebration of the Eucharist by way of showing him respect, so that they parted in peace one from the other, maintaining peace with the whole Church, both those who did observe this custom and those who did not.'

(Note that in the marked passage Irenaeus, who was working with Pothinus before the great persecution in AD 177, speaks of his predecessors who had handed down a custom long before.)

APPENDIX E

AD 199

TERTULLIAN, 'ADVERSUS JUDAEOS' (PATROLOGIA LATINA, VOL. II, p. 610)

I n quem enim alium universae gentes crediderunt nisi in Christum qui jam venit? Cui enim et aliae gentes crediderunt "Parthi, Medi, Elamitae et qui habitant Mesopotamiam, Armeniam, Phrygiam, Cappadociam, et incolentes Pontum, et Asiam et Pamphyliam, immorantes Aegyptum et regionem Africae quae est trans Cyrenem habitantes, Romanae et incolae: tunc et in Hierusalem Judaei (Act ii, 9, 10) et ceterae gentes: ut jam Getulorum varietates et Maurorum multi fines, Hispaniarum omnes termini, et Galliarum diversae nationes, et Britanorum inaccessa loca Romanis, Christo vera subdita et Sarmatarum et Dacorum et Germanorum et Scytharum et additarum multarum gentium et provinciarum et insularum multarum nobis ignotarum et quae enumerare minus prosumus? In quibus omnibus locis Christi nomen qui jam venit, regnat.'

TERTULLIAN, AD 199[1]

'For in whom else have all peoples believed except in Christ who has already come?'

'In whom have the diverse nations believed – Parthians, Medes, Elamites, and the dwellers in Mesopotamia, Armenia, Phrygia,

---

[1] *Life of Tertullian*, Patrologia Latina, vol. i.

Cappadocia, the inhabitants of Pontus, Asia, and Pamphylia, the dwellers in Egypt and the regions of Africa that is beyond Cyrene, both Romans and inhabitants and the Jews which are in Jerusalem, and now other nations also, such as the various peoples of the Getulae, many territories of the Moors, all the corners of the Spaniards, the diverse nations of the Gauls, and *the places of the Britons which are inaccessible to the Romans,* but all subdued to (the worship of) the true Christ? So, too, the people of the Sarmatians, and Dacians, and Germans, and Scythians, and many additional nations and provinces and islands unknown to us, and which we are scarcely able to enumerate? In all of which places the name of Christ (who now has come) reigns' (Personal Trans.).

FROM TERTULLIAN, *c.* AD 200

'To the rulers of the Roman Empire':
'We are but of yesterday and we have filled every place among you – cities, islands, fortresses, towns, market-places, the very camp, tribes, companions, palace, senate, forum – we have left nothing to you but the temples of your gods. For what wars should we not be fit, not eager, even with unequal forces, we who so willingly yield ourselves to the sword, if in our religion it were not counted better to be slain than to slay? Without arms even, and raising no insurrectionary banner, but simply in enmity to you, we could carry on the contest with you by an ill-willed severance alone. For if such multitudes of men were to break away from you and betake themselves to some remote corner of the world, why, the very loss of so many citizens, whatever sort they were, would cover the Empire with shame; nay, in the very forsaking, Vengeance would be inflicted.

'Why, you would be horror-struck at the solitude in which you would find yourself, at such an all-prevailing silence, and that stupor as

308

of a dead world. You would have to seek subjects to govern. You would have more enemies than citizens remaining. For now it is the immense number of Christians which makes your enemies so few, almost all the inhabitants of your various cities being followers of Christ' ('Apologeticus' of Tertullian, cap. 37).

APPENDIX F

AD 250-254

EXTRACT OF LETTER FROM ST. CYPRIAN 'TO HIS BROTHER STEPHEN' (POPE STEPHEN)

Faustinus, our colleague, stationed at Lyons, has . . . written to me . . . informing me . . . that Marcianus, who is stationed at Arles, has joined himself to Novatian. . . . Wherefore it behoves you to write a very full letter *to our fellow-bishops established in Gaul,* that they no longer suffer the forward and proud Marcianus who this long while boasts and publishes that . . . he has separated himself from our communion.

'Let letters be addressed from thee to the Province and to the people dwelling at Arles, whereby Marcianus being excommunicated, another may be substituted in his room and the flock of Christ, which to this day is overlooked, scattered by him and wounded, be again collected together. Suffice it that many of our brethren in those parts have in these last year's departed without the peace . . . at all events, let the rest who survive be holpen, who both groan day and night, and, entreating the mercy of our God and Father, implore the solace of our help.

'. . . Signify plainly to us who has been substituted at Arles in the place of Marcianus that we know to whom we should direct our brethren' (Letters of S. Cyprian, No. 68. Library of Fathers, Parker, Oxford, 1884).

Note – 'This epistle (No. 68) is found in six old MSS., and is ascertained to have existed in four others of which one was the very oldest. Its style is throughout Cyprian's, so that the question of its genuineness raised by Launoy was a mere theory' (Library of Fathers).

APPENDIX G

SIGNATORIES OF THE COUNCIL OF ARLES IN 314

(Mansi, vol. II pp. 476-477)

Chrestus	Bishop	Florus	Deacon	ex civitate Syracusanorum (Sicilia)
Proterius	"	Agrippa & Pinus	Deacons	de civitate Capuensium (Campania)
Pardus	"	Crescens	Deacon	de civitate Arpienism (Apulia)
Theodorus	"	Agathon	"	de civitate Aquilejensi (Dalmatia)
Claudianus	Presbyter	Eugenius	"	"ex urbe Roma missi a Silvestro episc" (Rome) (sent by Pope Silvester)
Vitus	"	Cyriacus	"	"
Merocles	Bishop	Severus	"	de civitate Mediolanensi (Italia)
Oresius	"	Nazarius	Lector	de civitate Massiliensi (Marseilles)
Marinus	"	Salamas	Presbyter	de civitate Arelatensium (Arles)
		Nicasius	Deacon	"
		Aser	"	"
		Ursin	"	"
		Petrus	"	"
Verus	"	Bedas	Exorcist	de civitate Viennensi (Vienne)
Daphnus	"	Victor	"	de civitate Vasensi
		Faustinus	Presbyter	de civitate Arausicorum
		Innocentius	Deacon	de civitate Nicaensi
		Agapius	Exorcist	"
		Romanus	Presbyter	
		Victor	Exorcist	de civitate Aptensium

Item de Galliis

Imbetausius	Bishop	Primigenius	Deacon	de civitate Rhemorum
Avitianus	"	Nicetus	"	de civitate Rotomagensium
Reticius	"	Amandus	Presbyter	de civitate Augustodunensium (Autun)
		Philomatius	Deacon	"
Vocius	"	Petulinus	Exorcist	de civitate Lugdunensium (Lyons)

311

Maternus	"	Macrinus	Deacon	de civitate Agrippinensium
		Genialis	"	de civitate Gabalum
Orientalis	"	Flavius	"	de civitate Burdegalensi
Agraesius	"	Felix	Exorcist	de civitate Treverorum (Trèves)
Mamertinus	"	Leontius	Deacon	de civitate Elosatium
Eborius	"			de civitate Eboracensi, Provincia Britannia
Restitutus	"			de civitate Londiniensi
Adelphius	"	Arminius	"	de civitate Colonia Londiniensium
Liberius	"	Florentius	"	de civitate Emerita, Provincia Hispania
		Sabinus	Presbyter	de civitate Baetica
		Natalis	"	de civitate Ursolensium
		Cytherinus	Deacon	"
		Probatius	Presbyter	de civitate Tarracone
		Castorius	Deacon	"
		Clementius	Presbyter	de civitate Caesaraugusta
		Rufinus	Exorcist	"
		Termatius	Presbyter	de civitate Bastigensium
		Victor	Lector	"
Fortunatus	"	Deuterius	Deacon	de civitate Caesariensi, Provincia Mauritania
Quintasius	"	Ammonius	Presbyter	de civitate Caralis, Sardinia

Item Provincia Africa

Caecilianus	Bishop	Sperantius	Deacon	de civitate Carthaginensi
Lampadius	"			de civitate Utina
Victor	"			de civitate Utica
Anastasius	"			de civitate Beneventina
Faustus	"			de civitate Tuborbitana
Surgentius	"			de civitate Pocofeltis
Victor	"			de civitate Legisvolumini
Vitalis	"			de civitate Verensium
Gregor	"			"de loca qui est in portu Romae"
Epictetus	"			Centumcellis
		Leontius	Presbyter	ab Ostiis
		Mercurius	"	"

APPENDIX H

AD 400

The Confession of St. Patrick was written by himself and directly copied in AD 807 by a scribe, 'Ferdomnach.' It is preserved in the Book of Armagh. It begins:

'I, Patrick, a sinner, the rudest and least of all the faithful and the most despicable among most men, had for my father Calpornius, a deacon, son of the late Potitus, a presbyter, who was of the town of Bonaven Taberniae; for he had a farm in the neighbourhood where I was taken captive. I was then sixteen years old. I knew not the true God, and I was carried into captivity to Hiberio with many thousands of men according to our deserts, because we had gone back from God and had not kept His commandments, and were not obedient to our priests, who used to warn us for our salvation.'

APPENDIX I

AD 417

E xtract from a letter of Zosimus the Pope to the bishops of Gaul, stating: 'One must not derogate from the old privileges of the metropolitan of Arles, to which Trophimus, a bishop of the first rank, was first sent from this see and from whom the faith spread like a river through the whole of Gaul' (Epistola Zosimi Papae ad Episcopos Galliae de privilegiis ecclesiae Arelatensi, AD 417).

'. . . Sane quoniam metropolitanae Arelatensum urbi vetus privilegium minime derogandum est, ad quam primum ex hac sede Trophimus, summus antistes, ex cujus fonte totae Galliae fidei rivulos acceperunt' (Mansi, vol. iv, pp. 359, 360).

APPENDIX J

AD 450

Extracts and signatories of a letter from nineteen bishops addressed to Pope Leo in AD 450, maintaining that Arles was the proper metropolitan of the Viennoise sees – that the Church was founded here by St. Trophimus, in apostolic times, and that he was commissioned by the Apostle Peter (Patrol. Lat., vol. liv, pp. 880, 881).

'. . . Omnibus etenim regionibus Gallicanis notum est, sed nec sacrosanctae Ecclesiae Romanae habetur incognitum quod prima intra Gallias Arelatensis civitas missum a beatissimo Petro Apostolo sanctum Trophimum habere meruit sacerdotum. . . .'

'. . . quae in Sancto Trophimo primitias nostrae religionis prima suscepit. . . .'

'. . . ut sicut per beatissimum Petrum Apostolorum principem Sacrosancta Ecclesia Romana tenerit supra omnes totius mundi Ecclesias principatum, ita etiam intra Gallias Arelatensis Ecclesiae, quae Sanctum Trophimum ab Apostolis missum sacerdotum habere meruisset, ordiandi pontificium vindicaret.'

'1. Constantinus (of Carpentras).
2. Armentarius (of Antibes).
3. Audentius (of Die).
4. Severianus (of Thorame).
5. Valerianus (of Cimiez).
6. Ursus.
7. Stephanus.

8. Nectarius (of Avignon).

9. Constantius.

10. Maximus (of Riez).

11. Asclepius (of Cavaillon).

12. Theodorus (of Frejus).

13. Justus (of Orange).

14. Ingenuus (of Embrum).

15. Augustalis (of Toulon).

16. Superventor.

17. Ynantius.

18. Fonteius (of Vaison).

19. Palladius.'

NOTE. – The signatories are taken from the reply of the Pope, this being addressed to the nineteen by name as above.

APPENDIX K

ELEUTHERII PAPAE RESCRIPTUM AD LUCIUM BRITANNIAE REGEM
(QUOMODE GERERE SE DEBEAT IN REGNO BRITANNIAE)

Petiistis a noblis leges Romanas, et Caesaris vobis transmitti, quibus in regno Britanniae uti voluistis. Leges Romanas, et Caesaris semper reprobare possumus; legem Dei nequaquam. Suscepistis enim nuper miseratione Divina in regno Britanniae legem, et fidem Christi. Habetis penes vos in regno utramque paginam: ex illiis Dei gratia per consilium regni vestri sume legem, et per illam Dei patientia vestrum rege Britanniae regnum. Vicarius vero Dei estis in regno juxta prophetam regem 'Domini est terra et plenitudo ejus, orbis terrarum et universi, qui habitant in eo'; et rursum juxta prophetam regem 'Dilexisti justitiam et odisti iniquitatem, propterea unxit te, Deus, Deus tuus, oleo laetitiae prae confortibus tuis,' et rursum juxta prophetam regem: 'Deus judicium tuum, &c.' Non enim dixit judicium, neque justitiam Caesaris.

Filii enim regis gentes Christianae et populi regni sunt, qui sub vestra protectione, et pace in regno degunt, et consistunt juxta Evangelium: 'Quemadmodum Gallint congregat pullos sub alis.' Gentes vero regni Britanniae et populi regni sunt; quos divisos debetis in unum ad concordiam, et pacem et ad fidem, et ad legem Christi, et ad Sanctum Ecclesiam congregare, revocare, fovere, manu tenere, protegere, tegere et ab injuriosis et malitiosis et ah inimicis semper defendere. Voe regno, cujus rex puer est, et cujus principes mane comedunt.' Non voco regem, propter parvam, et minimam aetatem sed propter stultitiam et iniquitatem, et insanitatem juxta prophetam regem: 'Viri sanguinum, et dolosi non dimidiabunt dies suos, &c.,' per comestionem intelligimus gulam, per gulam luxuriam, per luxuriam omni turpia et perversa et mala. Juxta Salomonem Regem, 'in malevolam animam non introibit sapientiae, nec habitabit in corpore subdito peccatis.' Rex dicitur a regendo, non a regno. Rex eris, dum bene regis; quod nisi feceris, nomen regis non in te constabit et nomen regis perdes: quod absit. Det vobis omnipotens Deus regnum Britanniae sic regere, ut possis cum eo regnare in aeternum, cujus vicarius estis in regno praedito ('Mansi,' vol. i, p. 698).

Answer of the Pope Eleutherius to Lucius, King of Britain, concerning the way he should conduct himself in the kingdom of Britain:

'You have asked us to send you the Roman laws and those of Caesar, which you are anxious to use in the kingdom of Britain. We are always at liberty to reject the Roman laws and those of Caesar, not so the law of God. By the Divine mercy you have recently received this law and the faith of Christ in the kingdom of Britain. You have both parts in your power in the kingdom: from these by the grace of God, through the council of your kingdom select the law; and by this, in the patience of God, rule the kingdom of Britain. You are assuredly the deputy or vicar of God in your kingdom, for King David saith, "The earth is the Lord's, and the fulness thereof, the round world and they that dwell therein"; and again, "I have loved righteousness and hated iniquity, therefore God, even thy God, hath anointed thee with the oil of gladness above thy fellows"; and yet again, "Give the king Thy judgment, O God, and Thy righteousness to the king's son." Certainly he does not say (any) judgment nor the justice of Caesar.

'Assuredly the Christian peoples and nation of the kingdom are sons of the king. They are under your protection and live at peace in the kingdom, and remain (according to the Gospel) as the chickens gathered under your wings. Indeed, these are the people of the kingdom of Britain, and the nation of the kingdom whom, though separated, you ought to hold together, bound in concord and peace to the faith and law of Christ and holy Church, to unite, to recall, to cherish, to hold in your hand, to protect, to shelter, and always to defend from wrongs and evils and enemies.

'"Woe to the kingdom whose king is a child, and whose princes eat in the morning" (*Ecclesiastes* 10:16). I do not call (such a man) a king, not on account of his youth and inexperience but on account of his folly and wickedness and unhealthy habits, for, as King David saith, "The bloody and deceitful man shall not live out half his days," and we recognize that from over-eating comes gluttony, from gluttony, luxury, and from luxury all filthy, perverse and evil habits. Solomon the king saith, "Into a malicious soul wisdom shall not enter, nor dwell in the body that is subject to sin." A king is known by his government, not by his kingdom. While you govern well you will be a king: unless you do this, the name of king endures not and you lose the name of king: which (God) forbid.

'God Almighty grant you so to reign in your kingdom of Britain, that you may reign with Him in eternity, whose vicar you are in the kingdom He hath given you.' (Personal Trans.)

APPENDIX L

The earliest known reference regarding the claim of St. Peter's Church, Cornhill, as being

(a) The first Christian Church in London,

(b) The original archiepiscopal seat in the South, and (presumably)

(c) The see from which Bishop Restitutus came in 314 to attend the Council of Arles,

appears to be that of *Jocelyn of Furness*, a writer of the twelfth century (Lethaby's *London*, Macmillan, 1902, pp. 24, 165).

The main details of the tradition are said to have been preserved in the Church of St. Paul-upon-Cornhill on hanging tablets, and the inscription on these is given by Archbishop Ussher in his published works (vol. v).

The reference is as follows:

'Similia habentur in tabula pensili, quae in aeda ilia St. Petri de monte frumentario, sive Cornhill (Cornwell vulgus appellat) adhuc cernitur:

'Anno Domino clxxix.

'Lucius, primus Christianus rex hujus terrae, Brittaniae tunc appellatae, fundavit primam ecclesiam Londoniae, scilicet ecclesiam S. Petri in Cornhill: et fundavit illic archipiscopalem sedem, et fecit illam ecclesiam metropolitanam, et primam ecclesiam hujus regni: et sic durvait spatio cccc. annorum, usque ad adventum S. Augustini Angliae

320

apostoli, qui in hanc terram missus est a S. Gregorio, Ecclesiae doctore, tempore regis Ethelberti. Tum vero archiepiscopi sedes et pallium a dicta ecclesia S. Petri in Cornhill translata fuit Doroberniam, quae jam vocatur Canuaria, ibique manet ad hunc usque diem. Et Miletus, monachus, qui cum S. Augustino in terram venit factus est primus episcopus Londinensis: et sedes ejus in Paulina ecclesia constituta est. Et ille Lucius rex fuit primus fundator ecclesiae S. Petri in Cornhill. Et regnavit in terra hac post Brutum (?) mccxlv. annis.' (Ussher's Works, vol. i, p. 88, 1639.)

[TRANSLATION]

'On hanging tablets in a chamber of St. Peter in Cornhill one may decipher the following:

'In the year of our Lord 179.

'Lucius, the first Christian king of this island now called Britain founded the first Church of London, well known as the Church of St. Peter in Cornhill: and founded there the Archiepiscopal seat and made it the metropolitan church and first church of his kingdom. So it remained for the space of four hundred years until the coming of St. Augustine, the apostle of the Angles, who was sent into this land by Gregory, a Doctor of the Church in the time of King Ethelbert. Then, indeed, the seat and pallium of the Archbishopric was translated from the said Church of St. Peter in Cornhill to Dorobernia, which is now called Canterbury, where it remains to this day. And Miletus the monk, who came into the land with St. Augustine, was made first bishop of London (Londinensis), and his seat was appointed in the Church of St. Paul. And he, Lucius, the King, was the first founder of the Church of St. Peter in Cornhill. And he reigned in this land 1245 years after Brutus' (?)

Another account is as follows:

'The tablet was preserved from the Great Fire, and is now hung over the chimney-piece of the vestry-room.'

The inscription is as follows:

'Bee it knowne to all men that the yeare of our Lord God 179, Lucius, the first Christian King of the land, then called Britaine, founded the first church in London, that is to say, the church of St. Peter upon Cornehill. And hee founded there an Archbishop's see and made the church the metropolitaine and chief church of this kingdome: and so indured the space of 400 years unto the coming of St. Austin the apostle of England, the which was sent into the land by S. Gregoire, the doctor of the church in the time of King Ethelbert. And then was the Archbishop's See and Pall removed from the foresaid church of St. Peter upon Cornehill into Dorobernia that now is called Canterburie and there it remaineth to this day. And Millet a monke which came into this land with St. Austin, hee was made the first Bishop of London and his See was made in Paul's church. And this Lucius king was the first founder of S. Peter's Church upon Cornehill. And he reigned in this land after Brute 1245 yeares. And in the yeare of our Lord God, 124, Lucius was crowned king and the yeares of his reign were 77 yeares.

'And he was buried after some Chronicles at London: and after some Chronicles hee was buried at Glocester where the order of St. Francis standeth now' (*London City Churches*, by A. E. Daniell. Westminster: Constable and Co., 1896).

APPENDIX M

FROM THE *HIGH HISTORY OF THE HOLY GRAIL* PROBABLY COMPILED ABOUT 1220, PROFESSEDLY FROM AN OLDER MS. OF THE 'CLERK JOSEPHUS'

(Of Sir Perceval.)

Good knight was he of right, for he was of the lineage of Joseph of Abarimacie, and this Joseph was his mother's uncle that had been a soldier of Pilate's seven years, nor asked he of him none other guerdon of his service, but only to take down the body of our Saviour from hanging on the cross. The boon him seemed full great when it was granted him and full little to Pilate seemed the guerdon; for right well had Joseph served him, and had he asked to have gold or land thereof, willingly would he have given it to him. And for this did Pilate make him a gift of the Saviour's body, for he supposed that Joseph should have dragged the same shamefully through the city of Jerusalem when it had been taken down from the Cross, and should have left it without the City in some mean place. But the Good Soldier had no mind thereto but rather honoured the body the most he might, rather laid it along in the Holy Sepulchre and kept safe the lance whereof He was smitten in the side and the most Holy Vessel wherein they that believed on Him received with awe the blood that ran down from His wounds when He was set upon the rood.

'Of this lineage was the Good Knight for whose sake is this High History treated. Yglais was his mother's name; King Fisherman was his uncle, and the King of the Lower Folk that was named Pelles, and the King that was named of the Castle Mortal, in whom was there as much bad as there was good in the other twain, and much good was there in them; and these three were his uncles on the side of his mother Yglais, that was a right good lady and a loyal: and the Good Knight had one sister, that hight Dindrane. He that was head of the lineage on his father's side was named Nichodemus.

'Gais li Gros of the Hermit's Cross was father of Alain li Gros. This Alain had eleven brethren right good Knights, like as he was himself. And none of them all lived in his Knighthood but twelve years, and they all died in arms, for their great hardiment in setting forward of the Law that was made anew.

'There were twelve brethren:
Alain li Gros, was the eldest.[1]
Gorgalians was next.
Bruns Brandalis was the third.
Bertholez li Chanz the fourth.
Brandalus of Wales was the fifth.
Elinant of Escavalon was the sixth.
Calobrutus was the seventh.
Meralis of the Palace Meadow was the eighth.
Fortunes of the Red Launde was the ninth.
Melaarmaus of Abanie was the tenth.
Galians of the White Tower was the eleventh.
Alibans of the Waste City was the twelfth.

'All these died in the arms of the service of the Holy Prophet that had renewed the law by His death and smote His enemies to the utmost of their power. Of these two manner of folk, whose names and records you have heard, Josephus the good clerk telleth us, was come the Good

---

[1] According to the Grand St. Graal, the series of "Grail-keepers" from St. Joseph (AD 90) to King Arthur (AD 500?) appears to have been as follows: Joseph of Arimathaea, Josephes, Brons, Alain, Josue, Aminadab, Catheloys, Manaal, Zambor, Pelleaus, Pelles (Pelles' daughter), Galahad.

Knight of whom you shall well hear the name and the manner presently.'
(First chapter of the first book of the High History, translated by
Sebastian Evans.)

'Just as they were about to pass beyond the Castle wall, behold yon
where a Knight cometh forth of a privy postern of the castle, and he was
sitting upon a tall horse, his spear in his fist, and at his neck had he a red
shield whereon was figured a golden eagle. "Sir Knight," saith he to
Messire Gawain, "I pray you bide." "What is your pleasure?" "You must
needs joust with me," saith he, "and conquer this shield or otherwise I
shall conquer you." "And full precious is the shield, insomuch as that
great pains ought you to take to have it and to conquer it, for it belonged
to the best knight of this faith that was ever, and the most puissant and
the wisest." "Who then was he?" saith Messire Gawain.

'"*Judas Machabee* was he, and he it was that first wrought how by
one bird to take another." "You say true," saith Messire Gawain, "a good
knight was he."' (Vol. i, pp. 49, 50.)

'"And what is your name?" said Messire Gawain. "Sir, my name is
Joseus, and I am of the lineage of Joseph of Abarimacie. King Pelles is
my father, that is in this forest, and King Fisherman my uncle, and the
King of Castle Mortal, and the Widow lady of Camelot my aunt, and the
Good Knight Par-lui-fet is of this lineage as near akin as I."' (Vol. i, pp,
97, 98).

'"Sir," said he to the hermit, "of what age is the knight and of what
lineage?" "Of the lineage of Joseph of Abarimacie the Good Soldier."'
(Vol. i, p. 99.)

'You have heard tell how Perceval was of the lineage of Joseph of
Abarimacie, whom God so greatly loved for that he took down His body
hanging on the Cross, which he would not should lie in the prison there
where Pilate had set it. For the highness of the lineage whereof the Good
Knight was descended ought one willingly to hear brought to mind and

recorded the words that are of him.' (Vol. i, p. 182.)

(Of Perceval and Lancelot.)

'"Fair sir, saith the Hermit, "and you, who are you?" "Sir," saith the Knight (Lancelot), "I will tell you. I am the son of King Ban of Banoic." "Ha, fair nephew," saith King Hermit to Perceval, "See here your cousin, for King Ban of Benoic was your father's cousin-german. Make him right good cheer!"' (Vol. i, p. 172.)

(Of Lancelot and Joseus.)

'"And what, sir, is your name?" 'Sir," saith he, "my name is Joseus, and yours, what?" "Sir," saith he, "I am called Lancelot of the Lake." "Sir," saith the hermit, "right close are we akin, I and you."' (Vol. i, p. 204.)

"Messire Gawain . . . came, as you have heard, of the most holy lineage of Josephus and the good King Fisherman.' (Vol. i, p. 251.)

From the prayer of Dindrane (in St. Mary's Chapel at Glastonbury?).

'Lord . . . lend force to the knight. . . that for your love and pity is fain to succour and aid my mother . . . You are her affiance and her succour and therefore ought You to remember that the good Knight, Joseph of Abarimacie, that took down Your Body when it hung upon the rood, was her own uncle. Lord . . . he took You in his arms beside the rood and laid Your Body in the Holy Sepulchre wherein you were covered of the sovran cloth for the which I have come in hither. Lord, grant it be your pleasure that I may have it, for love of the Knight by whom it was set in this Chapel: sith that I am of his lineage it ought well to manifest itself in this sore need, so it come according to Your pleasure.' (Vol. i, pp. 288, 289.)

(Of the King of Castle Mortal.)

'Josephus recordeth us by this evil King that was so traitorous and false and yet was of the lineage of the Good Soldier, Joseph of Abarimacie. This Joseph, as the Scripture witnesseth, was his uncle, and this evil King was brother-german of King Fisherman and brother of the good King Pelles that had abandoned his land, in order that he might serve God, and brother of the widow lady that was Perceval's mother, the most loyal that was ever in Great Britain. All these lineages were in the service of our Lord from the beginning of their lives unto the end save only this evil King that perished so evilly as you have heard.' (Vol. ii, p. 34.)

'Josephus telleth us that as at this time was there no bell, neither in Great Britain nor in Lesser; but folk were called together by a horn, and in many places there were sheets of steel, and in other places clappers of wood. King Arthur marvelled him much of this sound, so clear and sweet was it, and it well seemed him that it came on God's behalf, and right fain was he to see a bell and so he might.' (Vol. ii, 6, 71.)

'Then he (King Arthur) asked the hermit that bore the bell whence this thing came? "Sir," saith he to Messire Gawain, "I am the King for whom you slew the giant whereby you had the sword wherewith St. John was beheaded, that I see this on altar. . . . Thereafter I went to a hermitage by the sea. . . . I rose one night at matins and looked under my hermitage and saw that a ship had taken haven there. I went thither when the sea was retreated and found within the ship three priests and their clerks that told me their names, and how they were called in baptism. All . . . came from the land of Promise, and told me that Solomon had cast three bells, one for the Saviour of the World and one for His sweet Mother, and one for the honour of His Saints, wherefore they had brought this hither by His commandment into this kingdom for that we had none here."' (Vol. ii, p. 113.)

(Of Lancelot at Glastonbury.)

'He saluted them and then asked of them what place was this? And they told him that the place there was Avalon. They make stable his horse. He left his arms without the chapel and entereth therein, and saith that never hath he seen none so fair, nor so rich. There were within, three other places, right fair and seemly dight of rich cloths and silk and rich covers and fringes of gold. He seeth the images and the crucifixes all newly fashioned and the chapel illumined of rich colours: and moreover in the midst thereof were two coffins, one against the other, and at the four corners four tall wax tapers burning that were right rich in four rich candlesticks. The coffins were covered with two palls, and there were clerks that chanted psalms in turn on the one side and the other. "Sir," said Lancelot, to one of the hermits, "for whom were these coffins made?" "For King Arthur and Queen Guinevre." "King Arthur is not yet dead," saith Lancelot. "No, in truth, please God! but the body of the Queen lieth in the coffin before us and in the other is the head of her son, until such time as the king shall be ended, to whom God grant long life! But the Queen bade at her death that his body should be set beside her own when he shall end. Hereof have we the letters and her seal in this chapel, and this place made she be builded new on this wise or ever she died.'" (Vol. ii, pp. 133. 134.)

'Josephus telleth us in the scripture he recordeth for us, whereof this history was drawn only of Latin into Romance, that none need be in doubt that these adventures befell at that time in Great Britain and in all the other Kingdoms, and plenty enow more befell than I record, but these were the most certain.' (Vol. ii, p. 208.)

'"Sir," say they, . . . "well knew we the knight that bare this shield before you." "Lords, know ye then how he was named?" Say they, "Joseph of Abarimacie, but no cross was there on the shield before the death of Jesus Christ. But he had it set thereon after the crucifixion of Jesus Christ for the sake of the Saviour that he loved so well."' (Vol. ii, p. 245.)

(Of how the History of the Holy Grail came from Glastonbury.)

'Here endeth the story of the most Holy Grail. Josephus, by whom it is placed on record, giveth the benison of our Lord to all that hear and honour it. The Latin from whence this history was drawn into romance was taken in the Isle of Avalon, in a holy house of religion that standeth at the head of the Moors Adventurous, there, where King Arthur and where Queen Guinevre lie, according to the witness of the good men religious that are therein that have the whole history thereof, true from the beginning even to the end.' (Vol. ii, p. 279.)

INDEX

A

Aaron (martyr), 209

Achaia, 75

Acta Sanctorum, 75, 135, 140, 224

Adelphius, 162, 211, 312

Agrippa, 101

Aix, 137, 140

Alban, 209

Alexander and Rufus, 65

Alexander (martyr), 297

Alexandria, 94

Aliscamps, Les, 175

Ambrose, 46

Amphibalus, 209

Amplias, 150

Andrew, St., 27, 116

Andronicus, 69, 150

Anicetus, 153

Antioch, 62, 65, 70, 78

Antonia, fortress of, 43, 50

Apelles, Apollos, 150

Apostles, pre-Christian, 82, 183

Aquila and Priscilla, 150

Aquileia, 85

Archelaus, 45, 182

Aristarchus, 92, 99, 100, 179

Aristobulus, 150, 206

D

E

F

G

FURTHER READING

The Drama of the Lost Disciples by G.F. Jowett

The Early British Church by L.G. Roberts

Did our Lord visit Britain? by C.C. Dobson

Our Neglected Heritage by G. Taylor

St. Paul in Britain by R. Morgan

All books from Covenant Publishing